THE IMPORTANCE

—— • OF • ——

FEELING ENGLISH

THE IMPORTANCE

— OF —

FEELING ENGLISH

American Literature and

the British Diaspora, 1750–1850

LEONARD TENNENHOUSE

PRINCETON UNIVERSITY PRESS

PRINCETON AND OXFORD

Copyright © 2007 by Princeton University Press

Published by Princeton University Press, 41 William Street,
Princeton, New Jersey 08540
In the United Kingdom: Princeton University Press, 3 Market Place,
Woodstock, Oxfordshire OX20 1SY

ISBN-13: 978-0-691-09681-0

Library of Congress Control Number: 2006939046

British Library Cataloging-in-Publication Data is available

This book has been composed in Minion Typeface

Printed on acid-free paper. ∞

press.princeton.edu

Printed in the United States of America

1   3   5   7   9   10   8   6   4   2

For Nancy

CONTENTS

ACKNOWLEDGMENTS

T HIS PROJECT began as a paper presented at the first meeting of the
Society of Early Americanists and grew stronger and subtler in the
exciting intellectual milieu of that fledgling organization. SEA members
raised the questions that punctuate my argument; their many articles and
books helped to determine the final direction and scope of this work. Elizabeth Dillon, Sandra Gustafson, Ed Larkin, Carla Mulford, Susan Scott
Parrish, Ivy Schweitzer, David Shields, and Eric Slauter deserve special
mention for sharing their own work in progress and providing valuable
bibliographical leads.

Over the past few years, my introduction has been transformed by ener-
getic conversations with Khachig Tölöyan, editor of *Diaspora*. His capa-
cious knowledge of diaspora studies allowed me to arrive at a clear sense
of the various debates organizing that field. Wil Verhoeven and Marie Irene
de Sousa Santos provided forums at the University of Groenigen and at
the University of Coimbra, respectively, where I tested the conceptual
model for this book.

When I decided to write a book about the transatlantic literary relations
that created what we now call "American literature," I had the great good
fortune to find myself at Brown University, undoubtedly the best place in
the country to undertake such a study. Here, I have been blessed with such
colleagues as Rey Chow, William Keach, Kevin McLaughlin, and Michael
Silverman, who generously encouraged this project from the start and at
crucial moments provided institutional support for my undertaking. Colleagues in each of my three departments helped me think through aspects
of this argument. For that I owe particular thanks to Michel-André Bossy,
Jim Egan, and Olakunle George. To Phil Gould I am indebted at every
stage of this project. An unflagging enthusiast and a walking repository of
knowledge about transatlantic relations in the colonial period, he went
over every chapter with a keen eye and returned drafts to me with copious
notes scribbled in the margins. I owe him special thanks.

I have benefited from the collegiality of two graduate students with an
enduring appetite for antebellum American literature: Sian Silyn-Roberts
and Brian Sweeney. Sian served as an invaluable research assistant as well.
Two former graduate students, Ezra Tawil and Jason Solinger, did me the
great service of reading portions of the manuscript. Perhaps my most important insights—the fact that there is a distinctively American *Clarissa*,

for example—came to me while reading in the collections of the John Carter Brown Library and the John Hay Library. Brown also provided me with these truly unique research facilities, staffed with experts to guide me to the most wonderful material.

A portion of Chapter Three appeared in a previous version as "The American Richardson," *Yale Journal of Criticism* 12 (1998): 177–96. I wish to thank The Johns Hopkins University Press for permission to reprint the material. A modified version of chapter 2 appeared as "A Language for a Nation: A Transatlantic Problematic," in W. M. Verhoeven, ed. *Transatlantic Revolutions* (New York: Palgrave Macmillan, 2002), 62–84 and is reproduced with permission of Palgrave Macmillan.

Clifford Siskin, Elizabeth Dillon, and Daniel Cottom read the entire manuscript at various stages and together forced me to say what I meant. I revised earnestly in light of their comments. I am indebted to Hanne Winarsky of Princeton University Press for her unflagging support of this project.

Finally, this book germinated and grew in the warm environment of daily conversations with Nancy Armstrong, my most welcome critic.

THE IMPORTANCE
—— · OF · ——
FEELING ENGLISH

1

DIASPORA AND EMPIRE

AT THE RISK of stating the obvious, let me begin by asserting that any discussion of American literature will at some point have to address the questions of how soon and in what respects British Americans began to think of themselves as American rather than British. Instead of assuming that different national governments mean different national literatures, I come to this problem from the contrary perspective: that the separation of American from British literatures is still at issue and was therefore nothing like the clean break that we tend to project backward onto the late eighteenth century.[1] I plan to look at a wide body of Anglophone literature from the late seventeenth, eighteenth, and early nineteenth centuries for the purpose of discovering when it began to divide internally into recognizable British and American traditions. With this material, I move back and forth across the Atlantic, explaining how the American tradition defined itself in an ongoing and yet changing relation to the British. In this respect, my project participates in the growing body of scholarship concerned with transatlantic literary relations.[2]

My argument begins with the proposition that during the period from 1750–1850 American authors and readers were more interested in producing and consuming English literature than in creating, to borrow Elaine Showalter's phrase, "a literature of their own."[3] The literary evidence indeed suggests that during this period, most writers and readers in America considered themselves to be members of the generic English culture that we generally mean by "British culture," and they thought of their literature as products of such a culture. But this hardly means that anything written before political independence was British. Nor can we assume that a drive for cultural autonomy must have accompanied political independence. Such a view regards American literature as a coherent body of writing whose colonial-era production sounded themes that resonated with the writers of the American Renaissance. Hence the continuous search within a field constituted solely by American texts to find "profound continuities between early American literary expression and the classic literature of the United States in the mid-nineteenth century."[4] An alternative view argued most forcefully by William Spengemann claims that literary history should not be confused with the history of the national culture. Writing in the English language, particularly when writers in British America lacked political autonomy, should in his view be read as British since it is of a piece with other British writings.[5] To my way of thinking, both views are only half true.

During the period leading up to the Revolutionary War, British America was indeed composed of British colonies. On the other hand, most colonists from the British Isles were all too aware of the fact that they no longer lived there. Even though, and perhaps because, they had to do so under conditions that differed sharply from those that fostered literature back in England, from captivity narratives through the earliest sentimental fiction produced on this side of the Atlantic, colonial authors generally wanted to write as Englishmen.[6] In the face of the French threat during the Seven Years War, they indeed felt especially inspired to reaffirm their British identification. Benjamin Franklin confessed to Lord Kames in 1760 that "no one can rejoice more sincerely than I do, on the Reduction of Canada; and this not merely as I am a Colonist, but as I am a Briton."[7] In 1765 John Adams felt the need to ask, "Is there not something extremely fallacious in the common-place images of mother country and children colonies? Are we the children of Great Britain any more than the cities of London, Exeter, and Bath? Are we not brethren and fellow subjects with those in Britain, only under a somewhat different method of legislation, and a totally different method of taxation?"[8] For a colonist in America to declare himself a Briton was evidently to make a reasonable claim to national identity. Although they were called "Americans," that term did not in any way cancel out the more fundamental British identity that tied them to their nation of origin.[9] Indeed, until the decade of the Revolution, each colony observed separate lines of economic and cultural ties to the metropolitan center. As a result, Michael Zuckerman notes, "Americans were still very far from being a people bonded by a shared sense of purpose and identity." What self-awareness we see is that of people who, he contends, have "come to think of themselves as Pennsylvanians or Virginians rather than as Americans."[10]

After the War of Independence, there is every reason to believe that citizens of the new United States knew—and felt keenly—that they were no longer subjects of Great Britain. But it does not necessarily follow from this that the colonists renounced their British identity in other respects simply because they rejected British government. Political separation did not in fact cancel out the importance of one's having come to America from Great Britain. Indeed, the literary evidence indicates that the newly liberated colonists became if anything more intent on keeping the new homeland as much as possible like the old one in terms of its language, literature, and any number of cultural practices. To the degree that it subjected Englishness to circumstances that could not be imagined back in England, literature written by, for, or about British America was never really British. But to the degree that those who authored and read such literature not only tried to maintain an English cultural identity but also sought to put the stamp of Englishness on the new nation, neither can that literature be called American in any pure and simple way. I take issue, in other words, with the critical practice that for a hundred years has used J. Hector St. John de Crèvecoeur's "What is an American" (Letter III, *Letters From an American Farmer*) as the delineation of a new national culture. Despite the many helpful insights to be gained from recent attempts to compare the literature of the new republic to modern postcolonial literature written in South Asian, Caribbean, or African countries, there was no oppressed or colonized English-language culture of British North America waiting to emerge as soon as decolonization began.[11] Literature produced under the conditions I am describing requires an explanatory model that acknowledges a perplexed but continuing relationship between nation-state and national culture.[12] With some important adjustments, I propose, the cultural logic of diaspora offers such a model.

A Culturalist View of Diaspora

It is common to think of diasporic communities as made up of a homogeneous people who have fled war, hunger, religious persecution, or economic hardships in the mother country and so exist as distinct minorities in an adopted homeland. For many years, the term diaspora was applied to four great dispersions of this kind: Jewish, Greek, Armenian, and African. Recently, as many as eighty other groups have either taken on the term to describe their status or have been classified as a diaspora by social scientists. In addition to the dispersion itself, members of a diaspora share some collective memory of the motherland as the diasporic group is scattered across more than one geographical location. This memory affords the motive and basis for maintaining a relationship to the nation of origin, and its consciousness of that relationship becomes central to the identity of the diasporic group. We might think of Franklin's claim that he is a Briton as an example of just this kind of identification. There are several other points on which most scholars of diaspora agree: despite their various dislocations, members of a diaspora maintain cultural ties to their nation of origin and believe someday they will return there. Members of one diasporic group may also maintain ties to other such groups, provided they share the same attachment to their nation of origin. When this double tie breaks down, we can say that the group ceases to be a diaspora and becomes a subculture of the host nation.[13]

The prevailing critical tendency, as I see it, has been to understand diaspora as something on the order of a refusal to assimilate that preserves the ways of the mother country in defiance of the host culture. I want to extend the concept to the situation in British North America, where the culture of one diasporic group—namely the British—assumed hegemony over several others. We have every reason to think that many of the British men and women in North America held onto the idea that they could return to Great Britain. At the very least, they imagined that they were sufficiently English to fit in among their kinsmen back in England. Certainly throughout the seventeenth and early eighteenth centuries, the pattern of immigration and emigration had its ebbs and flows. As political conditions changed, some immigrants to New England did in fact return home—as happened, most notably, during King Philip's War. In other cases, sermons and writings imagined New England as a haven for the reformers of the church who would return to England either in person or as an example to continue the reformation of the church in England. Cotton Mather predicted as much, when he compared "the English Christians" cast in "the Dark Regions of America" to "the *Light*, which from the midst of this *Outer Darkeness*, is now to be Darted over unto the other side of the *Atlantick Ocean*."[14] Even those destined never to return to England, many of whom wrote in America, first published their sermons and their poetry in England and for an English readership. As Michael Warner observes, "Virtually every colonial writer looks both homeward to the seat of imperial culture and outward to the localities that would remain for them subordinate."[15] The other side of the same cultural coin was the colonists' fear of going native in the wilderness of America and so losing the cultural alternatives that made one recognizably English. The possibility of permanent separation from the English community is especially evident in captivity narratives that portray death as far preferable to either assimilating to Indian ways or undergoing conversion to Catholicism should the captive be turned over to the French.[16]

It may seem a stretch to equate colonial Americans with such classic diasporic groups as Jews or Armenians, not to mention Africans violently ripped from their natal lands and shipped to the Americas in chains. It is more common to assume that once the colonists achieved political and economic independence from England, they became a nation in their own right and were no longer concerned with returning to the nation of their origin. Were I actually committed to the classic definition of "diaspora," I would have to agree that the term does not apply to British Americans. To understand how the cultural logic of diaspora might indeed hold true for the colonists in America, especially in the years leading up to and immediately following the War for Independence, one must develop a somewhat looser concept. This second notion of "diaspora" neither depends on the dispersed group's direct memory of a single place of origin nor does it require members to remain intent on returning there. Quite the contrary, in order for this second model of diaspora to prove useful, the homeland has to disappear as a geopolitical site to which the diasporic group can entertain the possibility of actually returning.

There are several reasons why a site of national origin might vanish. It could be displaced several times over by the migrations of the dispersed groups. As the Jews were removed from ancient Israel to Babylon, Assyria, then Persia, the Roman Empire, and, later, to the Abbasid and Ottoman Empires, they developed centers of learning dedicated to remembering the homeland. Jonathan and Daniel Boyarim remind us that the place remembered as Zion underwent significant revision as it was reimagined and reproduced through ritual practices over time and in different places throughout the world.[17] The same principle holds true, even moreso perhaps, for the African diaspora. Dispersed by the international commerce in slaves during the sixteenth, seventeenth, eighteenth, and nineteenth centuries, Africans had little opportunity to develop commemorative institutions over four centuries and a series of removals. With successive generations, the memory of Africa was displaced by cultural practices designed perhaps at first to commemorate the place of origin but soon enough to recall subsequent displacements—Brazil, the Caribbean, the rural American South, northern urban ghettoes, and so forth.

As the actual memory of the motherland undergoes successive displacements, the members of the diaspora pursue a narrative trajectory that is less a departure and return and more of an extended detour. That is to say, the members of the diaspora move farther from the homeland with each attempt to return or recapture it. Moreover no two branches of a given diaspora undergo precisely the same sequence of displacements or detours; each hangs onto some features of the mother culture and abandons others as these features succeed or fail to accommodate to the new cultural milieu. Over the course of time, the various acts of commemoration that make each group cohere and give it a distinctive identity within a host culture produce a purely imaginary construct that replaces the sense of home grounded on experience and perpetuated by actual memory. In many instances the place of origin no longer exists as a geopolitical reality. Thus, for example, the notion of Zion serves as a kind of placeholder for the original homeland for many Jews with quite different points of origins. So, too, a generic pan-Africa represents the place of origin for many African Americans.

Let us assume there is an implicit cultural limit to the centrifugal dynamic whereby a diasporic culture develops internal differences through the process of dispersal. If the diaspora is going to maintain its foreignness rather than turn into one of so many subcultures within a host nation, horizontal affiliations must develop among its various branches; this happens as together various groups exchange commemorative practices and generalize the homeland, performing acts of community held in common by all Jews or Africans, even at the expense of local practices that serve as relics of actual memory. As various groups of a particular diaspora produce such a purely cultural common ground, a kind of centripetal cultural force begins to counter their geopolitical dispersal. The centripetal force, I must hasten to add, pulls the dispersed groups not back to the place of origin but toward an imagined cultural source that has in fact displaced that origin. This centripetal force is generated by the production of a generic homeland and results in a new sense of collectivity. In *The Black Atlantic*, Paul Gilroy develops a model along precisely these lines to explain how "Africa" became an imaginary homeland for many groups belonging to the African diaspora.[18] His model offers what I regard as the best way to date to understand most modern diasporas, because it bases a group's ability to maintain a semblance of autonomy and collective identity over time on its cultural practices, not on its ability to trace its genealogy back to some point of origin.

Instead of formulating a continuous tradition that aims at retrieving a lost past, an intellectual process Gilroy identifies with the chronotope of the road, he prefers to think within the chronotope of the crossroad. Let me offer one especially telling example of this alternative notion of cultural transmission that reveals the importance of detours, disruptions, circularity, and exchanges in keeping a diaspora alive and vital even under the conditions of globalization. Gilroy retells the story of musician James Brown's visit to West Africa in the 1960s. The American failed to find what he went there looking for or indeed anything that could be called "authentic" African music. Instead, Brown encountered African musicians who had listened to his African American band and began imitating his music. He was particularly impressed with Fela Ransome Kuti, whom he describes as "kind of like the African James Brown" (199). While Kuti and his band evidently felt they were discovering their Africanness in James Brown, Brown's own band was picking up material from the Nigerian musicians. "Some of the ideas my band was getting from that band had come from me in the first place," he reports, "but that was okay with me. It made the music that much stronger" (199). One can read diasporic cultural materials for the continuities that connect African American music and literature to an "authentic" origin in Africa. Rather than perform an imaginary return, one can look at points of exchange where the groups meet and agree on common ground. What these musicians shared was not the purity of some African origin, but something created in and through cultural exchanges across historical time and geographical space. Both African and African American obviously discovered their Africanness in the other's performance. Gilroy claims that such an exchange "explodes the dualistic structure which puts Africa, authenticity, purity, and origin in crude opposition to the Americas, hybridity, creolisation, and rootlessness" (199).

I want to draw a direct parallel between the relationship of modern and antimodern African diasporic cultural traditions, as Gilroy describes them, and the case of American literature. From the earliest attempts to canonize American literature in the nineteenth century to the present day, the tendency has been to trace a lineage of truly American authors either back through the American Renaissance to the Puritan fathers or, alternatively, back through the sentimental tradition to captivity narratives. The scholar-critic who participates in such a project looks for continuities between present-day cultural production and one or the other of these origins. To illustrate the difference with regard to American literature between the classic essentialist model of diaspora and a culturalist model like Gilroy's, we must keep in mind the difference between writing in seventeenth-century colonial America and the literature produced in America during the second half of the eighteenth century. Mary Rowlandson's captivity narrative, for example, equates her situation as an English woman captive to natives of North America with that of a Christian whose faith is tested in the wilderness. That the traces of what she identified as "English cattle" and an "English path" were equivalent to signs of God's presence should tell us that Rowlandson was writing as an English woman, who wanted to maintain her ties to other English people and ultimately her fitness to return to the community of her origin, or if not that, then the kingdom of heaven.[19] One hundred years later, such authors as Philip Freneau, Timothy Dwight, and Joel Barlow write as Americans reproducing English literature for and about a new nation—whose culture, they insisted, was no less English for having been transferred to and reproduced in North America. In other words, the kind of writer who emerges in America during the second half of the eighteenth century represents a decisive shift away from that of the transplanted English man or woman.

In the last decades of the eighteenth century, American authors reinvented the homeland by producing a generic notion of Englishness particularly adapted to the North American situation. In what is considered one of the first American novels, William Hill Brown's *The Power of Sympathy* (1789), the American protagonist can conduct a successful courtship because he is familiar with English letters. By way of contrast, his English predecessors tended to squander the same cultural capital in relationships that read like tawdry tales of seduction. What distinguishes Worthy from the European libertine is a taste in literature that manifests itself in a capacity not only to feel the proper sentiments but also to put them in writing; Worthy wins a wife by means of his skill as a letter writer. We can also see a generalized Englishness produced in the works of Charles Brockden Brown, who was keen on writing a body of American letters that would achieve recognition in England. The protagonist of Brown's *Clara Howard* displays a single-minded devotion to English literature that would classify his British counterpart as a dilettante. This same devotion on the part of an American artisan makes him worthy of marrying the daughter of an English gentleman. Rather than preserve an ancient tie to the land from which Englishmen immigrated to America, this novelistic notion of Englishness transforms the concept into one that can travel. "English" is no longer a state of being, nor is it a matter of who one is so much as a performance and a question of what one does. There is abundant historical evidence to back up what these literary examples suggest: that by the last half of the eighteenth century, an increasing number of Americans were thinking of themselves as generically English. T. H. Breen ascribes a notable rise in the consumption of English goods to a "re-Anglicization" of America.[20] Differences between the English in Virginia and those in Massachusetts apparently began to matter less than their common cultural ground as British colonials, thanks to what historian Colin Kidd has described as the process of "anglicizing homogenization," a process that became pervasive from 1760 on.[21]

To remain English—and we have every reason to think most colonial Englishmen wished to do so—they would have had to reproduce certain elements of their Englishness in North America. By ensuring the reproduction of that culture in subsequent generations—which is, I believe, the implicit purpose of any literature, but especially a literature produced in a colonial situation—Anglo-America was reproducing itself. That "self" was a reproduction, not of the mother culture, but of what had from the very beginning been an adaptation of the mother culture to a diasporic setting. From this it follows that a certain adaptation of English culture came to dominate the American colonies because the British did a better job of reproducing the culture of the homeland away from home than, say, the Germans did in Pennsylvania, the French in northern New England, or the Dutch in New York. I am not suggesting that British immigrants were especially good at retaining their sense of themselves overseas. I am only saying that they were especially good at reproducing cultural practices at once adapted for the colonial setting and yet able at once to distinguish Anglo-Americans from every other group and to subordinate other cultures to a pervasively normative and yet curiously elastic definition of Englishness. It is the ability of English culture to travel, take root elsewhere, and subordinate other groups, even to the envy of its competitors, that fascinates me, an ability peculiar not only to the fashion and food ways linked to English culture but to the literature as well. On these grounds, if for no other reason, I argue that we stand to learn something new about American literature and its curious relation to English culture by thinking of it in terms of a diasporic literature—one aimed at reproducing certain traits of Englishness in a radically non-European environment.

Central to my purpose is the separation of the nation as a political entity from the nation as a culture, which allows us to focus on the relationship between the two, rather than read them as two aspects of a single entity.[22] Indeed, the literature of the crucial period leading up to the Revolution indicates that English speakers believed they shared a culture with Great Britain. What is more, the literature of the new republic indicates that this concern for maintaining an English identity only intensified after the colonists fought and won political independence from Great Britain. Does seeing the situation this way make our literature any less American? According to the logic of diaspora, not at all. What makes our literature distinctly and indelibly American is our literature's insistence on reproducing those aspects of Englishness that do not require one to be in England so much as among English people. British Americans put their distinctive stamp on the new nation, not because they succeeded in reproducing English culture outside of England so much as because their way of imagining England was more truly American, in the specific sense I have been elaborating, than the signature practices of any other immigrant culture.

Keeping in mind just this much of what I will call the cultural logic of diaspora, we no longer read literature to determine when and how American culture achieved monolithic coherence. Rather than assume that what is most American is some product indigenous to the new United States, I argue that what we mean by American is most likely a reproduction of cultural practices that originated somewhere else. Thinking of the problem this way, we can understand the literature and culture of the United States as a relationship among several diasporic cultures. This relationship is hierarchical and varies not only from one literary epoch to another but also according to region, as new groups acquire the power to represent themselves in literature as distinctive within an internally conflicted and heterogeneous nation. More specifically, we can see how the English diaspora began as a struggle in which relationships among competing immigrant communities, races, and ethnicities allowed each such group to imagine itself politically situated in a differential relation to others.

The American Appetite for British Books

To gather a clear sense of the degree to which transplanted Englishmen and women sought to maintain their cultural ties with the mother country by means of the printed word, we need to look at the history of the book in America. Throughout the more than two hundred years from the colonial period to the early republic, the story of who printed and reprinted British texts, as well as which texts were imported and in what quantities, tells of deep and continuous cultural ties with Great Britain. From Isaiah Thomas's first account of this story in his *History of Printing in America*

(1810) to the on-going multivolume project unfolding under the general title of *The History of the Book in America,* all versions acknowledge that "throughout most of the colonial period most books had to be shipped in whatever the capabilities of the publishing and reprinting in North America."[23] The reasons for colonial dependence on imported culture are pretty clear. British legal constraints during much of the colonial period, the cost of paper, the availability of presses, the limited size of a readership in any given urban area—all made it easier for booksellers to rely on imported material. Throughout the eighteenth century, as domestic book production grew, American printers devoted their presses to almanacs, sermons (in declining numbers), session law reports, and the like. As a result, colonial booksellers and their customers continued to rely largely on British imports for books on politics and history, belles lettres, and much that was considered useful knowledge.

Until the 1790s, imported English novels remained cheaper than editions reprinted in America. Benjamin Franklin learned that lesson the hard way when he lost money in 1742 on reprinting an edition of *Pamela.*[24] Imported British magazines were especially popular, and their material was often reprinted—sometimes without acknowledgment—in American periodical publications. During the last two decades of the eighteenth century, as domestic production of books, magazines, and newspapers increased, Americans consumed imported books and magazines from Great Britain at an ever-increasing rate. Following a decline during the war years, the number of imports of British books quickly returned to prewar levels once the Treaty of Paris was signed. Going by the number of advertisements in American books and newspapers for reprints of British titles, and ignoring all those books that were pirated, imported, or purchased through British book agents, Hugh Amory and David D. Hall report that there were "133 editions down to 1749, 163 from 1750–1774, and 982 in the final quarter of the century."[25] James Raven describes the paradox in this way:

> By 1770, more books were exported annually from England to the American colonies than to Europe and the rest of the world combined, albeit with limited demand on the Continent for books in English. We are unlikely to be surprised that the importation of books from the mother country was the mainstay of bookselling in the early, sparsely populated years of colonial settlement, but that this volume should have increased rather than declined with the growth of colonial production is not so easily explained.[26]

Along with an increase in the importation of books from Great Britain, there was a decided shift in the kinds of items imported, including not only "belles lettres and novels . . . but also learned literatures, periodicals, and newspapers."[27] This increase was not a phenomenon peculiar to the Northeast alone but prevailed throughout the colonies.

Contributing to the number of books coming into America from British booksellers was the immigration of Scots and Irish printers and booksellers who drew on business and family contacts back home to aid in creating and satisfying the demand for the latest British books.[28] In his study of the book trade in the South, Calhoun Winton writes, "Scotland was a major exporter of people in the eighteenth century; important among those groups seeking opportunity abroad were members of the book and printing trades. David Hall, Franklin's Philadelphia partner, was a Scot as was Robert Bell, the reprinter."[29] Another Scot, Robert Wells, set up shop in Charleston, where according to Winton "in 1774 and 75, Wells advertised in his paper more than twenty titles of books then selling well in the English-speaking market, Goldsmith's *Vicar of Wakefield*, for example. This tracking of London publications represented an augmentation of his business; clearly, he felt that the market for such books was improving" (237). In addition to summaries of law books and histories imported from Britain and many works of belles lettres by such writers as Edward Young, James Thomson, Alexander Pope, Henry Fielding, Laurence Sterne, and Tobias Smollett, weekly journals were especially popular with southern readers. These weeklies "contained much international and intercolonial and local news," Richard Beale Davis notes, adding, "they were also literary journals, presenting essays formal and familiar and borrowed from each other or from British sources, British poems, and even (occasionally) British plays."[30] His summary account of the personal libraries and book purchases in the colonial South prompts Davis to comment, "The southern colonial and early national bookshelf . . . probably resembled libraries in the farmhouses or small manor houses of rural England" (130).

The South was not alone in its preference for British literature or in booksellers who claimed to be the best or most reliable source of British books. In this respect, the book market in northern cities resembled that of Charleston. James N. Green quotes the bookseller James Rivington, with bookstores in New York, Philadelphia, and Boston, who proclaimed in 1762 that he was "the only London bookseller in America."[31] This claim was intended to guarantee that his were the latest London imports. In describing the customers and the market for books, Elizabeth Carroll Reilly and David D. Hall note, "The pattern of sales in [Jeremy] Condy's store [in Boston] seems to prevail elsewhere. . . . Most of the books (counted by the number of titles) in these stores came from Britain, most were expensive, and most were available in very small quantities" (389).[32] As for less expensive books, Reilly and Hall explain, "Many chapbooks or other kinds of cheap books were produced overseas; in the 1770s Henry Knox was importing thousands of chapbooks costing 2d. wholesale from the London trade, some of them copies of children's books issued by the London bookseller John Newbery, others abridged versions of novels such as Samuel Richardson's *Pamela* and *Clarissa Harlowe*" (391). "One surprising cons

quence of American independence from the British Empire," write David Hall and Hugh Amory, "was to reinforce the anglicization of print that culturally was a strong feature of the pre-war decades."[33]

At the very least, these numbers give us cause to rethink Benedict Anderson's well-known account of the origin of nationalism as the rise of an imagined community of novel readers.[34] According to Anderson, fiction and newspapers enabled colonial readers to imagine themselves as part of a community of people much like themselves who would probably never meet or exchange a word of conversation but who could nevertheless imagine others like themselves engaged in reading the same materials, sharing the same views, and reacting in similar ways to the fate of a character. Such readers would consequently think of themselves as members of a community that may be socially dispersed but who shared the same culture. Much as I have been indebted to this model, I have come to realize that it simply will not hold up under the weight of evidence that indicates American readers preferred British books and magazines even, and especially, when they were struggling for political independence from England. Were we to take at its word Anderson's argument concerning the impact of literacy, we would have to conclude from my sampling of evidence from the history of the book in America that the colonial American readership imagined itself as a nation of English readers.

This comes close to what Raymond Williams means by "hegemony," a culture's capacity to dominate—and remain "the culture"—without imposing its rule everywhere and at all times.[35] To maintain the authority of a national culture, a particular set of ethnic practices has to dominate the discourses that matter, literature chief among them. To insist on national difference, various users of the language must reproduce it, often in its most authoritative or prestigious forms. Only by reproducing the terms of their own domination, according to the model I am using, can new groups introduce the differences that may, at some point, add up to their cultural emergence—in the case at hand, a different way of thinking in English that elevates American features of the culture over those designated as deriving from Britain.[36] America's brand of Englishness, I am suggesting, is precisely what made it American.

Colonial American Poetry as a Descriptive Theory of Diaspora

Now, for a practical example familiar to every scholar of early American literature. Among the figures that British letters made available to American authors and readers, "The Rising Glory of America" was especially appealing, I believe, because it could be read in two ways: one, as a way of insisting that the center of civilization shifted from Rome to England with

the decline of the Roman Empire and therefore celebrated English culture; and two, as a way of insisting that English culture improved as it shifted again westward to America and away from Europe. By invoking this trope, American authors could think of themselves as English even though they were not British. "The Rising Glory" could perform this legerdemain because it was in fact two tropes in one.

Developed by Roman poets to account for the transfer of imperial power from Athens to Rome, and imitated by poets over time as learning migrated from Rome to later imperial centers, the first trope under consideration, *translatio imperii*, predicted the westward transfer of imperial authority. During the Middle Ages, *translatio imperii* was used to imagine the transfer of such authority from Rome to Charlemagne's Paris and later to various Italian city-states. By the High Renaissance, poets were already making the case that France, England, or one of a number of other European candidates was the true heir of Roman *imperium*.[37] In making this point, such British poets as Dryden, Denham, Pope, Dyer, Dennis, Prior, Collins, Gray, Thomson, and Goldsmith emphasized the traditional link between *translatio imperii* and a second trope, *translatio studii*.[38] This second figure described the transfer of learning and the arts, or cultural authority, to the new imperial center. Hence, the lines from Pope's *An Essay on Criticism*: "Learning and Rome alike in empire grew; / And Arts still follow'd where her eagles flew."[39]

Among eighteenth-century writers, Bishop Berkeley alone has been credited by many scholars with declaring that the westward movement of empire heralded the certain transfer to America of imperial authority along with art and learning, as indicated quite clearly by his title "Verses on the Prospect of Planting Arts and Learning in America" (1752). "There," he claims, "shall be sung another golden Age, / The rise of Empire and of Arts" (13–14).[40] Then—in what only later became the most famous lines of the poem—Berkeley predicts that the transfer of imperial authority shall not continue further west but culminate triumphantly in what American poets would call "the rising glory of America":

> Westward the Course of Empire takes its Way;
>   The four first Acts already past,
> A fifth shall close the Drama with the Day;
>   Time's noblest Offspring is the last. (21–24)

First written in 1724 and published in a revised form in 1752, Berkeley's poem had a curious reception in North America. Modern literary critics have been quick to note its influence on any number of colonial American writers.[41] The scholars have not been so quick to note that except for one or two Latin poems that appeared in *Pietas et Gratulatio* (1761) lamenting the death of George II, Berkeley's combination of the two tropes into one did not make its appearance in American letters until 1770.[42] Rather than deal with this time lag, scholars tend to chalk up its prominent appearance to the figure's obvious jingoistic potential, citing its appearance in such poems as John Trumbull's "Prospect of the Future Glory of America" (1770), Hugh Henry Brackenridge and Philip Freneau's *Rising Glory of America* (1771), the version Freneau rewrote after the Revolution, Timothy Dwight's *America* (1780), David Humphreys "On the Future Glory of America," (1780), Joel Barlow's "The Prospect of Peace" (1778) and his *Vision of Columbus* (1787), which was revised and published as the *Columbiad* (1807).[43] If Berkeley's poem, as critics claim, offered such poets a way to express their Americanness, one must ask, then why did so many American writers neglect to take advantage of that fact during the very years leading up to the break with Britain?

Two reasons come to mind—one fairly obvious and the other requiring us to assemble the pieces of a rather interesting historical puzzle. I think it's quite possible that in the 1750s and 1760s British Americans intent on preserving their ties to a British culture of origins were less than thrilled with the idea that the muse was disgusted with England in its present state.[44] From this it follows that a revolutionary readership of the 1770s might well have enjoyed the idea that America was sure to become the new locus of art and learning. So much for the obvious and on to the historical details I consider more interesting.

Berkeley insisted that his "Verses on the Planting of Arts and Learning in America" be read alongside his well known *Proposal for the Better Supplying of Churches in Our Foreign Plantations, and for Converting the Savage Americans to Christianity, By a College to be Erected in the Summer Islands, Otherwise Called the Isles of Bermuda* (1725). He emphasized the necessary relation between the two texts explicitly in a letter to Lord Percival, to whom he sent the poem, and implicitly, when he later published his poem in 1752 on the two pages immediately preceding the reprinted text of his *Proposal*.[45] While the poem itself may, from our present vantage point, appear to flatter America, the *Proposal* openly insults the English colonists in North America. Here, Berkeley proposes that a college be built in Bermuda for the expressed purpose of civilizing English colonists, whom he as much as accuses of having gone native. As he puts it, "there is at this Day, but little Sense of Religion, and a most notorious Corruption of Manners, in the *English* Colonies settled on the Continent of America, and the Islands."[46] For Berkeley, the fact that neither the planters, nor their slaves, nor the indigenous peoples living in proximity to the settlements seem to be particularly Christian makes America a spiritual wasteland. To correct this situation, he proposes a school that will equip the sons of planters to minister to their brethren and convert their slaves who, in his opinion, "would only become better Slaves by being Christian" (346).[47]

When read alongside his *Proposal*, Berkeley's poetic celebration of the transfer of learning to America would have conveyed the unflattering message to Americans that they were greatly in need of cultural remediation. But it is only when he aims education at a second group within the colonial population that we see how truly retrograde his project was likely to have seemed to colonial Americans. In proposing that his college would train "savage Americans" to evangelize among their people, he as much as endorses the conquest and conversion policy that was James I's original rationale for colonial expansion. Berkeley reminds his readers that James I had ordered the colonists to propagate "the Gospel and civil Life among the savage Nations of *America*" (357). And if Native American students cannot be "procured by peaceable methods," he contends, then colonists should take "captive the Children of our Enemies" (347). There is little to indicate the poem was well received when it was published with *The Proposal*, but its apathetic reception in 1752 does not tell us whether English colonists found Berkeley's concept of colonialism offensive or whether it struck them as simply irrelevant. Within twenty years, the question was moot.

By the 1770s and 1780s, the policy of "conquest and conversion" that Berkeley had advocated in his *Proposal* would certainly have struck the American reader as both savage and decidedly un-English. Anthony Pagden points out that eighteenth-century authors saw British colonialism as a civilizing project in contrast to the evangelical missions of the French and Spanish, which were intended to conquer and convert the heathens. "In time," according to Pagden "the British dropped all but the minimal pretence to an overseas mission, although their claim to be exporting their own version of 'civilization' survived well into the nineteenth century" (37). Still identifying themselves as English, American readers in all likelihood found in Berkeley's use of *translatio studii* a model of education quite contrary to everything they considered base and decadent about their counterparts in Britain. As Philip Freneau wrote in 1775:

> Who could have thought that Britons bore a heart,
> Or British troops to act so base a part?
> Britons of old renown'd, can they descend
> T'enslave their brethren in a foreign land?[48]

On grounds that they were truer to British tradition than any Continental writer, American authors of all stripes embraced the poetics of *translatio studii*. To capitalize on the trope of the "rising glory" for their own purposes, from the 1770s they detached the poem from Berkeley's proposal and published it separately. Once the poem could be read independently, I am suggesting, it began to enjoy wide circulation. When in 1783, for example, Philip Freneau translated l'Abbé Claude Robin's *New Travels Through North America*, he inserted Berkeley's poem as the second page of the front matter, even though the French original included no such poem.[49] Freneau reprinted the pair of texts in 1784, and again in 1797 when Robin's text was serialized in Freneau's magazine the *Time-Piece*.

Yes, the historical conditions had certainly changed in favor of its reception, but in order to become the signature trope of American literature, "The Rising Glory" had to be significantly revised. In reproducing the trope, American writers sought to reverse the priorities that Berkeley established by subordinating learning to the goals of empire. They insisted that English colonists came to America, not as conquerors, but like latter-day Israelites who were punished for their (Puritan) literacy and their faith. Freneau and Brackenridge give voice to these sentiments when they contend that "By persecution wrong'd/ And popish cruelty, our father's came/ From Europe's shores to this blest abode" ("Rising Glory," 239–41). Timothy Dwight chimes in with the claim, "Forc'd from the pleasures of their native soil . . . / To these far-distant climes our fathers came" (*America* 4).[50] In "Columbia," the peaceful ambitions of "our fathers" exist in striking contrast to a Europe that aspires "To conquest, and slaughter" (9). In his "Oration, Delivered July 4th, 1783," John Warren echoes Dwight, as well as Freneau and Brackenridge, in claiming that "religious tyranny had forced from the unnatural bosom of a parent, a race of hardy sons, who chose rather to dwell in the deserts of America with the savage natives, than in the splendid habitations of *more* savage men."[51] Once such poems and orations had offered up lengthy historical accounts differentiating the benign motives of English colonists in North America from the imperialism of "rapacious Spain," it took but a line or two for later poets and orators to invoke the trope as it had been revised. This insistence that English colonialism was not an expression of British imperialism, but quite the reverse, allowed American writers to disavow any similarity between the Spanish practice so regularly condemned in this poetry and the American treatment of Indians by settlers on the frontier. Nor, by the same token, were Americans asked to acknowledge any resemblance between their own Indian policies formulated by Henry Knox and those formulated by Spain a century earlier.[52]

That American writers were as troubled by forced religious conversion as by military conquest is evident in the frequent references to cultivation that underscore the peaceful nature of their venture in the colonies. Such lines as "Labour fearless rear'd the nodding grain" (Dwight, *America*, 85) and "rough-brow'd Labour every care beguiled" (Dwight, *America*, 68) summon up a Lockean account of territorial acquisition through labor to ward off any resemblance to the Spanish and French practices of conquest, capture, and conversion. This notion of acquisition through the labor of cultivation presupposes that land in the colonies should be considered a *terra nullius*, a territory neither occupied nor under any nation's dominion.

Cultivation of such land provides a purely secular notion of improvement that adds value to it, and in turn bestows ownership on those who work the land. It is with this argument in mind that Freneau and Brackenridge contrast the aggression of Native Americans—acting in the name of French imperial authority—to the peaceful toiling of the members of "the hapless colonies":

> Yes, while they overturn'd the soil untill'd,
> . . . . fierce Indian tribes
> With deadly malice arm'd and black design,
> Oft murder'd half the haples colonies.
> Encourag'd too by that inglorious race
> False Gallia's sons . . . (263–69)

Cultivation of the soil, like education, falls within the Enlightenment category of improvement, which American writers considered the domain of *translatio studii.*

Through repeated usage, American authors shifted the source of imperial authority from political policy, or *translatio imperii,* to education—the domain of *translatio studii.* David Humphreys has exactly this change of emphasis in mind when he tells his readers that "happier days" for America "by hallow'd bards foretold, /Shall far surpass the fabled age of gold."[53] For Humphreys the "rising glory of America" is one and the same as the ascent of education over political force: "The human mind its noblest pow'rs display, /And knowledge, rising to meridian day, /Shine like the lib'ral sun" (557–58). Thus the transfer of learning, as he imagines it, works dialectically to displace government by conquest and conversion with government by education and commerce. The same inversion of Berkeley's tropes was soon played out by so many hands in so many different texts that it became rather commonplace and was likely to be hauled out for such occasions as Enos Hitchcock's oration for July 4, 1793. In Hitchcock's words, "To the early care of our ancestors to establish literary, and encourage religious institutions, are we much indebted for the accomplishment of the late revolution, which shows us the vast importance of paying great attention to the rising sons and daughters of America, by giving them an enlightened and a virtuous education."[54] In all these instances, the trope of the rising glory does not suggest that the new site where learning flourishes has moved farther from its source. To the contrary, English culture has simply been purified as it moved westward. As Berkeley had promised, America is not only "Time's noblest Offspring" but also "the last."

In claiming to be more English than their English counterparts, American authors were arguably no longer British. They were in fact mounting a challenge to the authority of the mother culture. This in a nutshell is the logic of diaspora: a displaced people, in imaginatively asserting their identity as if it were their culture of origin, transforms that culture into one capable of reproducing itself outside the mother culture. Even as the American colonies in British North America moved toward separation and independence, they increased their consumption of English culture and reproduced their own version of Englishness. This logic was figured as the very notion of *imperii studii*, which corresponds, I would argue, to a model of diaspora that depends less on a specific place of origin than on reinventing a cultural homeland that appeals to a group of immigrants and settlers requiring a new basis of identity to draw them together. The culture that was produced in response to such a need among the British in North America turned out to be one that could travel and adapt to new economic circumstances. Thus, I am suggesting, the trope of "the rising glory" contains a theory of cultural renewal as repetition with a difference and links that theory implicitly to the making of a modern nation. In arriving at this conclusion, I want to insist that American authors not only used Berkeley's trope to carry out this transformation but also imagined English literature as the instrument of change.

2

WRITING ENGLISH IN AMERICA

F ROM the Declaration of Independence until well after the War of 1812, authors and intellectuals writing in English in the United States debated the relationship between language and national identity. This debate ranged widely over philological, linguistic, and aesthetic matters and took up the question of what consequences might ensue from the political break with Britain: Was the Revolution only a political rupture, or did it require revolutionary arts of cultural and linguistic self-definition as well? The majority of modern scholars take the position that, yes, in order to be a nation, an emergent political order must establish its own language or languages. This language should not only serve the purpose of conducting state business but, equally important, it should also be able to produce a national literature or literatures.[1] But, I would argue, it is more in keeping with eighteenth-century thinking to say that revolution effects a return or restoration of national origins.[2] This concept of revolution did not entail breaking all cultural and linguistic ties with the imperial nation, but only those considered corrupt and corrupting. David Simpson characterizes this well-known position with regard to language usage: "there were many, aside from the committed Anglophiles who would sanction no deviation from the rules set down in London, who were open to the prospect of some particularly American modification of the language, but who were at the same time uncomfortable about making a completely new beginning."[3] From this position can be inferred yet a third, which I will put forth in this chapter—namely, that the language debates in the new United States continued a process of national redefinition that were underway in Great Britain from the mid-eighteenth century on. Independence was indeed a motive for the debate in America, and the result was an American language and literature. Even so, there is reason to pause before concluding that this process of redefinition was a distinctively American phenomenon, which can be understood as a departure from the European-English model. To the contrary it was in their respective attempts to do the same thing as the English—namely, stabilize English usage—that an American difference emerged.

During the long eighteenth century, both England and America experienced a sudden expansion of literacy and an explosion in the number and kinds of materials that appeared in print. The political revolution in England was relatively short-lived and ended with the restoration of the monarchy in 1660, but as Raymond Williams has argued, a "long revolution" in print had just begun. This revolution gained extraordinary impetus in 1695 when Parliament refused to renew the Licensing Act of 1662.[4] With one stroke, that refusal to continue government censorship removed both the limit on the number of printing presses that could operate and the constraints on what kind of material could be printed. Between 1695 and 1730, Williams writes, "a public press of three kinds became firmly established: daily newspapers, provincial weekly newspapers, and periodicals" (181). Literacy expanded to meet the supply of information in the print vernacular.

There is a similar story to tell about America. During the first half of the eighteenth century, literacy rates increased along the Atlantic seaboard of North America. We would expect the smaller number of potential readers, their diffusion across a much larger landscape, and the expense of paper to have made it difficult if not impossible for the expansion of print culture in the colonies to keep pace with the long revolution in England, but keep pace it did. "What makes this transformation of the press particularly remarkable," writes Michael Warner, "is that, unlike the press explosion of the nineteenth century, it involved virtually no technological improvements in the trade."[5] Despite the material constraints on production that remained constant until the end of the eighteenth century, "printing changed both in character and in volume, after 1720 growing much faster even than the population" (32). The sudden increase in print following close on the heels of the War for Independence becomes all the more impressive when we consider how extensive the new literacy already was. As Warner reminds us, "More newspapers were founded in the 1790s than had been started in the entire century preceding" (125). There was also a substantial, if not quite as dramatic, increase in the number of magazines and weeklies founded in the years following the war. In view of this print revolution, it should come as no surprise that by the late eighteenth century authors and intellectuals on both sides of the Atlantic set out to establish a standard vernacular.[6] Let us consider why the same project produced such different results in Great Britain from those in the new United States.

The Problem of Dialects

In his preface to the *Dictionary* (1755), Samuel Johnson represents his task as bringing order to a language whose spoken dialects were proliferating along with his nation's commercial ventures: "When I took the first survey of my undertaking, I found our speech copious without order."[7] In the preface, as in the *Dictionary* itself, Johnson abandons speech in favor of writing as the model of language. In what are perhaps the most quoted lines of this oft-quoted document, he explains, "As language was at its beginning merely oral, all words of necessary or common use were spoken before they were written; and while they were unfixed by any visible signs, must have been spoken with great diversity, as we now observe those who cannot read to catch sounds imperfectly, and utter them negligently" (308). It is "from this uncertain pronunciation" that we are to understand the rise of "the various dialects of the same country, which will always be observed to grow fewer and less different, as books are multiplied; and from this arbitrary representation of sounds by letters proceeds that diversity of spelling, observable in the Saxon remains" (308). Although speech once had a single origin and could be shared by the entire "Anglo-Saxon" community, Johnson explains, it has undergone dispersal and mixture with foreign elements, and he finds the result that one group of speakers is barely intelligible to another. Noting that this lack of intelligibility finds its counterpart in variant spellings, Johnson shifts his analysis almost imperceptibly from oral to written forms.

Once he resituates his model of language from speech to writing, it is a relatively simple step to establish a standard for acceptable practices because the variability of speakers no longer matters; differences in rank, region, work, and education can be subordinated to a uniform written standard. Johnson represents his lexicographic policy as a compromise between the dilettante and the populist: "where caprice has long wantoned without control, and vanity sought praise by petty reformation, I have endeavoured to proceed with a scholar's reverence for antiquity, and a grammarian's regard to the genius of our tongue" (310). To avoid "the corruptions of oral utterance" (310), on the one hand, and the excesses of contemporary written styles, on the other, he has, he says, "studiously endeavoured to collect examples and authorities from the writers before the Restoration, whose works I regard *as the wells of English undefiled*, as the pure sources of genuine diction" (319). Authorized by English tradition, Johnson comes down decisively on the side of a written standard over speech as the means of establishing a national vernacular.

In keeping with the exceptionalist ideology embraced by successive generations of American historians, most discussions of the American language debates treat the work of Noah Webster as uniquely suited to the colonies attempting to define themselves as a new nation. Webster himself thought of his work in that way. He begins his *Dissertations on the English Language* (1789) with the claim that the history of English pronunciation will show "the principle differences between the practice in England and America, and the differences in the several parts of America."[8] He believes the moment is right for establishing "a national language and [for] giving

... uniformity and perspicuity" to American culture (36). In attempting to do so, however, he confronts the same problem that Johnson wrestled with in compiling his dictionary—namely, how to deal with the variations in speech dialects throughout the nation. As a resolution to this problem, Webster considers it a lost cause to impose a written standard, as Johnson sought to do. For centuries, English grammarians attempted to introduce the subjunctive into English; they conspicuously failed, Webster reminds us, because "people in practice pay no regard to it" (viii). The grammarians should have known that no attempt to impose a Latin rule could overrule the "common practice, even among the unlearned" (viii). If "the people are right" in England, he concludes, then they are even more so in America.

Johnson looked to a written standard as the means of hierarchizing different dialects and retarding the rate of change that naturally prevails in speech. As David Simpson notes, Webster "is the first major challenger of the linguistic hegemony of the British in general and of Johnson in particular," and after Webster it is impossible "to be unaware of the argument about language as a *national* argument" (24). Webster's republican ideology makes him lean in the opposite direction from Johnson, that is, toward speech as the basis for any model of a national vernacular. Although his dictionary will offer a written standard, that standard must be built from the ground up so as not to overrule speech: "The body of the people governed by habit will still retain their respective peculiarities of speaking" (19). Moreover, a standard American English must allow for variants introduced by immigration. As Jefferson explained, new words are needed to accompany the discovery of new ideas as well as terms to identify new flora and fauna in an expanding America.[9] In keeping with the republican ideology of Webster's theory of language, American English should be known for its inclusiveness.[10]

The same ideology prompts Webster to single out certain features of the prestige dialect of spoken English that must not be reproduced in American writing. Most regrettable is speech that preserves British class distinctions: "In many parts of America, people at present attempt to copy the English phrases and pronunciations," which has traditionally distinguished "the language of the higher [from that of] the common ranks; and indeed between the same ranks in different states" (23–24). In looking to language to overcome traditional class distinctions, Webster echoes the sentiments of John Adams, Thomas Paine, Benjamin Franklin, and Jefferson, all of whom wanted to rid American English of the terminology of rank and aristocratic privilege. Here, then, was the dilemma Webster confronted in compiling his dictionary: how to standardize American differences based on region while, at the same time, canceling out British differences based on rank and station. Despite the problems of a language subject to the influence of various immigrants, but a language already embedded with class distinctions, he insists that "as an independent nation, our honor requires us to have a system of our own, in language as well as in government" (20). He believes that "the *general practice of the nation*, constitute[s] propriety in speaking" (27), and that such a practice will set a uniquely American standard. But Webster also admits that American speakers observe very different local standards, so that any standard inferred from speech will necessarily be eroded by spoken dialects. Having exposed the self-eroding character of any standard based on spoken English, he nevertheless arrives at the conclusion that "the unanimous consent of a nation, and a fixed principle interwoven with the very construction of a language, coeval and coextensive with it" provides the basis for a national standard (29).

It should come as no surprise that to identify the "fixed principle" of American English Webster turns to the logic of *translatio studii*. As it was transported and took root in America, he reasons, the English language was magically stripped of corrupted elements and restored to something like its original purity: "On examining the language, and comparing the practice of speaking among the yeomanry of this country, with the stile of Shakespear [*sic*] and Addison, I am constrained to declare that the people of America, in particular the English descendants, speak the most pure English now known in the world" (288). Thanks to the homogeneity of the American "yeomanry," Webster feels he can declare that there are "in the extent of twelve hundred miles in America . . . a [mere] hundred words . . . which are not universally intelligible" (289). It is important to note just who these yeomen actually were. In contrast with "the illiterate peasantry" of England, Webster's yeomen "have considerable education." Indeed, they are property owners who write, keep accounts, read newspapers and the Bible, and fill their heads with "the best English sermons and treatises upon religion, ethics, geography and history" (288–89). Having migrated to America, they established "public schools sufficient to instruct every man's children, and most of the children are actually benefited by these institutions" (289). By way of contrast, he maintains, people in England "can hardly understand one another, so various are their dialects" (289). By restricting his sample group of Americans to the nation's "yeomanry," Webster can identify a common standard of literacy that includes writing as well as reading, and this literacy shall set the standard for speech. The speech of the American yeoman allows Webster to maintain his difference from Johnson even as he settles on the print vernacular as his model for both writing and the prestige dialect of spoken English in the new United States. Because this model assumes the material form of a dictionary, it will necessarily privilege the dialect that comes closest to the written standard. This being the case, we must ask, what is the American difference?

To arrive at an answer, we must look briefly at the romantic rebuttal to Johnson's argument for a written standard. Wordsworth's "Advertisement" to the *Lyrical Ballads* (1798) declares that the poems in that collection "were written chiefly with a view to ascertain how far the language of conversation in the middle and lower classes of society is adapted to the purposes of poetic pleasure."[11] I think we should take seriously his claim that speech based on the spoken language is preferable to writing that conforms to a written standard, because speech offers a "natural delineation of human passions, human characters, and human incidents" (591).[12] I am less interested in the psychological, epistemological, or linguistic issues at stake here than in the very literal meaning of Wordsworth's expressed claim that writing should be based on "incidents and situations from common life" and that those incidents should be represented in the "language really used by men" (596–97). To counter the prevailing theory that speech should model itself on English prose, in my opinion, Wordsworth proposed a theory of language that in watered-down form eventually wormed its way into the very core of nineteenth-century liberal ideology: writing should model itself on speech that has its source in the practice of the individual. How, if not by adapting common speech, could writing be indigenous to a nation?

In this one respect, the romantic manifesto of 1798 echoes Webster's statement in his *Dissertations on the English Language* (1789). Both claim that speech is closer to the authentic source of the English language and therefore more democratic than the standard set by print. In both cases, however, we have to ask ourselves, who are these people who speak the pure, that is, dialect-free, English? For such "speakers," Wordsworth turns to what he calls "boundary beings," regional aboriginal types whose speech is recorded in folklore and preserved in poetry. Like Webster and Johnson, Wordsworth goes to written sources to find the true language of the nation; like Webster, he establishes a new, indigenous source of national literature in doing so. But there, I would argue, the similarity ends. Webster's yeomanry are a far cry from Wordsworth's illiterate boundary beings; Webster's yeomen are highly literate, freehold farmers whose English is similarly transplanted and regrounded in American soil. There is nothing quite like them in the British language debates.

The Americanization of British Letters

The so-called Connecticut Wits—Joel Barlow, Timothy Dwight, John Trumbull, David Humphreys, and Lemuel Hopkins—offer individual and collaborative instances of writers who use British literary forms together with a distinctively American vocabulary to assert their paradoxical position as American authors writing English literature for an American readership. The *Anarchiad* (1786–87) by Hopkins, Barlow, Humphreys, and others quite self-consciously borrows the English mock-heroic form of *The Rolliad* in order to translate what had been an English attack on Tory politics into an explicitly American assault on such domestic issues as the paper money crisis and the mob violence associated with Shays Rebellion. Barlow's *The Vision of Columbus* (1787) is another example of how English literature was remodeled to make a statement. In his introduction, Barlow calls his epic "an American production."[13] Made with Miltonic language, this version of the poem remodels the scene Milton borrowed from Exodus in which Moses is taken to the top of Mount Pisgah and shown the Promised Land as it will be inhabited by the twelve tribes. In Milton's poem, the angel gives the fallen Adam a view of the future. Barlow employs the same kind of language Milton gave the angel Michael and substitutes an ailing and imprisoned Columbus for the fallen Adam. Barlow even has Michael offer the discouraged voyager "a Pisgah view" of his journey to the New World rendered as a version of the fortunate fall. Where in books X and XI of *Paradise Lost*, Michael reveals to Adam the unfolding of human history that will conclude with the Second Coming of Christ, Barlow's angel shows Columbus how his voyage will set in motion a historical process that culminates in the creation of the United States. Book 7 of *The Vision* ends with an extended use of the *translatio studii* trope that celebrates American science, learning, religion, and art, as the angel comforts Columbus with the knowledge that Barlow's own contemporaries, the Connecticut poets, will improve upon their British forebears who, following Milton's death, declined in quality. The angel cites John Trumbull's "Skillful hand" in order to assure Columbus that "Proud Albion's sons, victorious now no more, / In guilt retiring from the wasted shore, / Strive their curst cruelties to hide in vain" (lines 343–45).

For those who think the political break from England generated a poetic revolution that allowed a distinctive American literary language to emerge, Timothy Dwight's *Greenfield Hill* (1794) offers a particularly compelling case. In addition to offering explanatory notes calling attention to his use of American terms, Dwight characterizes his poem as a kind of semiotic struggle with the tradition of English landscape and prospect poetry represented by Denham's *Cooper's Hill*, Pope's *Windsor Forest*, Goldsmith's *The Deserted Village*, and the traditional country-house poetry before them. Dwight apparently struck upon the Americanizing of English prototypes as a way of arguing against the uses to which such poetry had been put in England. Particularly popular on both sides of the Atlantic, Goldsmith's poem had gone through four editions in the first year of its publication (1770). The poem famously begins by recalling the village in an earlier time: "Sweet Auburn, loveliest village of the plain, / Where health and plenty cheared the labouring swain, / Where smiling spring its earliest visit paid, / And parting summer's lingering blooms delayed."[14] Section 2 of Dwight's poem echoes these very lines so as to suggest that the village whose passing Goldsmith laments has actually rematerialized and is flourishing in America: "Fair Verna! loveliest village of the west;/ Of every joy, and every charm, possess'd/ How pleas'd amid thy varied walks I rove, / Sweet, cheerful walks of innocence and love."[15] Where Goldsmith describes "bowers of innocence" now gone or at least found in the distant poetic past, Dwight sees "walks of innocence" as part of the present American landscape. And where Goldsmith regrets the relentless economic and social change that inevitably destroys such a way of life, Dwight celebrates the qualities of industry and competence that invigorate American culture and make his village thrive. This poetic logic assumes that what has faded into memory and metaphor in England has become vibrant and fully realized in the United States, so that Dwight's village provides the referent toward which Goldsmith's poem gestures.

Dwight certainly suggests as much in his "NOTES to PART II," where he claims that this part of the poem is designed "to illustrate the effects of the state of property, which is the counter part to that, so beautifully exhibited by Dr. Goldsmith in the Deserted Village" (530). By no means, however, does Dwight acknowledge all that he appropriated from his English counterpart. Goldsmith mourns the depopulation that accompanied emigration "To distant climes," to "the wild Altama" (11. 341). Goldsmith also describes the region of the Altamaha river in Georgia, as a wilderness, "Where at each step the stranger fears to wake/ The rattling terrors of the vengeful snake;/ Where crouching tigers wait their hapless prey;/And savage men more murderous still than they" (11. 353–56). Unlike his predecessor who laments westward migrations, Dwight celebrates the prospect of voyages still further westward and America's entry into the China trade. Although on this occasion he turns English elegy into patriotic celebrations of the United States, he elsewhere adapts Goldsmith's elegiac lines to acknowledge the decimation of the Amerindian population and rationalizes their genocide as retribution for legendary atrocities:

> Through the war path the Indian creep no more;
> No midnight scout the slumbering village fire;
> Nor the scalp'd infant stain his gasping sire:
> But peace, and truth, illume the twilight mind,
> The gospel's sunshine, and the purpose kind. (2: 724–28)

It is interesting that here, as in Goldsmith's poem, the agent of the decimation is significantly missing, as the American author celebrates the indigenous Americans as boundary beings left behind by history and Enlightenment. On the basis of these literary borrowings, it is tempting to conclude that the Connecticut Wits were contesting traditions dear to English culture and in this way striving to complete a process begun with the War for Independence.

I will take up the less obvious implication that by appropriating English literary forms, these poets were insisting on their status as authors of English poetry. Indeed, though American, it seems perfectly evident that they saw themselves in terms of the logic of *translatio studii*, as more truly English than those from whom they borrowed. What is Dwight's point in making his village the literal manifestation and referent for Goldsmith's if not to invert the expected relationship of copy to original, making his poem more English than Goldsmith's? Of Dwight's attempt in the notes to *Greenfield Hill* to call attention to such Americanisms as "Nutwood" for Hickory or "spring bird" for a New England songbird, David Simpson observes that the poet explains just as many terms that are not Americanisms. For his American readership, according to Simpson, Dwight "is explaining standard poetic diction to a potentially plain-speaking audience" (96). I am simply saying that despite their thematic assault on British politics and ingenious attempts to write American versions of English poetic forms, the Connecticut Wits had no intention of doing away with such forms.

That this use of English verse forms was understood as a way of preserving an English poetic tradition becomes all too evident when viewed through the critical lens of Hugh Henry Brackenridge. His long satiric novel *Modern Chivalry* (1792–97) launches a pro-dialect attack on American attempts to write British literature. Although his wandering protagonist speaks the standard dialect, neither his servant, an Irishman, nor any of the people he encounters on his journey seem capable of doing so. As a result, standard English becomes just another dialect. In the introduction to his first volume, Brackenridge acknowledges his participation, as a poet, in the language debates, where Webster became the prominent spokesman: "It has been a question for some time past, what would be the best means to fix the English language."[16] Rather than have an academy settle the issue, Brackenridge would prefer that "some great master of stile . . . arise, and without regarding sentiment, or subject, give an example of good language in his composition." The work of such an author might well "fix the orthography, choice of words, idiom of phrase, and structure of sentence, [better] than all the Dictionaries and Institutes that have been ever made." This work would also provide "a model or rule of good writing," a model that aims at being, in the words of Horace, "simple, and [about] one thing only" (4). Patterned on *Don Quixote* and imitations of Cervantes, Butler's *Hudibras*, as well as a number of other narratives both classical and European, *Modern Chivalry* includes a marvelous range of linguistic, literary, legal, economic, and political positions. Brackenridge incorporates this range of European literatures, however, only to exaggerate certain features of the languages in which they were written. As if the reader could have thought otherwise, Brackenridge concludes his first volume with this postscript: "The truth is, as I have said, I value this book for little but the stile. This I have formed on the model of Xenopohon, and Swift's Tale of a Tub, and Gulliver's Travels" (77).

Having had great fun at the expense of any search for a single written style, he kicks off his third volume by promising to offer such a model: "Proceeding with my object; the giving an example of a perfect stile in writing, I come now to the third volume of the work. I well know, that it will not all at once, and by all persons, be thought to be the model of a perfect stile, for it is only the perfectly instructed, and delicately discerning that can discover its beauties" (161).[17] But *Modern Chivalry* should not be taken as anything less than a partisan position with regard to the national language. Brackenridge designs this cacophony of voices and writing styles as an assault on the position held by Dwight and Barlow.[18] In poking fun at the idea of his rivals' plan for a single style of American English, Brackenridge implies that such a plan would significantly impoverish the language. Indeed, so hostile is that plan to American interests, he contends, that it must have been formulated by the English, who are only too aware of how much better Americans would write in the mother tongue: "The English language is undoubtedly written better in America than in England, especially since the time of that literary dunce, Samuel Johnson, who was totally destitute of taste for the vrai naturelle or simplicity of nature" (78).

From the history of the debate as dramatized by Dwight and Brackenridge, it is impossible to say which, if any, of the two positions actually won. What is important for my purposes is the debate itself: what shared assumptions allowed such men to disagree in terms that their readers found meaningful? Both sides assumed an instrumental relationship between language and nation. Where the one insisted that a standard written English would stabilize, standardize, and give shape to the polity, the other stressed the diversity of English voices in America. Together they created a tautology. Although someone like Dwight certainly favored high literary poetic diction, he also felt compelled to include specifically American terms that he glossed in his notes to *Greenfield Hill*. Moreover, for all the pleasure Brackenridge obviously took in collecting English variants, he still relied on what was obviously becoming the prestige dialect of English to make this point because he had his narrator speak according to the written standard. The intelligibility of Brackenridge's novel depends on the theory of language informing *Greenfield Hill*, just as the meaning of that poem depends on the position Brackenridge takes on language in *Modern Chivalry*. If it takes a field of variants to create a normative style, then dialects become meaningful as such only in relationship to a traditional English standard. Out of this paradox, I am suggesting, what might be called a "national language" was born.

As we have seen, in choosing to ground his vernacular standard on the literate individual, Webster resorted to much the same principle as both Johnson and Wordsworth. If there was an important difference in the speech on which Webster based his written standard, then, that difference resided in his commitment to a polite but practical standard represented by the American "yeomanry." With much the same commitment to the practical vocabulary associated with the Englishmen transplanted to the colonies, the Connecticut Wits adapted English verse forms to an American context.

This commitment to the present, the practical, and the normative also made American culture particularly receptive to the writings of John Locke, who had these same industrious freeholders in mind when he wrote "in the beginning all the World was *America*."[19] The idea of harvesting the untapped resources of the New World was his figure for the origins of private property. Americans returned the favor by adopting his model of the social contract. But given this receptivity to Locke's theory of government, it is only reasonable to consider why colonial Americans swerved so sharply from his attitude toward rhetoric. In order to tell the truth, Locke insisted, language should jettison metaphor, embellishment, and figurative language of all sorts. My reading of Webster implies that American English was not only based on speech but was also meant to be spoken: hence, the distinctively American tradition of eloquence. Despite their commitment to the practical language of yeomen, early American writers did not follow Locke in avoiding rhetoric, but rather openly embraced figurative language. Let us trace the curious process by means of which American rhetoricians reconciled figuration with practicality.

Locke in America

John Locke's notion of truth depends on language's fidelity to the object world, a fidelity that by definition is opposed to rhetoric. His epistemology assumes that all men, if given a chance to see the world directly, will see it in approximately the same way. This notion of consensual—indeed, commonsensical—knowledge of the world rests on the absence of distortion, mediation, ideology, call it what you will. Language in such a model is necessarily an intrusion and serves reason best when it would persuade us least. Because it uses allegory, metaphor, metonymy, irony, and other substitutions of one object for another, "the Art of Rhetorick [and] . . . all the artificial and figurative application of Words Eloquence hath invented,"

Locke writes, "are for nothing else but to insinuate wrong Ideas."[20] Well before the end of the eighteenth century, this distinctively modern theory of knowledge effectively displaced the Renaissance equation of reason with syllogistic rhetoric and set English letters on the road to realism.

Colonial American intellectuals heavily influenced by Locke also believed in the efficacy of rhetoric, or "oratory" as it was usually called. By 1768, John Witherspoon, newly arrived from Scotland to assume the presidency of the College of New Jersey, later renamed Princeton University, had begun to deliver his famous lectures on eloquence. According to Witherspoon, to communicate the truth effectively, one must use every trick of rhetoric at his command. With this justification, he proceeded to explain the use of metaphor, metonymy, allegory, irony, and catachresis. Meanwhile, his former classmate at Edinburgh, Hugh Blair, had been lecturing on rhetoric and belles lettres to many of the young Scotsmen who would immigrate to America and take up positions in the professions. Thanks largely to their influence, by the 1780s rhetoric was a staple of the American educational system. If truth, according to Locke, depended on eliminating rhetoric, it is important to ask how American Lockeans came up with a way of telling the truth that both met the Lockean standard and used rhetoric to do so. How, in other words, did Americans use Locke to produce what John Adams described as a revolution that began in oratory?[21]

Let us consider, first, the grounds on which Locke's *An Essay Concerning Human Understanding* outlawed an older theory of rhetoric while creating the basis for a new theory compatible with his epistemology. His task was twofold. To rationalize truth, Locke had to get rid of all ideas that were assumed to have come from God. In his effort to kill off the notion that human beings are born with innate ideas, he famously describes the mind as "white Paper, void of all characters, without any *Ideas*" (II.i.2). Then, abruptly switching metaphors, he proceeds to pose the question of the century: "How comes [the mind] to be furnished? Whence comes it by that vast store, which the busy and boundless Fancy of Man has painted on it, with an almost endless variety? Whence has it all the materials of Reason and Knowledge?" (II.i.2). Locke's answer is as revolutionary as his question. Having erased God from the page and swept the storehouse of the mind clean of the vestiges of early modern culture, he offers what was in his day a radically materialistic definition of knowledge. Most of our ideas, Locke contends, come into the mind from outside through the senses and are then translated into a form of information that he calls "sensation" (II.i.3). Supplied with a sufficient number of sensations, he reasons, the mind begins to perceive its own operations. It reflects on the material it has accumulated by way of the senses and considers how those sensations should be differentiated, arranged, assessed, and generalized. This capacity for reflection is, in Locke's words, something that "Man has wholly in himself" (II.i.4). Ideas received from this second source, or pure reflection, intermix with and often pass for sensations derived directly from the outside world, as when we see a globe of any uniform color and automatically know that it is not only red but also round.

Locke's lengthy catalogue of erroneous ideas reveals the degree to which his empirical model of human reason depends on negating everything that fails to meet that standard. As we accumulate sensations, Locke explains, we have to abstract an essence from particular members of each species, often without knowing that such an essence is the product of our own reflection, rather than a property of the thing itself. The problem of remaining faithful to our original sense of the thing while classifying and arranging it on the "white Paper" of the mind is compounded when we reproduce that information in words for purposes of sharing it with other people. To share information garnered from our own sensations requires us "to abstract" that information so that it can embrace sensations as they are experienced by others. Language is the product of such abstraction. The "Imperfection that is naturally in Language" tends to be so bad even under the best of circumstances, Locke insists, that reasonable men must no longer tolerate the "wilful Faults and Neglect" of good communication (III.x.1). On this basis, Locke denounces subtlety, wit, figurative language, rhetorical flourishes, and all signs of originality in language. Only where we are certain that our "Ideas . . . agree to the reality of things," he contends, can we be sure we have real knowledge (II.xxx.2).

To defend such a rational model of cognition against the irrational incursions of traditional rhetoric, Locke undertakes a lengthy discussion of the abuses of language (III.x–xi). Having thus presented and defended his model, Locke must nonetheless acknowledge the validity of some ideas that come neither from the sensations of the physical senses nor from our reflection upon the internal operations of the mind (IV). How else, for instance, does one come to know God, or any abstract idea that requires such language as Locke uses when he compares the mind to a blank piece of paper or an empty storehouse? Locke concludes his grand project by opening the door to a way of knowing those things we cannot know by way of the senses, a way of knowing that meets the test of reason. "Reasoning from Analogy," he contends, "leads us often into the discovery of Truths, and useful Productions which would otherwise lie concealed" (IV.xvi.12). What he offers up is a proof of the existence of God derived by analogy to mundane acts of creation: "I judge it as certain and clear a Truth, as can any where be delivered, *That the invisible Things of God are clearly seen from the Creation of the World, being understood by the Things that are made, even his Eternal Power, and God-head*" (IV.x.7). What is this if not the Deist godhead whose presence hovers over the English Enlightenment.

To translate a Locke who is clearly antirhetorical in England into a Locke who is the father of American eloquence, one must take the highway north from London to Scotland. There, in the early decades of the eighteenth century, Francis Hutcheson demonstrated in his *Inquiry into the Original of Beauty and Virtue in Two Treatises* (1725) how Locke would later be adapted for a colonial readership. Hutcheson begins with the Lockean notion that the mind begins as white paper "void of all characters." This enables him to open the first treatise of his *Inquiry Concerning Beauty*, with the premise that all our knowledge begins as sensations that come into the mind through the physical senses: "Those ideas which are raised in the mind upon the presence of external objects and their acting upon our Bodys, are call'd *Sensations*. We find that the Mind in such cases is passive, and has not Power directly to prevent the Perception or Idea, or to vary it at its Reception."[22] Where Locke begins with our sensations of the visible world to arrive at an understanding of the invisible godhead, Hutcheson looks at our sensational responses to the visible world and arrives at another faculty of mind—or "internal sense"—distinct from rational judgment. This faculty is what allows us to understand beauty or virtue. Using the principle of analogy, Hutcheson proceeds to argue for an internal sense that receives the sensation of pleasure upon perceiving beauty in proportion and harmony. He writes, "The internal Sense is, a passive Power of Receiving Ideas of Beauty from all Objects in which there is uniformity amidst variety" (67). Where Locke worked by analogy to the visible order to explain our knowledge of the invisible Godhead, Hutcheson proceeds from sensory perception of the visible world to the pleasurable sensation of beauty. By so modifying Locke, he can fill out the analogy and posit "internal senses" that transmit sensations to the mind much as the five physical senses do.

A rational creature whose pleasant sensations were produced by the external senses alone in his estimation could not achieve happiness. Even if the external sense were joined to the internal sense of beauty, order, and harmony, we could not experience the moral pleasures of friendship, love, and beneficence. Hutcheson thus answers the question that Locke left dangling: what beside the threat of injury from other individuals disposes individuals to enter into social relations? Having established the existence of an internal sense, Hutcheson proceeds in the second of his two treatises, *Concerning Moral Good and Evil*, to push the analogy further: just as there is a sensation of pleasure in receiving beauty, so, too, there must be another internal sense that produces the sensation of pleasure we feel on perceiving a virtuous action. He makes it clear that "these moral perceptions arise in us as necessarily as any other sensations; nor can we alter or stop them."[23]

It is at this point in his treatise *Concerning Moral Good and Evil* that Hutcheson turns to the power of oration: "Upon this moral sense is founded all the power of the orator. The various Figures of Speech are the several Manners which a lively genius, warm'd with Passions suitable to the Occasion naturally runs into" (165). To resurrect rhetoric from the ignominious grave in which Locke placed it, Hutchinson rethinks Locke's argument that words are untrustworthy when they do not serve the end of accurate communication. "They only move the Hearers," he writes, "by giving a lively Representation of the Passions of the Speaker" (165). Words excite the same idea in a hearer that is in the mind of the orator, but only if the orator speaks a moral truth; the orator must produce sensations that strike the moral sense. Given that "the Passions which the Orator attempts to raise are all founded on moral qualities," Hutchinson explains, "all the bold Metaphors, or Descriptions, all the artificial Manners of Expostula-tion, Arguing, and Addressing the Audience, all the appeals to Mankind, are but more lively Methods of giving the Audience a stronger impression of the moral Qualities of the Person accus'd or defended" (165). Beginning at Harvard in 1725, Hutchinson's theory of rhetoric was widely dissemin-ated in colonial America along with his moral philosophy.[24]

John Witherspoon not only taught Hutcheson's arguments but also took issue with them, further adapting them to the colonial situation. In his lectures on eloquence and morality, which began soon after he arrived in 1768 at what is now Princeton University, Witherspoon proved himself a dyed-in-the-wool Lockean and a stronger proponent of rhetoric even than Hutcheson. Witherspoon begins his lectures on morality as Hutcheson had done, by laying down a Lockean foundation: "There are but two ways in which we come to the knowledge of things, viz. first, sensation, second, reflection."[25] Then, briefly tipping his hat to Hutcheson, Witherspoon reit-erates his predecessor's claim for an internal or finer sense that is "very different from the grosser perceptions of external sense" (161). But With-erspoon moves swiftly and incisively from there to trump Hutcheson's notion of beauty with a separate and distinct inner sense of morality.

Evidently Witherspoon was uncomfortable with Hutcheson's easy anal-ogy between beauty and virtue. We understand beauty in much the same way that we understand the external world, he reasons, while the moral sense is "what in scripture and common language we call conscience"(161). In his estimation, by "the gratification of external senses . . . we are led to desire what is pleasing and to avoid what is disgustful to them" (162). But superior by far to those mental faculties that respond to physical sensations "is a sense of moral excellence and a pleasure arising from doing what is dictated by the moral sense" (162). Why is conscience not only fundamen-tally different from, but also superior to, the aesthetic sense? Because the conscience, according to Witherspoon, issues a call to duty or obligation that requires one to act rather than simply react to stimuli.[26] Not content to rely for morality on the difference between how our external and internal faculties respond to objects in the world, Witherspoon places stress on the kind of stimulus or source of the sensation to which we respond. Is it external, as in the case of our response to beauty, or is it purely internal, as in the prick of conscience?

The creation of an internal faculty devoted exclusively to moral understanding alters the relationship between rhetoric and human reason. According to Hutcheson, to describe an object fully, one must use language that expresses both external and internal sensations received from the object. Witherspoon does not dispute that principle. What he objects to is the equality Hutcheson grants to beauty as the analogue, kindred spirit, and vehicle of morality. To set his own internal sense of morality apart from Hutcheson's notion of beauty, Witherspoon classifies the rhetoric that expresses that sense as "sublime." In place of "the lively genius" of Hutcheson's ideal orator, Witherspoon advocates a "greatness or elevation of mind" that lends speech the sublimity necessary to stimulate the moral sense (260). Where Hutcheson calls upon rhetoric to provide "a more lively method of giving the audience a stronger impression of the person accused or defended," Witherspoon requires rhetoric at once to transform reason by means of passion and to incite us to moral action or, as he puts it, "to move the passions of others so as to incline their choice or to alter their purpose" (263). Rhetoric, in this respect, enters the mind of the listener and operates on that mind exactly like the faculty of conscience.

Tied now to an internal sensation that speaks to moral obligation, "rhetoric" in no way resembles the early modern notion of the term as a form of self-fashioning.[27] As if to emphasize this difference between the concept of "rhetoric" to which Locke so objected and his own, Witherspoon uses a distinctively colonial figure for "rhetoric" that displaces the trope of copiousness that had been the traditional figure of choice for the Renaissance courtier. It is common, he explains, for uncultivated people to speak in a manner "narrow, short and simple" (251). Instead of adjectives, such peoples as the Hebrews of old and the modern Chinese tend to substitute one noun for another, thereby offering the listener an object that communicates figuratively. Indians in America are a fine demonstration of this principle, as they speak largely in metaphors.[28] In his simple fidelity to truth, the Indian provides Witherspoon with an indigenous figure for the orator who uses a "descriptive manner of speaking to paint scenes and objects strongly and set them before the eyes of the hearers" (263).

The primary purpose for American English is to put objects before the eyes of hearers, as it did in Locke's England. It is not good enough simply to hear words in order to know objects, for oratory has to paint scenes and objects in order to put them before the listener. The listener must see the object in order to understand the full truth. I am tempted to say that the difference between accurately describing objects and painting them as strongly as required for this purpose is the difference between the tradition of realism for which English literature is known and the romance tradition that famously characterizes American literature. In realism, meaning appears to reside in a world outside of language, a world in which that language is best that is most clearly mimetic. It tells you what the observer sees; thus in the hearing of words the audience knows the truth. But in Witherspoon's account, the object of mimesis has itself changed. Pried loose from its empirical grounding or referent, the scene or object can fully come into being only through a speech-act that transmits the full sensations of one speaker to another. That is to say, the object is not fully itself until it incorporates the internal sense of the orator or poet.

Although rhetoric had been taught in America since the early colonial period, John Witherspoon was, in Jay Fliegelman's words, "the first important American teacher of rhetoric."[29] Witherspoon's lectures represent something of a sea change in American education, whereby not only did the most influential teachers in America of rhetoric come from Scotland, but so did the most widely adopted texts as well. Two such textbooks, George Campbell's *The Philosophy of Rhetoric* (1776) and Hugh Blair's *Lectures on Rhetoric and Belles Lettres* (1783), were published more frequently in America than in Britain. Although books on oratory by English authors remained popular in America, textbooks on rhetoric and belles lettres by Scottish authors were even more widely used by secondary schools and colleges.[30] Upon its publication, Blair's *Lectures* was immediately adopted by Brown University, and a number of colleges up and down the Atlantic seaboard soon followed suit.[31] Although England and Scotland underwent their own sea change during the 1750s and 1760s with renewed interest in rhetorics, Americans nevertheless preferred Scottish pedagogy and rhetoric books to those of the English. The number of teachers and ministers who took part in the Scottish immigration to America from 1760 until 1775, and then following 1781, certainly helped to foster the Scottish approach to rhetoric.[32] But the surplus of teachers alone does not explain why Americans embraced Scottish pedagogy and textbooks so enthusiastically.

On the face of it, there should have been little indeed to draw Americans to the Scottish rhetoricians. After the Act of Union (1707) and the Jacobite Rebellions, according to Robert Crawford, "many influential Scots believed that common British norms—which meant, generally, Anglocentric norms—were needed if Scotland were to prosper and win English approval."[33] Crawford sees this period as producing a gap between what was perceived as Englishness and what was yet to be defined as Britishness. This gap or historical space afforded an opportunity for what he calls a "devolution" of English literature. Clifford Siskin takes the argument a step further and suggests that the practices, including Scottish rhetoric, introduced in an effort to produce what amounted to a literate individual gave shape to something that would later be called "culture."[34] As part of a program of national improvement, the Scots were invested in the study of both rhetoric and English belles lettres as the means of establishing closer cultural ties with England. By the 1740s Scottish universities were committed to improving their students' conversational skills in the prestige dialect, to advance their level of English composition, and to cultivate their taste for English literature.[35] According to Crawford, producing a generation of young professionals who qualified for full participation in the English public sphere would dispel the notion that Scotland was a backward, tribal society.[36] While Scotland was experiencing the pangs of cultural unification with England, the British colonies in America were preparing for political separation from the mother country.

It is hard to believe that Americans were especially eager to assert their equality with Englishmen in a British public sphere during the years leading up to and following the War for Independence. Yet, following the war, books on English rhetoric and belles lettres by Scottish authors were as popular as ever, and it was not until the middle of the nineteenth century that "textbooks by American authors took the place of the Scottish rhetorics."[37] This leaves me with only one plausible conclusion to draw. The Scots had designed a means by which one could acquire English culture without living in England. In doing so, they had developed a model of English identity that was completely transportable. Neither geography nor family history would determine who could carry on a conversation in the prestige dialect, write an eloquent English sentence, enjoy English literature, and display English taste. Education trumped other qualifications for participating in the public sphere. Thus a model that the Scots had developed as outsiders who wished to perform well among Englishmen appealed to Americans who wanted to establish English as the dominant language and literature of a nation that now found itself permanently estranged from England.

The American Pope

Pope provides a convenient example of how the study of rhetoric was put into practice in the colonies and the early republic. If we were to go by the sheer number of publications and reprints, the most popular poet in America during the eighteenth century was Alexander Pope; the most popular poem in America was his *An Essay on Man*. We might say that this American Pope differed from his English namesake in ways that indicate something of the way a diasporic culture takes up material from the mother culture and turns it to a different use. The English Pope was Catholic in his faith and encased in a body twisted and misshapen from tubercular bone disease. His poetry earned this man renown, wealth, as well as considerable enmity. His earliest published work appeared in Jacob Tonson's 1709 edition of *A Poetical Miscellany the sixth part* alongside pieces by Swift and other, lesser hands, and probably sold no more than a couple of hundred copies. Within five years, however, readers' demand for his revised *Rape of the Lock*, (1714) would allow that work to sell what was then a whopping 3000 copies in four days. The subscription sales to his translation of the *Iliad* (1715–20) brought Pope further social prominence, enhanced his political connections, and made him financially independent. Rather than payment by the line, his entrepreneurial genius was such that he was able to negotiate a contract permitting him to sell by subscription the first 750 copies of each volume.[38] This move changed both the basis on which an author could earn a livelihood in England and the social status of the belletristic writer. Well known as the target of pamphlet attacks that charged him with greed, immorality, venality, plagiarism, and fraud, Pope's verse epistles, essays, and mock-epic *Dunciad* proved him the more successful combatant in the early eighteenth-century war of words. This contentious chapter in British literary history is much more thoroughly documented and explained than Pope's success in the United States.

In contrast to the British Pope, his American counterpart was famous from the start. His poetry was not only imported by numerous colonial booksellers but also reprinted from Maine to South Carolina in a variety of formats. Selections of his poetry appeared in collections of "celebrated authors," served as the very example of English versification in handbooks of rhetoric, and were widely quoted and imitated in American poetry. The fact that printings of at least 160 editions of *An Essay on Man* were published between 1747 and 1850 made Pope an extremely popular poet in America, second only perhaps to Isaac Watts.[39] *An Essay on Man* was advertised for sale in a variety of venues from some of America's most famous printers and booksellers to quite ordinary dry goods stores, where one could purchase chapbooks of the poem by the dozen along with linens, beer, and breeches. During Pope's own lifetime, some American readers followed his work closely. The belletristic writer and later mayor of Boston, Mather Byles, for one, sent fawning letters to the British Pope. Sales of his work in America indicate, however, that Pope's popularity increased dramatically in America only after he had been dead for several decades, precisely when his reputation in Britain was in decline. Where today's literary scholarship concerns itself primarily with the politics, religion, and aesthetics of the British Pope, scholars working on his American counterpart worry the question of which of Pope's literary forms and poetic lines colonial authors borrowed for purposes of imitation or quotation. How, they ask, could Pope have managed to appeal to loyalists and revolutionaries, Tories and Whigs, at a time when political factions in revolutionary America could agree on little else?

To explain the extraordinary number of American editions and imitations of Pope and his circle that appeared during the last decades of the eighteenth century, Richard Bushman leans heavily on the fact that this poetry was authored by satirists who thrived on political factionalism.[40] From this he infers that American interest in such writing would have increased markedly during the years leading up to and immediately following the Revolution. Lewis Simpson contends that the Federalists found in Pope a way of expressing their fear of anarchy and desire for restraint. Simpson attributes the apparent compatibility between Federalist and Augustan sensibilities to the fact that a "sense of progressive disorder haunted those who shared the temper of the Augustan mind with its strong feeling for structure and propriety and for the humanistic community of literature."[41] Stressing the satirist's criticism of Robert Walpole's administration and demand for moral reform, William Dowling argues for equally compelling "parallels between eighteenth-century Connecticut and the England of Pope and Swift."[42] Kenneth Silverman presses for an even more literal understanding of the political continuity between England at the beginning of the eighteenth century and America at the century's end. Timothy Dwight borrowed from Pope's "Messiah" to write his "America," according to Silverman, because Dwight's vision of the future of America, in 1771, "is largely the ideal England of 1712."[43] But such commentary begs the question of why a Calvinist minister like Dwight would represent the England of 1712 as his political ideal for the America of 1771. For that matter, why do literary scholars want to see Pope's popularity in America as somehow dependent on similarities between a later colonial America and an earlier Augustan England? Common sense should tell us that the contrast between a colony in the process of achieving political independence and a restored constitutional monarchy is clearly more important.

With this in mind, I want to consider how the literary environment for Pope's popularity in America during the last decades of the eighteenth century differed from the one in which he originally wrote. From the second decade of the eighteenth century, Pope's Catholicism laid him open to charges of Jacobitism, and the fact that he maintained close ties with Henry St. John, 1st Viscount Bolingbroke, only fed political suspicions. But in marked contrast with Pope's contemporaries and successors, his American admirers and imitators proved quite capable of uncoupling his verse forms from the politics of early eighteenth-century England. John Trumbull's use of the mock epic, Joseph Stansbury's and Philip Freneau's imitation of lines from *An Essay on Man* and the *Satires*, Jonathan Odell's adaptation of the *Dunciad*, Timothy Dwight's dependence on the *Satires* and *Moral Essays*, and Joel Barlow's borrowings of Pope's rhetoric indicate that, reworked by late eighteenth-century American writers, Pope's poetry spoke across a spectrum of local political interests. Who, after all, could be farther apart politically than staunch Loyalists like Stansbury and Odell and such passionate revolutionaries as Dwight, Freneau, and Trumbull?

A study of advertisements and prefatory material for various American editions of *An Essay on Man* reveals that most of the 120 printings from 1780 to 1820 filled one of three purposes, not one of which was overtly political. First, *An Essay on Man* was to be used, in the words of various advertisements, as a book that would impart concise moral truths to children.[44] Second, *An Essay on Man* appears to have been widely used in America as a textbook for teaching grammar and rhetoric. Accordingly, the title page of another edition reads: "*An Essay on Man* . . . by Alexander Pope. With Notes Illustrative of the Grammatical Construction. Designed as a Textbook for parsing."[45] Finally, Pope's poetry was considered particularly useful for purposes of teaching oratory. Along with selections from Shakespeare, Milton, Watts, and Young, among others, Pope's couplets show how, in the words of Ebenezer Porter's *Rhetorical Reader*, "a discriminating stress on a single word, determines the manner in which" a sing-song delivery can be avoided.[46] Nor can we ignore the many mentions of Pope in the various rhetoric books by Hugh Blair and Lord Kames printed in America both in unabridged as well as in highly redacted forms. The importance Pope assumes in these rhetoric books is especially noteworthy since Lord Kames's *Elements of Criticism* went through ten editions in America from 1796–1835 and Blair's *Lectures on Rhetoric* went through fifty-six editions from 1784–1823.[47] At least one American edition repeats Blair's declaration that "the ethical epistles of Pope are a model; and in them he shows the strength of his genius."[48]

In his essay on "Subjection and Subjectivation," Étienne Balibar explains why the discipline of poetry, and specifically a verse form that required a highly regulated meter, rhyme scheme, and internal logic, might be important to poets writing during and after the American Revolution.[49] For most of the eighteenth century, Balibar observes, political theory—especially contractual theories of government—tend to emphasize the expression of free subjectivity over and against the individual's subjection to the state. The literature of the period is generally on the side of this emergent notion of the subject, I would argue, especially literature so apparently rule-bound as neoclassical poetry. Although Pope's poetry invariably asserts the dominion of reason and hierarchy over the demands of an enthusiastic imagination and incipient democracy, we know that he was strikingly entrepreneurial in marketing that poetry and aggressively individualistic in asserting his unique qualifications as a critic of eighteenth-century life and letters. Though a Tory poet, he was shaped by, and helped to shape, the larger ideological imperatives of his time. The British Pope whiggishly insisted on his authority as an erudite and eloquent individual.

Balibar identifies the period of revolution in America and France with a shift in the relation between the two meanings of the term "subject": one's assertion of free subjectivity, on the one hand, and one's subjection to the state on the other. Generally speaking, Enlightenment culture is known for privileging the rights and expression of free subjectivity over and against the limits that monarchy placed on "the citizen." During the age of revolution, however, unleashed individualism no longer provided an imaginary solution to the problem of an oppressively hierarchical state. On the contrary, authors had to figure out how to harness imaginatively the energy of individualism for the greater good. In the new cultural environment, subjection provided the precondition—even the guarantee—of free subjectivity, or self-government rather than that imposed by the state. As Balibar explains, it was only "because they had abolished the principle of their subjection" that the men of 1776 and 1789 could imagine themselves as free subjects (11). Several cultural consequences ensue from a definition of freedom that depends on overcoming subjection. Individuality has to be understood neither as a given nor an essence but as something to be achieved through self-emancipation. From this it follows that freedom is not a state of being so much as something one does—namely, the performance or practice of freedom. In a culture that places a premium on literacy, individualism is something one acquires in relation to constraints imposed on speech by writing. To make a standard verse form into a form of self-expression, for example one could learn to perform writing in spoken English. By drawing on Pope and other neoclassical writers, rhetoric and grammar books provided late eighteenth-century Americans with the formal constraints necessary to carry out precisely this theory of verbal self-expression.

Imitating Augustan verse forms similarly allowed some of the best-known American poets of the time to stay within the British tradition of letters and yet define themselves as writing for an American readership. In 1803, the patriot poet David Humphreys claimed, "in the British dominions and the United States, every poet who aspires to celebrity, strives to approach the perfection of Pope in the sweetness of his versification."[50] It is perhaps this use of Pope that prompts Lawrence Buell's contention that "their appropriation of Pope in the service of a secularized Calvinism does not imply that New England writers of the early national period turned to Neo-classical modes exclusively, or even chiefly, for expressing their Puritan heritage." Quite the contrary, he continues, "Neo-classical style seems to have implied a freedom from such constraints."[51] Paul Giles makes a similar point when he insists, "By subverting Puritan eschatologies, Pope instituted an American poetic tradition of comic, carnivalesque scatology."[52] If, as Giles and Buell suggest, Americans equated Great Britain with subjection, under what conditions might American writers understand themselves as escaping the constraints of a Puritan tradition by imitating the British Pope? I would suggest, following Balibar, that these writers used the discipline provided by Pope's heroic couplet to make the tradition of British letters speak with a distinctively American voice. To this end, American poets of the late eighteenth century represent their poetry as British verse forms plus something more.

An example from Philip Freneau's well-known imitation of *The Dunciad*, "The Midnight Consultations or a Trip to Boston" provides a convenient illustration of my point. Writing of the Royal Governor of Massachusetts and Commander in Chief, General Gage, Freneau uses the heroic couplet to set up the target of satiric attack. The first line of the couplet gives Gage the chair of state with its symbolism marked by aristocratic crimson, and the second line deflates the honor of occupying that position to a substance of physical weight:

> First, Gage we saw—a crimson chair of state
> Receive'd the honour of his Honour's weight

In the next couplet, Freneau reduces the royal deputy to a mere scarecrow and elaborates his character in the same figural terms as Pope's dunces:

> This man of straw the regal purple bound,
> But dullness, deepest dullness, hover'd round.[53]

Here, as in the preceding couplet, Freneau uses the first line of the second couplet to set up a political mission—Gage wears the governor's sash—only to show in the second that the British general is simply too stupid to perform the functions of government. Freneau proceeds in this way to cast Gage down to the level of Pope's most dull-witted dunces.

Freneau repeats this tactic in the next stanza to establish the reason for Burgoyne's eventual defeat:

> Hard by, Burgoyne assumes an ample space,
> And seem'd to meditate with studious face,
> As if again he wishe'd our world to see
> Long, dull, dry letters writ to General Lee—
> Huge scrawls of words through endless circuits drawn,
> Unmeaning, as the errand he's upon.—
> Is he to conquer—he subdue our land?—
> This buckram hero, with his lady's hand?
> By Caesars to be vanquishe'd is a curse,
> But by a scribbling fop—by heaven, is worse! (81–90)

The march of iambic pentameter couplets slowly but surely transforms the idea that such a man is incapable of governing a rebellious colony into the idea that the British themselves are unable to make meaningful statements in writing. Although this "buckram hero, with his lady's hand" refers as much to the style of British governing as to their style of writing, Freneau is ultimately more interested in the fact that Burgoyne can no more use the English language to govern meaning than he can use his military might to control the colonies. By his own subjection to Pope's verse form, Freneau asserts masculine mastery over the circuitous scrawling of his British counterparts, mocks Burgoyne's well-known efforts at playwriting, and lays claim to a distinctively American voice.[54]

3

THE SENTIMENTAL LIBERTINE

T HE SENTIMENTAL tradition is central to American letters. For reasons that should become clear in this chapter, American writers chose, and perhaps still choose, to write either within that tradition or against it. Even when they wrote against it, such writers had to draw on the plots, characters, and language associated with the sentimental tradition in order to take issue with it. Literary criticism has attributed this appeal not only to sentimentalism's overt political import but also to its ability to divert attention from the public sphere. Critics have both celebrated sentimental literature for demonstrating democratic virtues by creating fellow feeling among its readers and chastized it for debasing democracy by appealing to the lowest common denominator of the readership. It is deemed central in figuring the family as a model for the nation and criticized for titillating the reader with violations of family relations.[1] Indeed, in sifting through the major criticism on sentimental literature, I can find only one point on which most critics agree; namely, that our sentimental literature not only originated in England but also took root in the North American colonies and assumed a shape that changed the British tradition. In this chapter, I will argue that much of what makes sentimentalism at once so central and so difficult to pin down politically derives from the fact that it was reshaped to accommodate what I am calling the "British diaspora."

It is with the notion of diaspora in mind that I will attend to what certain authors did to British materials to make them address specifically American concerns. Samuel Richardson's heroines offer an excellent example. The British author sought to make—and to a large extent succeeded—them desirable, when he gave Pamela and Clarissa a form of interiority whose verbal prowess challenged the libertine's powers of sexual enticement and intellectual mastery. By intercepting her letters and reading her nuanced accounts of the moral dilemmas in which he placed her, Mr. B comes to feel for Pamela much as Lovelace does for Clarissa. Unlike Lovelace, Mr. B renounces his libertinage after a protracted struggle that pits his seductive powers of wealth and position against the authority of her words and the force of tender emotion. Through this struggle, Pamela emerges as the embodiment of a new class ethos that measures an individual on the basis of the ability to express in words the emotions necessary to preserve her purity, thus her eligibility for marriage.[2] To understand how the American version of these sentimental heroines differed from their European prototype, let me begin by observing that the versions of *Pamela* and *Clarissa* printed in the United States in the 1790s were significantly shorter than those printed in Britain.

With the reduction in the number of pages to about one-tenth the length of the British text went the whole activity of writing, intercepting, and reading of letters that comprises the action of these novels. Stripped of their literariness, the American editions induce us to admire neither Pamela's literacy, nor Clarissa's fine sense of social decorum, nor either heroine's exquisite awareness of sexual propriety. With its epistolary dimension gone, the novel leaves us with the impolitic truth that impermissible desire is perfectly natural in a male so long as it is aimed at a woman he can eventually marry. Resembling the redactions of Richardson's novels in this respect, the overwhelming majority of the seduction stories appearing in American magazines during the 1790s tell us little about the heroine's unique interiority or why she, above all others, has become the object of libertine desire. Absolutely nothing seems to distinguish her from any other woman. But the minute we take this difference with the British text to heart as central to the American appeal of these stories, the lack of a literary interiority that characterizes the American heroine affords a clear sense of sentimentalism's appeal in the new United States. With the focus no longer on the exchange of letters and who reads what or by what means, we have to assume that the bare-bones plots dealing only with the vicissitudes of the heroine's body spoke specifically to the interests of an American readership. Let me suggest how.

The British diaspora in America was made up of a large number of partial families, transplanted second sons, as well as a disproportionately large ratio of single men to unmarried women who immigrated to America under a variety of contracts and conditions.[3] As a result, during and immediately following the very substantial emigrations from Britain from the 1750s to the 1770s, and again after 1781, there was a sizable population of fractured and makeshift families. To this should be added the many families who arrived in America intact only to be broken apart by disease, war, or economic deprivations. Nor can we ignore the great number of Africans brought to America as slaves and prohibited from forming families. In this environment, it is hardly surprising that readers of the late colonial period and early republic embraced fiction that dealt with the problem of broken families. Seduction narratives offered the perfect means to convert European sentimentalism into narratives that set up and resolved precisely this problem.

To understand the appeal of American sentimentalism, we must consider why, as Cathy Davidson has noted, the plots and subplots of most sentimental fiction in America—more than half of the novels of the early national period alone—were stories of seduction.[4] The same readers who embraced boiled-down versions of Richardson's novels were drawn to such homegrown seduction narratives as *The Power of Sympathy*, *Amelia*, and *The Coquette*. *Charlotte Temple*, a British transplant, garnered tepid praise when first published in England only to become a best-seller when reprinted in the United States. Such was the American demand for seduction narratives that even the distinguished monthlies of the period printed serial installments of novels and innumerable short stories dealing with seduction.[5] One cannot overstate the redundancy of these narratives. Whether British or American in origin, artful or banal, this fiction invariably featured the same array of cruel libertines, foolish coquettes, heartbroken parents, ruined women, stillborn babies, and destinies misshapen by desire. Indeed, the fact that seduction is such an oft-repeated story with only minor variations seems to be precisely the point. To explain this virtually limitless tolerance for repetition, I will first look briefly at the seduction stories that appeared in popular magazines published during the early republic. These stories set out to play on the readership's interest in sex, but that, I believe, was only an enticement, not the chief source of their extraordinary appeal. That appeal is owing to the machinations of the libertine, I will argue, as he disrupts the exchange of women that maintained the integrity of large landholdings and preserved patrilineage.

On this basis, the libertine might have been considered subversive, were it not for the fact that these stories associate the destruction of the patriarch with the wrong kind of emotion. Indeed, a longing for a reconstructed family with a father at its head characterizes American sentimentalism to this day.[6] No single story adequately explained where, on the one hand, the rules for exchanging women could be safely bent or even broken and where, on the other hand, they had to be obeyed lest the entire system of exchange between men come to an end. Nor did any single seduction story provide adequate compensation for the feeling of loss that attends the rupture of the family line. The characteristic lack of such a resolution tells us that the point is to leave the reader with a keen sense of loss and the desire to see the family remade. Seduction stories thus offered both British and American readerships experiments in imagining who could in fact marry whom. At stake in these experiments was the basis of civil society—the rules for exchanging women—that constituted kinship relations between men. It only makes sense that the longing for such a community should be especially strong in the diaspora, which is arguably held together by precisely such longing.

In England, the disintegration of the family provided grounds for imagining an expanded elite along the lines that Locke spelled out in his *Second Treatise of Government*. Thus *Clarissa* made the reader feel poignantly the absence of the kind of man who valued the heroine for her qualities of mind and emotion rather than the property she brought with her to the marriage market. The two male characters who do value her in sentimental terms—Belford and her cousin, Colonel Morden—are powerless to protect her and in this respect give the reader a clear sense of what to yearn for. Locke argued that such an affiliation of paternal men was preferred to the alternative of a patriarchal society, where power and property descended according to the principle of primogeniture.

American seduction stories suggest that what is needed is the person who can perform as the good father, no blood relationship required. The difference may appear slight, but as early as 1680 Locke well understood it when he wrote *The Second Treatise of Government*. His chapter entitled "Of Paternal Authority" specifies that if the head of an English household does not raise his son to be a citizen like his father, that parent forfeits his right as a parent, and some substitute should be sought. This is the same logic of an expanding ruling class that prompts Richardson to plant the suggestion that Colonel Morden under other circumstances could take the place of Clarissa's father. It is significant that when Locke comes to imagine what form of paternal power will work as a substitute, he thinks of British North America: "in those parts of America, . . . when the Husband and Wife part, which happens frequently, the Children are all left to the Mother, follow her, and are wholly under her Care and Provision."[7] Here, Locke imaginatively abandons lineage and argues that to the person who fills the role of father by nourishing and educating children should go the authority of the father over both them and their property. Sentimental fiction written in the United States used the seduction story not only to produce intense feeling for the family—the conviction that the individual was vulnerable without one—but also to direct that feeling at a new kind of family.

Seduce and Reform

We can see the American family emerge in and through the small differences among the body of seduction narratives published during the early republic. Between 1789 and 1796, the *Massachusetts Magazine* alone published well over one hundred stories, letters, and poems dealing with seduction. The formal variations are as few and predictable as the stories are diverse in topical material and uneven in literary quality. I want to consider briefly a pair of seduction stories that appeared in two successive issues of the *Massachusetts Magazine*, each of which leads us to expect that virtue will triumph over the lustful machinations of the libertine only to disappoint those expectations. In "Lothario: or, the Accomplished Villain," a libertine entices his victim to flee her father's home for London. For attempting to rescue her, the heroine's father is put to death with a handkerchief that his daughter's seducer has infected with smallpox.[8] The heroine and her mother soon follow the father to the grave, her brothers are thrown into jail, and "in less than six months the whole family were no more" (445). In stories written in the United States, the daughter's seduction often brings ruin to her entire family.

In the other stories imported from England, however, the daughter's seduction does not invite such dire consequences. While such stories were relatively rare in England, they loom large in American magazines, indicating an American appetite for this variant. In the very popular "Innocent Simplicity Betrayed," published in the same magazine the month after "Lothario" appeared and subsequently reprinted by two other American magazines, the virtuous daughter of Venoni flees her father's home in Italy for England with Sir Edward, who is cast in the role of the libertine.[9] Like the father of "Lothario," Venoni pursues his daughter to London, where he supports himself as a street musician. In failing health, the heroine hears his melodies, summons him to her rooms, and reunites with her father. Caught in the act, her seducer not only asks the father for the hand of the woman betrayed, but also follows through on the marriage, which miraculously mends her health and brings prosperity to an entire valley of Italian farms and villages. In contrast to what might be considered the prototype of this kind of narrative, Richardson's *Clarissa*, these heroines display little of the sensibility that might challenge a libertine's desire for mastery and provoke a reader's admiration. The daughter of Venoni may appreciate music and dislike the idea of an arranged marriage to the churlish man her father originally selected for her, but the story does not explain why she should be rewarded for succumbing to her desires; the same act on the part of the heroine in "Lothario" and indeed in many other stories would have spelled the ruin of her entire family. That the girl who runs off with the libertine may bring prosperity rather than misery to herself and her family indicates that something beside her lack of sexual restraint determines the outcome of this kind of narrative.

Some stories in both categories suggest that a girl's lack of education made her vulnerable to the libertine's wiles. In these, the daughter of a tenant farmer or a girl of simple tastes fails to understand the ways of the world.[10] But those who might rush to the conclusion that literacy emerges as a virtue in and of itself, as it does in the English tradition, must confront the fact that for all the stories in which the lack of a proper education delivers the heroine over to a libertine, there are a nearly equal number in which an education provides no protection from seduction at all.[11] Since there is in fact no rule of sexual conduct in one story that is not overturned by that of another, I want to turn our attention to what—if neither her virtue nor her education—is the basis of the appeal that draws the libertine to his victim.

American seduction stories are not as concerned as their British counterparts to stage class conflict as a battle of the sexes, a battle that appears to vanish with each successful marriage. Novels by Richardson or Austen suggest that whether or not a woman might achieve for her family the benefits usually reserved for those of lineage, property, and rank depends entirely on her self-control, but American seduction stories do not share this preoccupation. These stories are primarily concerned with how a man acquires a woman, from whom, and under what conditions, far more than they care about how a woman captures the heart and estate of a well-born man. Women in these American stories are the unvarnished medium for carrying on a relationship among men. A review of the stories reprinted from British sources and selected for republication in American magazines suggests that they were chosen precisely because they do not feature a feisty heroine in the Richardsonian mold but instead focus on the kinds of deals fathers might cut with their daughters' seducers. One such story, "The Duellist and the Libertine Reclaimed," has a libertine seduce the daughter of a man who is not his equal economically but just someone "whose fortune raised him above dependence."[12] The heroine's brother, a soldier, challenges the libertine only to have the duel quashed by a wise old officer, whose speech inspires the would-be duelists to break into tears and embrace. As if in recognition of their common manhood, the libertine asks the father for the hand of his daughter. Another story finds the libertine simply overcome by "shame and remorse" when caught in bed with his tenant's daughter.[13] He, too, promptly asks the girl's father for the hand of the daughter and proceeds to marry the woman in an act that flies in the face of the rules of kinship governed by blood and rank. That these British stories were printed and reprinted in America in the late 1780s and 1790s alongside those homegrown seduction stories in which the daughter's ruin spelled that of her family tells me that together the two kinds of narrative identify precisely what was at stake in refiguring the libertine in America.

I would like to consider what single statement the two narratives make as they combine in William Hill Brown's *The Power of Sympathy*, one of the first novels to be both written and published in America.[14] One can describe this novel as a seduction story with two interpolated tales of seduction, all three plots of which combine to dramatize how the machinery of libertinage transformed kinship relations. The main plot of Brown's novel features a confessed libertine, young Harrington, as he sets about to seduce the orphaned heroine, Harriot. The fact that she lacks a father means that Harriot has no one to give her in marriage, which in turn denies Harrington someone with whom to make the exchange. Under the prevailing system of British marriage rules, only the father or his surrogate can give the woman away. "I suppose you will be ready to ask, why, if I love *Harriot*, I do not marry her," her would-be seducer asks of his confidant, "But *who* shall I marry? That is the question. *Harriot* has no father—no mother—neither is there aunt, cousin, or kindred of any degree who claim any kind of relationship to her." Harrington goes on to answer his own question: "I am not so much of a republican as formally to wed any person of this class."[15] Had Harrington's son carried out the seduction, the novel might have turned out to be more like a Richardsonian novel focusing on the private thoughts of the libertine and an unfortunate woman. But this early American novel ultimately refuses to resolve the conflict between men of different ranks by translating that conflict into one between seducer and his steadfastly virtuous victim. Young Harrington decides to forgo seducing the woman and proposes marriage instead, only to have his father prohibit the union. He does so on grounds that Harriot happens to be the illicit daughter of a woman whom the elder Harrington had seduced many years earlier. Thus her father is perhaps the only man with whom the younger Harrington cannot enter into the kind of exchange that would expand the kin group, because that man is none other than his own father as well. Young Harrington's father cannot make a deal with himself. Having set up rank, property, and lineage as the basis for establishing kinship relations, the tale proceeds to reject each.

Two interpolated seduction stories reinforce in revealing ways the cultural logic of the main Harrington plot. As self-contained stories nestled within *The Power of Sympathy*, they tell readers how to read the novel in relation to the short stories they encountered in the popular magazines of the period. In a story whose incest plot echoes the main narrative, a seduced Ophelia delivers a child whom the narrator describes as "a child, at once the son and nephew of *Martin*" (38). This plot condemns that act of incest, not because incest is a crime in and of itself, but because it constitutes "a severe mortification to the proud spirit of *Shepherd*, the father of *Ophelia*" (38). So, too, in the case of the second interpolated tale the heroine's father is the real victim of her seduction. With his daughter seduced and her betrothed having committed suicide, thereby causing the woman herself to go mad, her father declares, "Is not [the libertine] cause of my woe, a melancholy instance of the baleful art of the SEDUCER? ... *They have taken away my staff in my old age*" (52). By giving the father this opportunity to lament his own emasculation, Brown makes the point that seduction is first and foremost a disruption of relations of exchange between men. Though the senior Harrington is himself a libertine, the inference is that Brown's readers would have considered him the major victim of libertinage. His son's suicide upon discovering his blood ties to Harriot spells the doom of the Harrington name.

Despite the extinction of the male line, however, *The Power of Sympathy* eventually reconstitutes the Harrington family through the daughter's marriage to her brother's confidant and counselor. In sharp contrast to the three seduction tales comprising the body of the novel, Worthy conducts his courtship of Myra through letters. While obviously a man with considerable leisure time on his hands, his taste in literature distinguishes Worthy from the other men in the story. This taste manifests itself in a capacity to feel. It also allows him to recognize in Myra's fine embroidery the taste of a woman who is his feminine counterpart. As he explains in a letter to her, "Removed as I am, from the amiable object of my tenderest affection, I have nothing to do but to admire this offspring of industry and art" (31). It is in and through their mutual taste as conveyed through their exchange of letters that a new and more worthy family subsumes and transforms an earlier basis for family relations. Indeed, the reader is offered the exchange of letters between Worthy and Myra as something on the order of a written contract that puts an end to the repetition of seduction that all but wiped out the Harrington line. This resolution seems to indicate that the unregulated desire of the libertine poses a threat to patrilineage in the new United States.

But if this is so, why do we encounter crueler and more abusive libertines as well as reformed and more penitent libertines in the fiction of the period than perhaps any other character type? Given that seduction stories were not only printed in magazines of the early republic but embedded in the novels of that period as well, it does not require a great leap of imagination to understand how seduction stories worked to displace a British ideal of the family.[16] In serving this purpose, the libertine underwent important changes as well.

Let us next consider what happened to this stock figure as British seduction stories were combined with American-authored stories published side by side in such popular magazines as the *Massachusetts Review,* the *Philadelphia Minerva,* the *New York Magazine or Literary Repository,* and the *Columbian Magazine* and incorporated as well into the novels of the early republic.[17] Where Richardson situated Mr. B and Lovelace within a finely calibrated social and economic grid, the origins of the American libertines are characteristically obscured. We know exactly where Mr. B's money comes from, and we meet his sister who has married well in terms of rank. By contrast, the American libertine tends to be a man of some breeding who comes from a family of some property. In the manner characteristic of a second son, he is sometimes forced to take a commission in the army. Most often he has leisure time in which to pursue his sexual inclinations, but his lack of income invariably prevents him from translating those inclinations into marriage. Major Sanford in *The Coquette* sums up the situation nicely. Although he has taken a fancy to Eliza, he is "much courted and caressed" by Mr. Lawrence, "a man of large property," who, Sanford reports, "intend[s] to shackle me in the bonds of matrimony."[18] Does this not sound as if Sanford were in danger of being trapped into marriage with Lawrence? The fact that the woman in the scenario is less than interesting only reinforces the distinct impression that marriage is primarily a relationship between men. Sanford admits that while his bride has "no soul," those concerns are overridden by the fact that she is "heiress . . . to a great fortune; and that is all the soul I wish for in a wife" (131). Once his economic needs have been met by a well-made marriage, Sanford is free to pursue his sexual desires elsewhere.

In contrast with British domestic fiction, American seduction stories condemn neither the seducer nor the woman seduced so much as the underlying cause of seduction, which it attributes to the disparity between desire and economic necessity. The American libertine finds himself trapped by the prevailing system of exchange, which neither provides a solid economic foundation for a family nor gratifies his sexual desire.[19] Charlotte Temple, Maria Fawcett, Amelia, even the notorious Coquette, Eliza, are all worthy objects of that desire. Indeed, the object of libertine desire is generally virtuous (the coquette being the exception that proves the rule), and she arouses something like natural desire in him. But marrying any one of these women would fail to bring the money he needs to maintain a gentry way of life. Richardson's Mr. B, by way of contrast, has already come into his inheritance before he attempts to seduce his servant, Pamela. It is as if American fiction incorporates the libertine in order to have him act on natural desires forbidden by an older system for exchanging women.

What end does such behavior serve? The omnipresence of the libertine as the embodiment of masculinity creates a situation hostile to an earlier system of arranged marriages implicitly, if not explicitly, attributed to the British. In *The Power of Sympathy*, the destruction of the Harrington line on account of libertine practices represents the withering away of the socioeconomic features binding the libertine to an earlier set of marriage rules that in turn bind property to blood. If we consider the prototypical British seduction story from this perspective, we are sure to notice that Richardson's Mr. B was made to feel shame, suffer remorse, and undergo a moral transformation as a result of reading Pamela's letters. In *Clarissa*, the rake is broken in two. Lovelace must die for his unrepentant libertinage, but his companion and confidant, Belford, suffers remorse and undergoes a transformation comparable to Mr. B's. While Worthy is a man of no clear rank, his sexual behavior distinguishes him from both of the Harrington men, for he observes only the rules of taste and sensibility—the rules governing the novel itself—in selecting a marriage partner. Through their written intercourse, Worthy emerges as the man of sensibility who will care for Myra. Such a quality of the heart has become the basis for marriage—neither bloodline nor property, but his capacity to care. The object of his desire undergoes a corresponding transformation that makes her his feminine counterpart, a writing subject, whose embroidery proves her capable of turning money into her own brand of domestic elegance. To put it as reductively as possible, their exchange of letters not only constitutes the marriage contract, but also constitutes the pair, male and female, as individuals capable of entering into such a contract of their own volition.

The Libertine Difference

Clearly the sheer number of late eighteenth-century stories, novels, and moral essays featuring the libertine begs the question of what kind of cultural work such a figure accomplished. At the very least, if the seduction narrative is part and parcel of a tradition of sentimental fiction in America, then the assumption that such fiction appealed primarily to women seems off the mark: as I have tried to suggest, the omnipresence of the libertine has chiefly to do with altering relations between men. We know that his presence almost guarantees that the story will challenge prevailing norms of class privilege that put some men at a distinct disadvantage in relation to others when it came to founding and perpetuating a household, but why did this challenge have such appeal in America in the 1790s? We need to consider what it was about the libertine that resonated with the American readership?

Some elements of the figure clearly engage the foundational myths of the new United States. To begin with, the libertine was associated with antitheological, critical, even speculative thinking. In the French tradition, the libertine was often an instructor and not necessarily only an instructor of erotic pleasure.[20] Because he was considered free from ordinary moral constraints, his habit of mind and his distinctive practices set him in opposition to established belief, and in the Sadean tradition, he performed as a parodic inversion of religion. But the kind of cultural authority arising out of wit and parody was not the material out of which good husbands are made.[21] More appealing to an American readership was the English meaning of the "libertine," which Johnson's *Dictionary* specified as "One unconfined, one at liberty."[22] Surely an individual who rejects moral orthodoxy, someone of a speculative disposition, a person with antireligious beliefs, one who appeared to be "at liberty," must have held special meaning for a class of people for whom religious freedom was the exalted rationale for the economic motives propelling emigration. The only difference between the American and European libertine was that rather than seek religious freedom in America, the libertine sought freedom from religion there. If a man's most important moral gesture were his choice of, and fidelity to, a recognized set of religious practices, the libertine was the very antithesis of such an embodiment of morals because he was obedient to none. Indeed, the libertines that populate the seduction stories of the 1790s cannot be considered moral in even the loosest sense. They bring with them the cultural baggage of immoral practices from European fiction. Through their machinations—detached from any moral purpose—an American family came to be defined as separate and apart from the family organized around British models of household and kinship. If there is a moral to the story of seduction featuring the elder Harrington in *The Power of Sympathy*, then it is that the older, more traditional British notion of kinship as defined by established rank is far too limited for the new United States.

In American culture more so than British, class affiliation was based on literacy, diversity of views religious and political, and more expansive— that is to say, more exogamous—marriage practices. Gordon Wood summarizes the situation in these terms: "If England had thirty different religions, then America had hundreds," and few were "traditionally organized." While it was theologically varied and sophisticated, Wood contends, "American society remained remarkably shallow and stunted by contemporary English standards."[23] My take on this paradox is that the fine gradations of social stratification that English marriage practices maintained were not and could not be guiding marriage choices in America. Why, if not because men refuse to adhere to rank in the new United States, does the male Harrington line die out and the female line prevail? Moreover, Worthy is no less worthy a member of the gentry because he does not seek Harrington senior's approval to marry Myra. We can extend this alternative to those stories in which the libertine is overcome with remorse and allowed to marry the object of his desire. Once married, these couples are just as important as anyone else. To show how the seduction story favored by American readers broke up the family only to bring disparate people together in a new contractual relationship, let me turn to what I call the "American Richardson."

The American Richardson

While William Bradford advertised an edition of *Pamela* in New York, September 1742, Benjamin Franklin is credited with printing the first American edition of Richardson's novel in 1742–43 and the following year was advertising his own edition. Advertisements for the novel appeared in Boston and New York as well as Philadelphia. Despite this demonstrable inter-

est in Richardson's novel, 1744 was also the year in which the printing of
Richardson's texts all but ceased in British America. The sheer number of
sheets that were required for an edition of the full text probably made the
cost of its publication too risky a venture; given that for those booksellers
who could afford them, copies were readily available from British booksellers as were pirated Irish editions, there was probably not sufficient demand
for full editions. That demand diminished in the decades before the Revolution makes it all the more puzzling that the novel became so popular
immediately after. The fact remains that after a forty-year period, editions
of novels printed in America whose author was identified as Samuel Richardson suddenly appeared in the United States.

The dates and titles of these editions speak for themselves.[24] In 1789,
Pamela, Clarissa, and *Sir Charles Grandison* were announced for sale in
Philadelphia, and two years later an edition of the *Clarissa* published under
the title *The Paths of Virtue Delineated; or the History . . . of the Celebrated
Clarissa Harlowe.* In 1792, *Pamela* appeared in Philadelphia. In 1793,
the same novel was published in Boston and the following year in both
Worcester and Philadelphia. An edition of *Clarissa* appeared in Boston in
1795, and that same year *The Paths of Virtue Delineated or . . . Clarissa*
was reprinted and offered for sale in Cooperstown, New York. In 1796,
Clarissa was published in Cooperstown, and *Pamela* appeared in print,
once in Lansingburgh, New York, and twice in New York City. In 1797,
Pamela was again published in Boston, and the following year saw printings
of *Clarissa* in Suffield, Connecticut, and Philadelphia, while *Pamela* was
printed four times in New York City. In 1799, *Pamela* came out in Fairha-
ven, Vermont, and Norristown, Pennsylvania, and *Clarissa* was published
in New Haven. Publications of both novels became somewhat more spo-
radic as the nineteenth century got underway, but evidence of a Richardson
boom is indisputable: in the last decade of the eighteenth century, after a
long hiatus, American printers found it profitable to produce American
editions of Richardson's novels in unprecedented numbers for an American readership.

To begin to distinguish Richardson's post–Revolutionary War popularity
from the more modest success enjoyed by his fiction in pre–Revolutionary
War British America, we must add another and perhaps more startling set
of facts to these publication data. When *Pamela* was first published in London in 1740 and then several years later in North America by Franklin, the
novel ran to about 250,000 words, and when *Clarissa* was first published
in London in 1747–48, it ran to well over 1,000,000 words. These versions
continued to be published in England throughout the eighteenth and well
into the nineteenth century. In striking contrast, the *Pamela* that appeared
in Philadelphia in 1792 totaled only about 27,000 words in length, and the
Clarissa that appeared in 1795 ran to somewhere around just 41,000 words,

or about the same length as Susannah Rowson's *Charlotte Temple.* Further-more, every edition of Richardson published in the United States from the late 1780s through the first two decades of the nineteenth century observed pretty much the same model of abridgment.

This model was based on an edition that appeared in London in 1756, reprinted in 1764, and entitled, *The Paths of Virtue Delineated; or the History in Miniature of the Celebrated Pamela, Clarissa Harlowe, and Sir Charles Grandison, familiarised and adapted to the Capacities of Youth.*[25] For obvious reasons, the phrase "youth" should not be taken to mean that these editions, with their accounts of seduction and rape, were necessarily intended for young children.[26] From the publication data, two conclusions may be drawn: the late 1780s and 1790s saw a sudden and intense explosion of the shorter Richardson into print, and the enormous popularity of the abridged Richardson was an American phenomenon. Although both the long and short versions were readily available on both sides of the Atlantic, eighteenth-century English readers much preferred their Richardson un-abridged. The English market not only consumed the many printings and editions of the unabridged Richardson that issued from the London presses, but snapped up the cheaper Irish editions as well.[27] A glance at the colonial book market further testifies to a widening gap in reading tastes. The unabridged, or English, Richardson continued to be available as an imported commodity to American readers throughout the forty-year period when it was out of print in the colonies. Indeed, following the Treaty of Paris (1783), an abundance of inexpensive Irish editions of British books were exported to America, and unabridged editions of Richardson were comparatively cheap. The abridged editions of Richardson nevertheless remained hands-down favorites among American readers.[28]

Nor, as the next section of this chapter will demonstrate at some length, were the editions of *Clarissa* and *Pamela* preferred by American readers simply truncated versions of the originals. The principle of abridgment used in these editions differs significantly from that guiding the more familiar chapbooks, which generally ran from around sixteen pages for something like *Robinson Crusoe* to about twenty-nine pages for an edition of *Tom Jones,* while the Richardson editions were invariably three to five times that length.[29] Americans expressed a similar inclination for an abridged edition of *Robinson Crusoe* that went through 125 printings from 1774–1825, ran to 138 pages, and diverged as much in narrative form from its chapbook counterpart as it did from the English original.[30] This publication data should prompt us to consider what the two different versions of Richardson can tell us about English and Anglo-American culture, respectively.

The case of Susannah Rowson's *Charlotte Temple* affords an instructive parallel. The literary critical tradition has long regarded *Charlotte Temple* as an inferior version of an English novel, on the grounds that it is a bad version of an English novel in the sentimental mode of Richardson.[31] And to be sure, *Charlotte Temple* is not very long, its characters are sketchily drawn, and the plot is everything. The book, in short, has all the marks of formula fiction. When published in England in 1791, *Charlotte Temple* met with only moderate success, but when it appeared in the United States some three years later this same novel turned out to be one of the nation's first best-sellers. Given the preference on the part of an American reader-ship for the short, plot-bound Richardson over the more literary English versions of *Pamela* and *Clarissa*, *Charlotte Temple* might well represent a significant improvement on the English Richardson, when measured against the generic expectations of a colonial readership. The fact that read-ers under British rule preferred the English Richardson over the abridg-ment indicates, moreover, that sentimental fiction was probably popular in America during the eighteenth century for many of the same reasons it was in vogue back in England, where fiction succeeded in modernizing the kinship rules observed by members of the literate classes without putting their Englishness in jeopardy. After the Revolution, however, narratives of courtship and marriage would have to adapt those same rules for a reader-ship that was no longer English in political terms, one that therefore had good reason to be anxious about its national identity in every other respect.

Clarissa's Americanness

Having proposed this ideological divergence between the English and American versions of Richardson, let me now consider the formal differ-ences between the two narratives to see if they can tell us how the American Richardson addressed American interests. Since Ian Watt's definitive study, criticism of the English novel tends to assume that Richardson either initi-ated or helped to establish the predominant form of the English novel.[32] Whether one claims, as Watt did, that a certain kind of realism rose to dominance because it addressed the interests of a middle class on the rise or whether one argues, alternatively, that domestic romance helped to bring that class into being, the fact remains that such novels as *Pamela* and *Clarissa* established the form of domestic fiction reproduced by the so-called great tradition of English fiction. It is now commonplace to say that from its inception, the mainstream novelistic tradition not only counted women among its readership, but also authorized women to articulate the beliefs and values of the readership as a whole. For literate classes com-posed of both men and women, Richardson made passive aggression—withholding of the self—into a sublime testament to selfhood: a source of self-worth and cultural authority that would go unrecognized were it not for the fact that such interiority expressed itself in written English. It apparently meant a great deal to a polite English readership, I am suggesting, that Richardson demonstrated at such elaborate length the necessity of casting one's interior life in written form. The publishing history of his novels indicates that a certain kind of verbosity—what might be called a protracted display of personal literariness—was essential to the English Richardson's success. The putative author—though a woman—was the model for "the individual," and her discourse presumed that virtually anyone with sufficient literacy could emulate a brand of interiority that denoted a superior quality of Englishness. As I have already suggested, all such signs of literariness and the cultural work that exhaustive letter writing accomplished was removed in the heavily edited versions that distinguished the American Richardson. If we look to what remains in the redacted version of *Clarissa,* we can see how it reconceptualized cultural reproduction in a way that addressed the needs of a population in diaspora.

Beginning in the early seventeenth century and for almost two centuries thereafter, colonial British subjects confronted the dilemma of maintaining their English identity outside of England. Living in North America required members of the English community to formulate new courtship practices and marriage rules that would define their offspring as English. Perhaps the first narrative form to deal with this problem, the captivity narrative, is a good place to look for formal precedents to the seduction novel. Produced in significant quantities and consumed before, as well as after, the Revolution, this narrative characteristically used daughters both to pose the problem of maintaining English identity in British North America and to offer a resolution: either the captive daughter was returned undefiled to her family, or else she died in captivity. In either case, her blood remained pure. In the well-known case of Mary Rowlandson, as Nancy Armstrong explains, "The exclusive nature of the patriarchal prerogative" makes it possible for Englishness to descend from the father to the daughter and through her into the family of another Englishman, "thereby preserving the Englishness of the colonial community."[33] In the colonies, Armstrong concludes, the daughter of a European serves as the special kind of fetish that Annette Weiner calls "an inalienable possession" in that she can neither be seized nor traded without endangering the group's identity.[34] Daughters who acquire this iconic status have to die when they leave their father's family. Identifying this cultural logic in narratives of the late eighteenth century, Armstrong points out that daughters who do leave the community without their father's blessing can return to that community either through death, as Richardson's Clarissa did, or "through their daughters, as in the case of Charlotte Temple."[35]

Why these narratives must carry out the principle of purity or death so ruthlessly becomes apparent in an alternative narrative tradition exemplified by the story of Mary Jemison, the captive girl who "went native," married a Native American, and reproduced an English household in captivity.[36] By reversing almost point by point the cultural logic of Rowlandson's account, Jemison's narrative indicates that during the eighteenth century accounts of captivity began to offer two competing narratives of national identity. One narrative equated the English family with English culture and unfolded as if perpetuating the Englishness of Anglo-America depended on restricting subsequent marriages to people who come from exactly such a family as their own. The alternative view, as encapsulated in the story of Mary Jemison's captivity, assumed that English culture is reproduced within and perpetuated by the household. The virtue of this second, and initially residual, model lay in the fact it takes for granted the mixed nature of the domestic unit. As Armstrong explains, "no matter who makes up this household or where they come from, it can incorporate, imitate, reenact . . . or otherwise replicate whatever appears to be most English about the English family. Such a household produces a family peculiar to the settler colonies."[37] When we think of the seduction novel as a later version of the captivity narrative, which was in fact read side by side with indigenous genres of American fiction, it will soon become clear that such novels were also about much more than the unmaking and remaking of a family. Approaching the problem from this perspective, we can see how the difference in length between the two Richardsons might have offered their respective readerships an even more radical difference in the formal means and methods of reproducing English culture.

All novels that take the form of a captivity narrative also put the rules for group identity on the line. As I have already suggested, the American *Clarissa* may be distinguished from its English counterpart by a minimal expression of emotions, and it pays even less attention to the exchange of personal letters. The narrator simply informs the reader that Clarissa "wrote to Mr. Lovelace, that as she had no other means of escaping her brother's tyranny, she would meet him the next Monday at the garden gate, and put herself under his protection." With this statement, letter writing ceases.[38] What had merely provided an occasion for the English Clarissa to carry on highly nuanced emotional performances in prose—namely, the seduction plot—takes charge of the American edition. The abridged Richardson dispenses with all but the most necessary verbal displays in order to concentrate on the conduct of the female body. To explain what this shift from the body as the source of emotive language to the body as the source of sexual experience does to the concept and fate of individual identity, let me briefly compare a few key episodes from each of the two versions of *Pamela* and *Clarissa* on this basis.

In what is arguably the most erotic moment of the English version of *Pamela*, we find the heroine's letters quite literally assuming the position of her body as the object of Mr. B's desire: "Artful slut," he calls her, as he gropes about her body in search of letters she has surreptitiously authored: "I never undressed a girl in my life; but I will now begin to strip my pretty Pamela; and I hope I shall not go far before I find [her letters]."[39] But when Mr. B tries to undress his reluctant servant in the American edition, as he does without success on quite a few occasions, it is solely for purposes of taking possession of her body; he takes little if any interest in Pamela's letters. Here, within three sentences, we encounter two such attempts on her virtue:

> The squire was dressed in women's clothes, but no sooner did he come up to Pamela's bed, than he began to use such indecent freedom, that she soon discovered what he was. The distress in which Pamela was, made her use every expression to induce him to withdraw, upon which he uttered several bitter imprecations upon himself that he had never intended her the least injury. Another attempt was made on her, but she was so much overpowered, that she was obliged to be put to bed.[40]

That the American version makes no effort to transfer value from Pamela's body to her writing makes most of the prose in the English edition unnecessary to the narratives preferred by American readers.

Like her English counterpart, the American Pamela insists on returning to her father the minute she figures out what lascivious designs her new master has in mind, and like his English counterpart, Mr. B reneges on his promise to comply. He sends her to his remote countryseat, the better to seduce her. Once squirreled away in his country house, however, the American pair neglects to carry on the full-fledged letter-writing war that preoccupied them in the English edition. Pamela rejects a bogus marriage offer out of hand and leaves her diary where Mr. B will discover that she indeed means what she says. Writing is just as basic to this heroine's identity, I am suggesting, but basic in a more protojuridical way. In that it verifies more primary practices of speech and conduct, thus her suitability for marriage as well as the sincerity with which she would enter into it, writing establishes the consensual basis for a successful relationship.[41] To put it another way, Pamela must demonstrate that she can say no before she can be invested with the authority to say yes.

If the American Richardson deletes certain features from the English Richardson and modifies the role they play in determining whether a poor serving girl can marry a member of the gentry, then the American version expands other features out of all proportion to the importance they commanded in the English edition. The episode dealing with Mr. B's illegitimate daughter, Sally Godfrey, is notable in this respect. The episode takes up a fraction of the longer English edition and seems to exist only for purposes of displaying Pamela's extraordinary kindness toward those less fortunate than she. Thus we must ask ourselves why this event, of all those comprising the tediously long description of Pamela's married life, looms proportionately so large in the American edition. A visit to the girl at boarding school in the abridged edition reveals that Miss Godfrey has acquired a quality of deportment and a degree of literacy capable of overriding the unfortunate circumstances of her birth, thus making her eligible for marriage into the respectable classes. Sally Godfrey resembles Charlotte Temple's illegitimate daughter in that she, too, has been raised in England by a surrogate family, while Sally's mother, more fortunate than poor Charlotte, is reported to be "doing well" in Jamaica. In both cases, the woman, once ruined, achieves social redemption to the extent that she observes the model of good conduct. That her redemption depends on her literacy as opposed to the purity of her lineage suggests that in the editions preferred in America following the Revolution, cultural reproduction was far more important to national identity than the continuation of a bloodline. Indeed, one American abridgment (Boston, 1793) even questions Pamela's lineage in celebrating her accomplishments: "Pamela Andrews was the daughter of John and Elizabeth Andrews, (or at least reputed so) who lived in a small village in the West of England, and who, by pinching themselves more than they were already by the narrowness of their circumstances, got her taught to read and write."[42] This statement calls attention to the paradox implied by the very existence of an American Richardson.

Even though the abridgment's rejection of the epistolary mode in favor of third-person narration is the most obvious stylistic difference between the American and English editions, the quote clearly indicates that Pamela's literacy is the first and most important fact we must know if we are to understand the events that lead to her fortunate marriage. What inferences may be drawn from this paradox? In England, as in the unabridged Richardson, the heroine's writing points back to a source residing in the body, a source linking her identity with a natural and unspoiled interiority. In a striking challenge to the ontology of British letters, the American version gives us no reason to think her writing either originates in her body or locates value in her origins. Indeed, the opening line of the 1793 Boston edition suggests that just the reverse is true. Rather than point back to qualities inherent in the body, the value of Pamela's body depends on that body conducting itself according to a written model. Because both Richardsons make the heroine's status dependent upon her relationship to writing, it behooves us to look more closely at the difference between the two in terms of what happens to writing at the moment of rape.

If Pamela's seduction provides the stuff of domestic comedy, Clarissa's rape can only be called a domestic tragedy. Far from overturning the logic of cultural reproduction spelled out in the abbreviated *Pamela*, however, the American *Clarissa* actually observes the same logic in a more exaggerated form. In marked contrast with what might be called the "damaged" writing with which the English novel registers the same act of violence in Letter 262, Paper X (893), the absence of her personal record in the abridged *Clarissa* recasts the heroine's rape from an assault on her sensibility into a devastating physical experience. As the narrator explains:[43]

> What followed was the most vile and inhuman acts of violence. The distressed lady, roused from the dreadful lethargy into which she was sinking, pleaded for mercy, and cried, I will be yours—, indeed, to obtain mercy, I will be yours! But no mercy could she find. Her strength, her intellects failed her. Fits upon fits followed, which procured her no compassion.[44]

More peculiar than this relatively explicit description of the rape is Clarissa's consent to the dirty deed—provided of course that Lovelace would first agree to marry her. The option of consent in some form is what must be inferred from her pathetic statement of surrender, "I will be yours." This description of the sexual encounter and her capitulation does appear in the English version, but the account is buried in one of the letters where Clarissa is trying to report what she remembers after having been drugged. She writes, "I grew worse and worse in my head; now stupid, now raving, now senseless." She reports the physical threats, her fears, and then in an effort to recall what she said, she writes, "I remember, I pleaded for mercy—I remember that I said *I would be his*—to obtain his mercy—But no mercy found I!"[45] The emphasis in the English version over several pages is on her confusion, her subsequent delirium, and the full range of emotions she experienced from drinking the tea that Lovelace had doctored. Given the extraordinary reduction in length of the American narrative, however, the statement "I will be yours" is given considerably more prominence as an offer that holds open the possibility of marriage even under the duress of sexual assault.

Because sham marriages were far more common among people lower on the social scale, the kind of ceremony Lovelace proposes was particularly unacceptable to an English readership that was beginning to think of an affective, companionate marriage as the only legitimate one. As the American version of the Sally Godfrey episode suggests, other forms of marriage came to be increasingly associated with a colonial culture where they apparently seemed necessary and more acceptable. In the English novel, down is the only direction in which a woman can go once she has been sexually compromised.[46] By contrast, an American heroine could be both virtuous and fallen, embodying Pamela and Sally Godfrey at once, the two no longer representing contradictory types. Indeed, the Sally Godfrey episode demonstrates the reversibility of a woman's sexual downfall in the version of the seduction narrative preferred by an American readership;

after her ruin she can even improve her social position. Where *Pamela* demonstrated the conditions under which one could avoid a fall in status, *Clarissa* worked in reverse, demonstrating the conditions under which one was destined to fall.

According to this model, the sexual purity of the daughter is much less important than her ability to form a household where the rules of good conduct—hence Englishness itself—can be reproduced in and by subsequent generations. This is not to say that the story of cultural reproduction according to Mary Jemison won out over the kind of captivity narrative exemplified by Mary Rowlandson, much less that the American seduction novel could allow its heroine to "go native." Not at all. I am simply suggesting that during the early republic sexual impurity does not necessarily cancel out Englishness, for remain English one must. After political separation from England, the popularity of the seduction novel suggests that it was more important than ever to have the kind of cultural identity that once came only from being born of English parents. The conditions under which one could acquire and maintain such an identity had simply changed.

This, I believe, is the reason why Clarissa's uncle Morden enters so intrusively into the abridged edition as a potential form of agency. The American Richardson assigns this absent relative a role resembling that played by Charlotte Temple's father. Her active apologist and would-be redeemer, her father arrives at Charlotte's side just in time for her to beg his pardon, receive it, and expire. Her father then returns to England with Charlotte's newborn daughter. Of the aftermath of this climactic episode, Rowson's narrator has this to say: "After the first tumult of grief was subsided, Mrs. Temple gave up the chief of her time to her grand-child, and as she grew up and improved, began to fancy she again possessed her Charlotte."[47] Colonel Morden's intervention on Clarissa's behalf increases in importance in the American edition, where his ministrations might have cancelled out the fact of her rape and excommunication from the Harlowe family. The American novel clearly empowers Morden as a father surrogate. Convinced of Clarissa's innocence, he pleads, we are told, with the girl's family to send a nurse to care for her. When brother James steps in to prevent his mother from offering any succor, Morden is reported to have declared, "In me shall the dear creature have the father, uncle, and brother she has lost."[48] Here, Morden represents himself as nothing so much as one of those surrogates for the father that Locke considered necessary in America. In view of the American adaptation of the Sally Godfrey episode, I am inclined to take this statement literally to mean that had Morden arrived in time, he might have eventually given Clarissa in marriage to another English gentleman, as certain to be smitten as Morden himself by her tragic beauty and genteel deportment. Indeed, it is fair to say that all such departures from the longer version of *Clarissa* place value on the quality of the copy in contrast to the original. What counts for an American readership, we must conclude, is not so much the loss of purity as one's fidelity to an idea of a home one imagined to be English. Nor does the heroine's conduct have to meet the father's approval any more than she has to marry the man whom he selects for her. In all cases, substitutes will do. Morden can assume the position of the true father simply by behaving like one, and by behaving like one, he might well have legitimated the ravished Clarissa—that is, had she only lasted a little longer.

The Importance of Remaining English

To understand American seduction narratives from this perspective is tantamount to thinking of the *Clarissa* preferred by an early republican readership as a lesser *Charlotte Temple* instead of assuming that *Charlotte Temple* was a bad imitation of *Clarissa*. *Charlotte Temple* fulfills precisely the cultural logic guiding the abridgments of the versions of Richardson that were preferred in America. What the shorter *Clarissa* sought and failed to accomplish—the redemption of a heroine who failed in Mary Rowlandson's terms—is realized in Rowson's novel, despite the fact that it plays out the English formula for punishing a fallen woman. Charlotte not only dies as the penalty for "going native" (or French, as the case may be), she is also reborn in her daughter.[49] Thus she combines in a rather literal way the fates respectively assigned to Clarissa Harlowe and Sally Godfrey—or, just as appropriately, Mary Rowlandson and Mary Jemison. Doubled in her daughter, Charlotte embodies the very contradiction that a sentimental British readership absolutely disallowed, no doubt because that duality challenged the model of monogamy on which an emergent middle class in England had based their claims to moral authority.

Charlotte's father simultaneously reproduces and displaces this model of the family, when he takes his daughter's daughter back to England, thereby reconstructing the original English household with a father, mother, and granddaughter. Charlotte's father, of course, is performing the role of a surrogate father in keeping with Locke's notion of paternalism. Indeed, despite her illegitimate birth in the colonies, the second ending of the novel indicates that Charlotte's daughter not only provides a perfect copy of her mother, but improves on the rebellious original as well. We are told that the formation of this individual will not be entrusted to the care of others but overseen by an English household that regulates her sexual conduct accordingly. The perfection of the copy in comparison with the original finesses the fundamental question of cultural identity posed by this novel: Are you Anglo-American because you are born of an English family, or are you Anglo-American because you live your life according to an English model?

It should not be all that difficult to imagine why it was necessary for a genre of fiction to raise and suppress this contradiction in familial terms if we take into account how conservative the revolutionary moment actually was. The break with England was a rejection of the monarch's authority in certain matters of economics and law. But as Gordon Wood has observed, "The revolutionary leaders never intended to make a national revolution in any modern sense."[50] Indeed, we have no evidence to suggest that they intended to break away from English letters, English science, English learning, or even English culture at the most common and pragmatic level. If the generation of men and women who detached their colonial government from England did in fact consider themselves English people, then it follows that they should desire to maintain that cultural identity during the same period when they were discussing the political principles constituting a modern, just, and independent state.

Narratives of seduction—or in many cases, rape—are peculiarly good at rationalizing the inherent contradiction between a progressive political agenda and a conservative cultural one. If Anglo-Americans imagined their culture as a woman—that is, as a Mary Rowlandson, a Charlotte Temple, or even a Clarissa Harlowe—then the perpetuity of that identity would depend on her remaining faithful to her origins. Seduction would threaten that bond, and rape would declare it had been forcibly broken. This was an old story, common to Europe and America. In the American Richardson, however, the same event that necessarily spelled the heroine's doom for English readers was in fact the beginning of an additional chapter for their American counterparts. No longer a question about what the heroine *is*—Does she embody the purity essential to command the position of an Englishwoman in the exchange of women?—the question turned on what the heroine *does*—Can she reproduce an English way of life outside of England? The colonial model exemplified by Mary Rowlandson would no longer do, for it refused to acknowledge the difference between an English subject and an Anglo-American one. The American seduction novel, in contrast, produced a break in the heroine's lineage in order to consider how one could remain English despite that break. Under these circumstances, avoiding seduction, as Pamela does, became just another way of repairing the rupture of lineage that Clarissa promises but fails to achieve by creating an English household away from home. The need to establish continuity with English culture was so overdetermined in the years following the American Revolution, I am suggesting, that it elevated the sentimental fiction imported from England into the fantasy of family reunion.

The Afterlife of the Libertine

As the novel sought to imagine a nation, it appropriated the European opposition between libertine and legitimate patriarch and put the seduction story to work on regional divisions within the population based on race and class in ways that strove to imagine the nation as a coherent people. By having the reproduction of an American family depend on setting aside British conventions regulating the traditional exchange of women among empowered families, the seduction stories of the late eighteenth century appeared to argue for a more inclusionary nation. That the marriage contract was nonetheless a figurative means of putting limits on the very social contract it appears to universalize becomes particularly apparent in novels that were written during the twenty- to thirty-year period leading up to the American Civil War. The contrast between nineteenth-century Latin American novels and novels by writers in the United States who were heirs of the English diaspora is instructive. In a groundbreaking account of the Latin American novel, Doris Sommer showed that in nineteenth-century Latin American fiction heterosexual desire provides the means of binding together racially differentiated groups as an internally coherent national culture.[51] The great national romances of the preboom period imply that the blood of the European colonizer was not indelibly tainted by cross-racial marriage with Indian heroines. Spanish blood is capable of ennobling those with whom it mixed.

Not so, however, for the strain of English culture transplanted in the new United States. The problem confronting the novelist who wrote for an American readership on the brink of the Civil War was compounded by a peculiarly English spin on the concept of race that found perhaps its most extreme expression in the notorious "one-drop" rule. When race was at issue, American novels could not observe the pattern of seduction stories and still have the libertine marry the woman he had deflowered. The owner of slaves simultaneously assaults the slave's father and defiles his own blood as he usurps that father's position. In this respect, his situation resembles that of the elder Harrington in *The Power of Sympathy*. There can be no recuperation of the family under these circumstances.

To demonstrate its enduring legacy in American fiction, I want to consider briefly how Harriet Beecher Stowe uses the seduction story to address the slavery question. Put in novelistic terms, that question goes something like this: how can an America divided by slavery be represented as one coherent kin group without triggering Anglo-American miscegenation? A single drop of African blood would set one outside the Anglo-identified nation. To imagine a racially divided nation as a single family, the novelist could decide, as Stowe did, that the bond holding the family together was a fragile emotional bond that would be shattered by physical expressions of sexual desire. Indeed, such a physical expression as incest flew directly in the face of family feeling. Stowe accordingly translated what had been the woman as object and property of men into a subject whose body was the vehicle of her own self-expression and could not therefore be used sexually without her consent. This notion of the woman was, of course, the centerpiece of all sentimental literature in the Richardsonian tradition. Literature that authorizes such an affective basis for social affiliation stripped the father of his prerogative for the trading of women. Indeed, such literature equated the father's right to dispose of the daughter's body not only with the libertine's seizure of another man's rightful property but also with the slave owner's treatment of women as his property.

Cassy's story in *Uncle Tom's Cabin* is made out of the seduction plots found in the popular magazine stories. She describes herself, for example, as "a woman delicately bred" who has fallen in the world.[52] Each of her previous owner-lovers resembles nothing so much as the typically faithless lover of the libertine literature. She speaks of her first owner in these terms: "I was his property,—I became his willingly, for I loved him. Loved!"(516). The only difference between this phase of her personal history and that of hundreds of other seduced and abandoned American heroines was the inscription of Cassy's body within the institution of slavery. She is no mere love slave. Slavery literalizes her bondage and makes her object status a painful legal and economic fact rather than a metaphor for her emotional bondage to the man who stole her from her father. Cassy's first owner resorts to the seducer's logic that although marriage was impossible, nevertheless, "he told me that, if we were only faithful to each other, it was a marriage before God" (517). Also true to form, this first lover-owner soon tires of the woman he has seduced and fastens on another.

Standing in opposition to the figure of the faithless lover is the sentimental libertine, whom Stowe uses to rescue George Harris's sister. As Emily explains, "I was bought by a good and generous man. He took me with him to the West Indies, set me free, and married me" (600). When her former owner returns power over her body to the ex-slave, he also grants her the means to become the kind of subject who could consent to marry and create a family. In stark contrast to both the faithless libertine and the sentimental libertine of earlier literature, Simon Legree emerges from Stowe's pen as a hyperbolic version of that relatively rare American phenomenon, the sadistic libertine. As we have seen, this figure is locked in a definitive struggle with those paternal figures who embody the prevailing rules of kinship. The seduced woman figure is simply a mediator through whom the libertine viciously assaults any rules not of his own making as he exercises the patriarchal prerogatives to treat his dependents like objects and dispose of them as he wishes.

To the degree that slavery literalizes the ownership of women, it renders the familial relations that form around the object of libertine desire not only purely figural but also more intense, precisely because those relations are based not on natural kinship but on the commonality of human suffering. Stowe has Cassy call Tom "Father Tom" three times within a mere page and a half (562–63). Because both Tom and Cassy have been denied their biological children, Emmeline easily slides into the position of substitute daughter to these parents. In threatening her, Legree simultaneously conceals this physical lack and reproduces it on the symbolic level as an emotional lack with which any parent or child, male or female, could identify. As she says to Cassy, "If the Lord gives us liberty, perhaps he'll give you back your daughter; at any rate, I'll be like a daughter to you" (580). Thus when Cassy and Emmeline succeed in fleeing their libertine oppressor, Legree is only being true to the conventions of the seduction narrative in directing his wrath at Tom. As metaphoric father of the always-absent girl, Tom emerges as the object of Legree's sadistic desires once the woman mediating the exchange between them vanishes.

By fashioning Legree from the materials of the libertine, Stowe has set up the seduction narrative in such a way that the emotional component of the family, or family feeling, can exist only in the absence of sexual desire that leads to the physical reproduction of the family. Consequently, none of those included in the American family—Eva, Tom, Emmeline, Topsy, or Ophelia—can experience such reproductive desire. In contrast to the elder Harrington of *The Power of Sympathy,* Legree elicits extraordinary moral outrage simply because he acts out sexually his position of patriarchal dominance over enslaved women. The earlier version of the libertine could convert or eventually reproduce itself as the more modern liberal father who saw his victims not as objects but as subjects possessing subjectivities equivalent to, if different from, his own. By the time we arrive at *Uncle Tom's Cabin,* however, the libertine no longer exists along a continuum that includes as its other extreme the worthy father and head of household because each has cancelled out the affect of the other. The desires of the seducer destroy the qualities required of the father who understands his dependents as autonomous subjects rather than as objects to be sexually exploited or sold. So necessary is this opposition between family feeling and sexual desire to the possibility of imagining an American family capable of including black and white, north and south, men and women, that Stowe allows family feeling to reunite with its physical expression only outside the United States—in Canada, the West Indies, France, or Liberia.

Stowe's novel makes clear that once race is entangled with kinship through the institution of slavery, there seems to be no way to legitimate the family produced by the libertine. Stowe seems to have understood full well that the two modes of the seduction story are ways of negating paternal authority. One version of the seduction tale, when adapted to the story of slavery, makes it impossible for an exchange to take place, because the father is the owner and cannot trade with himself. The second story is a form that negates the father by injuring or killing him. As a result, the only form of family feeling that Stowe can imagine is that embodied in the mother, specifically the Christian mother. By so transforming the terms of the sexual contract into one that focuses on the condition of women under slavery, Stowe does indeed displace the relationship among men that is at stake in the American versions of the seduction story. That is to say, by focusing on maternal feeling she obscures the fact that the seduction story is always a story about the conditions that enable men either to seize or to respect one another's property.

To conclude, I want to look briefly at *The House of the Seven Gables* and consider how Nathaniel Hawthorne worked with the same seduction narrative that organizes *Uncle Tom's Cabin*. I am especially interested in how he uses that material to differentiate the literature associated with the masculine authors of the American Renaissance from the sentimental tradition. Hawthorne not only uses the seduction narrative to set the autochthonous, if plebeian, claims of the Maules against the more traditional kinship practices of the Pyncheon family; he also makes the reformation of the libertine the means of resolving this opposition with the formation of a coherent family out of contending kin groups. Holgrave tells Phoebe the story of their respective forebears, Matthew Maule and Alice Pyncheon, as a version of the seduction story. Like the traditional libertine, Maule is a free thinker who holds "heretical tenets in matters of religion and polity."[53] His ability to mesmerize Alice is such that it allows Maule to gain "a subtle influence over the daughter of his enemy's house" (527). Her seduction leads Pyncheon in turn to claim that he has been "robbed" of his daughter (529).

If we simply substitute the Pyncheon house for the daughter's body, this seduction story, like the prototype, reveals itself as little more than a set of negotiations between men to acquire property from one another. Once mesmerized, Alice loses possession of herself and lives only to do Maule's bidding. Indeed, Hawthorne uses the figure of the slave to explain what is at stake in the subject thus handing over her choice of love object to another: "[W]hile Alice Pyncheon lived, she was Maule's slave, in a bondage more humiliating, a thousand-fold, than that which binds its chain around the body" (531–32). Much like Cassy, Alice cannot marry because she lacks the power of consent. Finally, like so many of the betrayed women of seduction stories, Alice is humiliated when Maule marries someone of his own rank—in this case, though, a laborer's daughter. "Penitent of her one earthly sin," Alice dies, in Holgrave's account, of "humiliation" (533).

But as much as Alice Pyncheon may remind us of the heroines of earlier seduction stories, the fate of the Pyncheons neither rises nor falls on her marriageability. Ruining her is Maule's retribution for a property battle with Pyncheon, a battle that Maule has unquestionably lost. It is none other than Pyncheon himself who allows his daughter to fall prey to his rival in hopes of recovering—through this perverse exchange with Maule—the deed to Indian lands in Maine that would make Pyncheon a wealthy man. Indeed, all the repetitions of this one basic story in *The House of the Seven Gables* have to do with who has legitimate claims to the Pyncheon property and, by extension, to the Indian lands that may or may not have been deeded to the Pyncheons. Should Maule deliver the deed, Pyncheon's fortune "would be worth an earldom," and he could, in the style of earlier libertines, live up to his aristocratic pretensions (523).

Throughout the novel, Hawthorne quite deliberately places Phoebe Pyncheon in a position structurally equivalent to that of her long-dead cousin Alice, where Holgrave "could complete his mastery over Phoebe's yet free and virgin spirit" (534), much as Matthew Maule had over Alice. Having established the possibility of repeating the tale he has just told, Holgrave chooses to renounce the mysterious power of seduction he appears to have inherited. His doing so differentiates Hawthorne's use of the family from Stowe's. To understand the sudden change in the Maule-Pyncheon relations, Hawthorne's narrator asks us to "concede to the Daguerreotypist the rare and high quality of reverence for another's individuality" (535). When Hawthorne inexplicably removes the young Phoebe from the novel for several weeks only to bring her back as if from the dead, she returns as a marriageable woman: "in the few intervening weeks, her experiences had made her graver, more womanly, and deeper-eyed, in token of a heart that had begun to suspect its depths—still there was the quiet glow of natural sunshine over her" (607). Hawthorne represents as temporary social death the mere threat of losing ownership of her individuated desire that distinguishes the modern individual from the object of another's desire.

Where Stowe felt compelled to kill off little Eva, Hawthorne returns Phoebe to the novel transformed and marries her off, symbolically healing the class division within his version of the American family. This resolution not only requires that the woman be an autonomous subject capable of genuinely consenting to Holgrave's offer of marriage, it also requires that Holgrave be in a position to understand the marriage contract as a social contract, and therefore as the means of inserting himself within the elite community of men formed and maintained by the exchange of women.

Hawthorne is unusually explicit on this point, for he has Holgrave say to Phoebe, "I have a presentiment, that, hereafter, it will be my lot to set out trees, to make fences ... in a word, to conform myself to laws, and the peaceful practice of society" (616). These words magically usher in a world where family feeling and sexual desire can intermix without conflict. This world, in the words of the novel, is "Eden again," and a new generation borne of Maule and Pyncheon provide "the two first dwellers in it" (616).

Both *Uncle Tom's Cabin* and *The House of the Seven Gables* draw on the seduction narrative that had been a staple of American reading since the eighteenth century. In marked contrast with his appearance in the American seduction stories of 1785–1818, the libertine provides Stowe with an instrument for arousing moral indignation. Tom's sacrifice at the hands of the lustful Legree divides the world into good and evil as perhaps no previous American seduction story had and repeats the moment when all those capable of such feeling—even the liminal character of Topsy—unite in a feeling of human loss around the deathbed of little Eva. How can one not abhor the agents and institutions that extinguish such condensed embodiments of humanity as daughters? But if Stowe uses the libertine to produce a sense of moral outrage, our revulsion at the crimes of passion that slavery authorizes fails to herald anything more than an uprising of moral sentiment. The novel envisions not a bit of change in the particular economic institutions that legitimate slavery. Stowe famously rests her case and ends the novel with a revolution of the heart that insists emotion is capable of crossing lines of both race and gender. At best, then, her novel arrives at an emotional resolution to a political problem, or family feeling that cannot translate into a household capable of containing racial difference, at least not within the boundaries of the United States.

By way of contrast, Hawthorne refuses to offer a family detached from economic and social fact as a purely affective model of the nation. Where Stowe's narrative sought and failed to reconcile racially, regionally, and economically incompatible oppositions dividing the nation as she imagined it, Hawthorne displaces all those divisions onto the difference between two New England families. Despite the narrow polarities in terms of which he chooses to define the problem of national unity, Hawthorne nevertheless requires repeated interventions by the libertine before the two families can exist on a socioeconomic footing that enables intermarriage. Unlike Stowe, Hawthorne will not effect a transformation of the heart without a change in the distribution of power and money; family feelings and family fortunes are mutually contingent. Thanks to his eighteenth-century heritage, in other words, Hawthorne can only countenance a marriage contract that is also a social contract. Despite the care with which he modifies the descendants of Maule and Pyncheon so that Holgrave and Phoebe may

come together as social equals differentiated only by their respective genders, Hawthorne finds it necessary to qualify the optimism suggested by
their union in a single family. First by a preface setting romance in opposition to history, then by Phoebe's figurative death and resurrection as a
mature woman, and finally by a union embellished by the language of
romance, their marriage is defined as an exception to the rule of history.
Given that Hawthorne's America is nothing if not a family history, there
is no way that the couple produced by this history can start anew without
a lot of baggage.

I have tried to show that eighteenth-century seduction stories used the
European libertine to think about the new nation as an aggregate of individuals capable of resolving differences of rank, status, and region through
marriage. When later American novelists like Stowe and Hawthorne took
up this same figure, try as they might, they failed to make the nation into
anything resembling the large, complex, and coherent family toward which
both their novels aspire. While it is true that both Stowe and Hawthorne
used the seduction story to imagine the nation as a coherent family, their
fiction leaves us with anything but a body of like-minded individuals who
could be imagined as members of a single family. The nation was no more
a coherent entity to individuals writing then, I am suggesting, than it is now
in the age of multiculturalism. For then, as now, any attempt to imagine the
nation as an all-inclusive family produces conspicuous acts of exclusion,
revealing in turn differences so fundamental that those differences can only
be resolved symbolically in the wishful form of romance. Stowe's Liberia
is no different from Hawthorne's "new Eden" in this respect. The United
States may exist as a relatively discrete polity, and even as an independent
economy, but its population has never been one that could be successfully
represented as a family as the people of Shakespeare's or even Victoria's
England could. From this perspective, to prefer Hawthorne's fantasy of an
Anglo-America as whole and ontologically consistent is as misguided as
the attempt to justify Stowe's fantasy of a heterogeneous population united
by feeling alone.

Because neither Stowe nor Hawthorne was the least bit lacking in literary
talent, much less in familiarity with the language and logic of the seduction
story that both were manipulating, we must assume that their mutual failure to produce a model of the nation—at once inclusive, autonomous, and
internally coherent—was not a failure so much as a mark of their success.
As citizens of the United States, they seem to say, we are hardly a family—
except under the most attenuated circumstances. We are something else,
for which there can be no literary convention, given the demands of domestic romance by means of which fiction reifies the idea of a nation. What
we give you instead of a durable synthesis is a sequence of disrupted and

failed families remodeled anew, thus more adequate, inclusive, and dura-ble. What if not the most rending internal divisions generate the fiction that there is a common collective body to save and infuses the reader with a desire to do so? The rhetorical disruptions that give rise to this affect are precisely the tropological activity I have ascribed to the American libertine. These disruptions allow seduction to generate sentiment by infusing the reconstructed family with a kind of urgency that lives on in contemporary political rhetoric.

4

THE HEART OF MASCULINITY

O N THE WAY to fulfilling the expectations of his European forebears, something happened to the libertine. While assaulting the marriage practices imported from Europe, the libertine set the stage for a new kind of masculinity. He did so by creating the need for a character to step forth as a father substitute. When the seduction narrative in which he figured so largely converged with sentimental literature in the new United States, the libertine himself could either assume such a position by renouncing his wicked ways or else cede that position to someone capable of heading up a reformed and revitalized English household. The libertine is, in this respect, simply the other side and facilitator of what might be called "true manhood." Worthy in *The Power of Sympathy* exemplifies the kind of man capable of rescuing the family. As such, he is the reason why William Hill Brown's novel should claim pride of place as the first American novel. But we have yet to establish what makes Worthy so worthy. The present chapter establishes the link between his brand of literacy—as displayed in the letters he writes to Myra Harrington—and the sentimental heroine of British fiction and her masculine counterpart, the man of feeling. Making this connection allows us to discern the all-important difference that converted the tremulous feelings of the prototype into the kind of masculinity for which the libertine created a need: in Worthy's hands, writing comes to serve as the means of containing and mediating, rather than inflating and spreading, emotion. Emotion consequently works within, and on behalf of, contractual exchange.

By 1800, feeling in a man had acquired the cultural capital with the United States readership that it had sought but never achieved in Europe, despite the popularity of novels like *Sir Charles Grandison*, *The Man of Feeling*, *The Fool of Quality*, and *The Sorrows of Young Werther*.[1] To assign the "man of feeling" its rightful role in the formation of a specifically American masculinity, one must understand how this figure maintained its traditional tie to British literacy, even as it produced the much-vaunted rugged individual who pushed the frontier westward across an entire continent.[2] Its dual capacity to be both British and American is the reason why the man of feeling succeeded in America where it initially failed to catch hold in England. But that is only half the story. To understand the full literary and cultural importance of the man of feeling is to follow its return to Europe in the fiction of Austen and Godwin; it was only after it was revised in North America that the man of feeling acquired a kind of symbolic currency in English fiction. No longer simply a foil to the "man of reason," the man of feeling came to be a necessary component of a new form of ruling-class masculinity. My point in this chapter is therefore to uncover the transatlantic crossings in which each nation put its mark on the masculinity of the other. If the publishing history of any single novel is capable of making this point, then that novel has to be Charles Brockden Brown's *Clara Howard*. Following its peculiar trajectory across two developing national cultures gives us a sense of what a literary history might look like were its goal to reveal how the two different national traditions developed in relation to each other rather than each in its own terms from different points of origin.

Initially entitled *Clara Howard in a Series of Letters*, Brockden Brown's epistolary novel of 1801 makes rather unsubtle reference to Henry Mackenzie's *Man of Feeling*, a novel belonging to a subgenre of fiction that flourished only briefly in the 1770s and fell out of favor in England around 1780. The fact that Brockden Brown names his protagonist Edward Hartley could not help but call to mind Mackenzie's Harley, the British prototype of the man of feeling.[3] True to the prototype, Brockden Brown's protagonist authors a protracted sequence of letters in which personal feelings and social obligations prove mutually paralyzing. But in marked contrast to the outcomes of either Mackenzie's novel or Goethe's rendition of the man of feeling in *The Sorrows of Young Werther*, each of which fails to unite the protagonist with the woman he loves, this form of frustration eventually leads to the marriage between the American Hartley and the British Clara Howard. This initial phase of the novel's publishing history raises two questions: 1) how did American culture manage to marry off the man of feeling where his European forebears did not find him marriageable?; and 2) Why did American readers continue to respond to this figure decades after the English apparently failed to find him interesting?

Six years after the American publication of *Clara Howard*, the Minerva Press, a press well known in England for publishing popular fiction written by women, published Brockden Brown's novel.[4] We might find it odd that a novel featuring a man of feeling should come out in America under the title *Clara Howard*, a name that would surely have resonated for readers with that of Clarissa Harlowe and so call attention to the female protagonist. It must seem even more peculiar that given its reputation as a press that published popular entertainment appealing in large measure to a female readership, the Minerva Press would change the hero's name to Philip Stanley and retitle the American novel *Philip Stanley: or the Enthusiasm of*

Love. Although the Minerva Press had published Brockden Brown's earlier *Ormond* (1800), *Arthur Mervyn* (1803), *Edgar Huntley* (1803), and *Jane Talbot* (1804), *Clara Howard* was the only novel by Brockden Brown that the Press retitled for publication in England.[5] Rather than preserve Brockden Brown's echo of the Richardson title, the British edition called attention to the importance of the hero and not the English woman he desires, while the subtitle "or the Enthusiasm of Love" identified this hero as a man of feeling. With the historical peregrination of this novel as my guide, I want to explain what had to happen to the man of feeling before the figure could be well received on both sides of the Atlantic.

The British Man of Feeling

While a great deal has been written about the eighteenth-century vogue for sensibility and the rise in the number of male characters who displayed its features, his capacity to feel strongly was not the only quality that made the man of feeling politically important. From the early modern period onward, literature routinely endowed aristocratic males with a depth of feeling that other characters lacked. A well-born character could experience grand feelings of sympathy or passion and still act heroically on the battlefield and wisely at court. In marked contrast to Renaissance or Baroque literature, however, eighteenth-century fiction provides male protagonists the majority of whom do not express their feelings in politically charged forms. Often cited as an eighteenth-century figure of male sensibility is Richardson's Sir Charles Grandison. Described by one critic as a man of "softened manhood," Grandison can, in Richardson's words, "weep for the distress of others."[6] While he rescues people in need of help, it is not his actions in the world that make him desirable, but his sensibility, a combination of his ability to appreciate art and literature, his polite and moral conversation, and, perhaps most important of all, his compassion. In addition to his tendency to weep, Richardson has given Grandison considerable wealth, which makes him eminently marriageable, where the stubborn fact about Mackenzie's or Goethe's man of feeling is that neither has anything like rank, property, or money. Neither is consequently allowed to marry. During the initial vogue for this character-type in the 1770s, it set a man's feelings and the forms of gratification available to him completely at odds. In theory, his inability to marry prevents the man of feeling from becoming a fully enfranchised individual.

In his *Second Treatise of Government,* Locke argued that among the many reasons patriarchalism was not a suitable model for British political or social practice was that it prevented young men from achieving full citizenship in a zero-sum game. They had to wait until their fathers relinquished that position to them at death. Under British law, Locke reminded his readers, sons should not have to wait for their fathers to die in order to become heads of household.[7] Specifically directed against Filmer's treatise on patriarchalism, Locke's argument draws on an operative assumption about masculinity to launch its attack: a male was fully a man only when he was no longer a dependent. One should not have to inherit manhood, Locke implies. To achieve it, he should only be twenty-one, know the law, and have the economic capacity to reproduce and maintain a household. Mackenzie's hero of sensibility poses a dilemma for this definition of masculinity; if one has the interiority reserved for a historically earlier elite, without the accoutrements of power, that individual is simply out of luck in eighteenth-century England. Unsubstantiated by wealth or position, his feelings alone cannot make Harley a citizen in Lockean terms.

I find it particularly interesting that in this respect the man of feeling resembles Richardson's Clarissa more than his Sir Charles Grandison. Both Clarissa and Harley are victims of a heartless masculinity in the form of fathers who will not give their daughters to men capable of intense feeling. As a result, both protagonists waste away from an unnamed disorder of mind that afflicts the body. The novels that Ian Watt canonized in his accounting of the so-called rise of the novel invariably assign men to a life in the world and allow women to enjoy a compensatory interior life with its own form of authority.[8] Thus when Mackenzie proposed to give his masculine protagonist a form of agency based on feeling alone, he was implicitly putting that protagonist in the position reserved for the heroines of eighteenth-century novels. Why do such a thing?

Throughout the eighteenth century, the novel, in contradistinction to the relatively fixed social relations implied by neoclassical tradition, offered stories that imagined loosening ever so slightly the rigid social hierarchy identified with the ancien régime and expanding its upper-middle levels to include individuals of energy, desire, and moral virtue. Characters unwilling to settle for their place among the middle ranks or a life destined for service could find a place above the one to which they were destined at birth. Henry Fielding has it both ways. He creates heroes who had been stolen as babies or misplaced at birth, but they are unable to adjust to social life at the lower levels. Although he restores them to their rightful places without changing the status quo, he makes the social order appear to relax just a bit. Tom Jones, though a bastard, does get his Sophia. In that these examples of the new masculinity possess an energy that will not allow them to stay in their place, they appear to contest the very system of rank, station, and blood at whose head stood the monarch. In the end, as his central placement in the editions of English fiction edited by Anna Laetitia Barbauld and Sir Walter Scott suggests, Fielding contributed to the formation of a national masculinity that argued for a more inclusive, flexible, and less hierarchical society.[9] Although, one might expect it to be more politically loaded for women to achieve this same effect solely by means of the Austen feelings, quite the reverse was the case. During the period encompassing the work of Richardson and Austen, we find numerous cases of women marrying above their social level. Richardson's Pamela marries up into the gentry when Mr. B finds her intrinsic qualities of mind coupled with her literacy equivalent to property. Once his wife, of course, Pamela never presumes to put herself on a par with her husband. That eighteenth-century readers found such upwardly mobile marriages relatively easy to imagine was surely because the woman was already subordinated by gender to the man whom she married.

By creating the man of feeling, Mackenzie asks the eighteenth-century reader to imagine a similar fate for a male protagonist, specifically a gentleman, whose chief assets are his sensibility and literacy. He is introduced to us as "bashful," with a sensibility "which the most delicate feelings produce, and the most extensive knowledge cannot always remove"(4). So tenuous is his grip on these feelings that his characteristic response to tales of human suffering is to lose any capacity for action and burst into tears. As prone to sensibility as a woman, Mackenzie's man of feeling is endowed with a verbal agency equal to women of a superior rank precisely because he is a man. Mackenzie tries, in other words, to make the gender asymmetry that Richardson used to perfection work on behalf of a man of no means but great sensibility. When Harley reluctantly visits Bedlam, he grows distraught at the first clanking of chains and cries of the inmates, and wants to leave even before the ladies of the group beg the guide to remove them from such scenes of anguish (19). We also discover that when Harley offers his benevolence and delicacy of feeling in exchange for the hand of Miss Waltham, her father rejects the exchange out of hand.

Mackenzie sets up various conditions, all the stock and trade of domestic fiction and any one of which could resolve the conflict between Harley's desire and his lack of means. If, for example, he could simply inherit from a distant relation he would have sufficient money and land to negotiate with Mr. Waltham for his daughter's hand. But from early on he never had the disposition to cultivate the rich relation's affections and thereby work himself into her favor. "In short," Mackenzie tells us, "he accommodated himself so ill to her humour, that she died, and did not leave him a farthing" (7). Having failed to win an inheritance, he might secure a lease for "some crown-lands which lay contiguous to his little paternal estate" (7), but to do so would require patronage "with the great, which Harley or his father never possessed" (7). Alternatively he could rent the land abutting the Waltham estate and turn it to a profit, but he fails to secure the necessary loan. With money to rent property, he could marry Miss Waltham and through her acquire her father's property. Had he inherited rank from his father but little money, on the other hand, he could marry her and through her gain an inheritance. Were he merely an ordinary man by birth but one who enjoyed substantial means, he could acquire social prestige through marriage to a woman of superior rank. A summary of the circles within circles of frustration around which Mackenzie unwinds his hero's tale shows the lengths to which the author goes in order demonstrate that no man can acquire a social position by what domestic fiction had classified as "feminine" means. Only men who can exchange property for the daughters of other men can become fully men, according to this tradition. Mackenzie overturns no ideological apple carts in asking his reader to sympathize with a man who embodies the combined excess of feelings and lack of independent means characterizing a sentimental heroine. In doing so, that reader must simply acknowledge that the man of feeling lacks precisely the masculine qualities required of Locke's new man.[10] The reader must also accept the fact that real capital and not symbolic capital is the precondition for living a life of sensibility.

In exposing the inadequacy of Harley's sensibility in the face of the masculine prerogatives of wealth and status, however, Mackenzie also suggests an alternative masculinity residual in eighteenth-century masculinity and comparable to the feminine power of feeling. If he does not succeed in persuading her father to give Miss Waltham to him in marriage, Harley does manage to make her desire him—indeed, desire him to the extent that she, like Clarissa, refuses the marriage that her father arranges. The net effect is that the man of feeling succeeds in throwing a monkey wrench into the traditional exchange of women, which limits the power of the hereditary landowner. By way of comparison, much as Goethe's Werther adores the fair Lotte, she is engaged and then married to the solidly bourgeois Albert. No feelings on Werther's or even Lotte's part—however intense and all-consuming—alter this outcome. Thus I find it significant that Harley's expressions of feeling succeed in removing Miss Waltham from the prevailing economy of exchange. By his very failure to marry, Harley achieves much the same political result that Clarissa did.

The American Man of Feeling

Whether one wants to claim that *Clara Howard* represents an entirely new departure for Brockden Brown or simply a variation of the sort of novel he had written several times before, the fact is that he was well aware *Clara Howard* was going to elicit a different response from those his previously published novels had produced.[11] As he indicated in a letter to his brother James, this novel was "dropping the doleful tone [of his earlier works] and assuming a cheerful one, or, at least substituting moral causes and daily incidents in place of the prodigious or the singular" (433). And so it does. To accomplish that end, Brockden Brown organized his novel around the figure of the man of feeling, a figure he adapted to his precise moment in American history. The European prototype was of questionable masculinity, burdened with a sensibility that rendered him incapable of action in the world and doomed him to meet a tragic end. Brockden Brown empowers his man of feeling to act on behalf of "moral causes." His capacity for action made this protagonist eligible to marry a woman of superior birth. Let us consider what Brockden Brown does to constitute an American brand of masculinity out of this highly unpromising material.

First, he reverses the traditional relation between sensibility and literacy. In contrast to his British counterpart, Edward Hartley does not come into the world with an exquisitely full-blown sensibility. Brockden Brown takes care to establish that the protagonist acquires his sensibility from literature belonging to and read under the tutelage of a transplanted Englishman, Mr. Howard. Hartley not only lacks economic means in that he has "no father" and "no property" (38), he also lacks the attributes of sensibility that Mackenzie's hero seemed to possess as a fluke of nature. "My temper was artless and impetuous" (38), Hartley explains, "I was a mere country lad, with little education but what was gained by myself; diffident and bashful as the rawest inexperience could make me" (37). ("Bashful" is the term that Mackenzie used to describe Harley.) Mr. Howard is willing to give Hartley a taste of British culture but nothing more; as Hartley tells us, "He never gave me money, nor ever suffered the slightest hint to escape him that he designed to carry his munificence any farther than to lend me his company, his conversation and his books" (38). Nor did Hartley in turn seek any material advantage from the relationship: "in my attachment to [Mr. Howard] there was nothing sordid or mercenary" (38). Indeed, we may attribute Mr. Howard's mentorship to his belief that a little British learning will teach this uncouth young American to stay in his place. "He was anxious to persuade me," Hartley writes, "that the farmer's life was the life of true dignity, and that, however desirable to me property might be, [I] would not strive to change it" (38). Will cultural capital operate as real capital and allow Hartley to move up socially? This is the question the novel addresses.

As if to answer in the affirmative, Hartley uses the language of debt to explain the education that he acquired under Mr. Howard's tutelage, an education that succeeded in changing the young man's status from the inside out. "To him I am indebted for whatever distinguishes me from the stone which I turned up with my plough, of the stock which I dissevered with my axe" (39). As a result of his education, Hartley suggests, he has ceased to be an object and become instead an Enlightenment subject: "My understanding was awakened, disciplined, informed; my affections were cherished, exercised and regulated by him" (39–40). With the emergence of his sensibility comes none of the sense of entitlement that we find in Mackenzie's man of feeling, who lacks any inclination to work for the money he needs. To the American man of feeling, cultural and economic capital are two sides of the same coin. Just as he enhanced his knowledge through the labor of reading, so Hartley plans to increase his property through the labor of his body. The objective is to achieve economic autonomy and acquire the status of head of household, much as Franklin had spelled out in his model of the economic possibility in America.[12] As he explains, "I had sisters who needed my protection, and for whose destiny I ought to labour to attain independence" (40). By way of contrast to his European predecessor, the American man of feeling is cast from a Lockean mold.

Thus it comes as something of a jolt when this same man of feeling suddenly disavows the British component of his acquired sensibility. Having labored as an apprentice to a watchmaker, he determines that he must continue to labor until he rids himself of the values acquired with a knowledge of British literature, which instills a prejudice against those who labor. As he explains: "The ideas annexed to the term *peasant*, are wholly inapplicable to the tillers of ground in America; but our notions are the offspring, more of the books we read, than of any other of our external circumstances. Our books are almost wholly the productions of Europe and the prejudices, which infect us, are derived chiefly from this source. (53)" Hartley clearly considers it anachronistic for citizens of the new republic to hang onto European notions of rank. Yet, he is still subject to this reverence for inherited position. Indeed, it is awareness of his own position, as seen from the British point of view, that fuels his aspirations to rise in American society: "My ambition of dignity and fortune grew of this supposed inferiority of rank" (53). In this respect, Hartley resembles those British protagonists who are unwilling or unable to accept the social position into which they have been born.

The American protagonist must labor in the best Lockean tradition to plant what begins as British sensibility—a sign of leisure more than labor—in newly cultivated American soil. American soil purifies, cures, and restores masculinity to the English man of feeling much as it restores family feeling to the European libertine. When he first lived in England, Hartley's mentor, Mr. Howard, resembled more a libertine in the mold of the elder Harrington in *The Power of Sympathy* than a man of reason. By the time he meets up with Hartley, Howard's life was singularly marred by an inability to remain faithful to any woman, inspiring the woman he loved most in the world to marry his less profligate cousin. After immigrating to America with his private library, however, Howard underwent a salutary transformation. As Hartley tells it, Howard's "residence here, at a distance from ancient companions, and from all the usual incitements to extravagance, completed a thorough change in his character. He became . . . temperate, studious, gentle, and sedate" (49). Howard brings what is best about British culture in the form of his library and returns with it to England when he is purged of the bad features of British culture. Only then is he qualified to marry his newly widowed beloved, Clara's mother. By repeating this same course of reading, Hartley's character undergoes a similar transformation. Through a British education, his Pygmalion-like patron shapes Hartley's character around the very qualities that Howard himself had come to possess in America. Thus it is telling that Howard describes the transformation of his client as the extension of qualities usually located in opposing British types: "You are the son," he tells Hartley," of my affections and my reason" (51).

The American may have acquired reason and sensibility, but to marry advantageously, he still needs some sort of magic to translate his judgments and feelings into something of tangible value. This magic resides in Clara Howard. It is for good reason that the title of the American edition calls attention to the central importance of the love object in a novel that focuses obsessively on Edward Hartley, his education in reason and sensibility, and his single-minded pursuit of that object. Clara is British-born, yet she is the only one in the novel who "estimates the characters of others," not by birth or fortune, "but by the intrinsic qualities of heart and head" (51). The reformed Howard—having inherited his late cousin's property and married his cousin's widow—must now act as paterfamilias and arrange an exchange of his wife's daughter Clara with someone who in some sense is his equal. Under these circumstances, he views Hartley's reason and sensibility as equivalent to Clara's rank, property, and income. "I mean to admit you," he tells Hartley, "as an inseparable member of my family, and to place you, in every respect, on the footing of my son" (51). Here, Brockden Brown deliberately removes what British fiction had seen as the major obstacle to the successful courtship of a man of feeling and a daughter of the landed gentry. He solves that problem, however, in order to place what seems to be a new and more troubling obstacle in the path of an ideal union of American masculinity and British feminity. Clara withholds her consent until Hartley meets *her* terms for marriage.[13]

This has to be an important moment in American fiction, where a British woman both embodies the British standard and changes that standard. She will not marry according to her stepfather's will any more than she would have married on the basis of rank. Indeed, Clara refuses to consider Hartley unless and until he fulfills his prior contractual obligations to another woman. The novel invites us to entertain the fantasy that having met a British woman who does not evaluate a man's worth according to his rank, Edward could simply marry her. But nothing could be farther from

Brockden Brown's purpose. Having created a feminine embodiment of British values free of the taint of British prejudice, the novel labors for another hundred pages to put a new cultural ideal in its place.

Before meeting Clara, Hartley had agreed to wed Mary Wilmot chiefly because she had five thousand dollars, which he would use to support his two sisters. The marriage was an honorable agreement, free of deceit, but still one of pure convenience. As Hartley explains, "I never loved Mary Wilmot. Disparity of age, the dignity and sedateness of her carriage, and perhaps the want of personal attractions, inspired me with a sentiment, very different from love" (43). On discovering that the money was not coming to her after all, Mary vanishes for all practical purposes. Hartley assumes, reasonably enough, that because she can no longer honor her side of the bargain, she will not insist that he carry through on his. But Clara Howard holds Edward Hartley to a strict notion of the contractual obligation to marry—the spirit, we might say, rather than the letter of the law. She insists paradoxically that for Hartley to be the kind of man that she would marry, he must faithfully carry out his obligation to his former fiancée. Where Goethe's Werther was perfectly willing to seize another man's intended, Hartley's education gives him the capacity both to feel, and to constrain his feelings and defer gratification for a very long time. In what feels like a version of the cycles of frustration organizing Mackenzie's novel, the lion's share of *Clara Howard* consists of a protracted quest for Mary Wilmot.

In order for the American man of feeling to marry, his feeling for the woman of his choice has to be transmuted into one compatible with the love of the law. "So far from wishing to rule others," Hartley writes in a letter, "it is my glory and my boast to submit to one whom I deem unerring and divine. Clara's will is my law" (90). In this way, Brockden Brown subordinates both individual desire and traditional class affiliations to alliances based on consensual agreement. He belabors this point by having Hartley track down his former fiancée in a fruitless quest that explores American geography through a network of rivers from the Atlantic to the Pacific and back again. Only after his protagonist has crisscrossed the entire continent—suggesting that is where Hartley's responsibility begins and ends—does Brockden Brown conjure up a man of means, the benefactor Sedley, as a preferable partner for Mary, freeing Hartley to marry Clara.

Mackenzie's man of feeling had timely appeal as a witness to injustice and suffering in a world undergoing rapid change. Traditional lines of clientage and patronage were disappearing—the story of Old Edwards and his family retells this all-too-familiar tale—and traditional relations between squire and tenant farmer were giving way to ruthlessly mercenary relations. Money in the hands of a new breed of landlords, coupled with nascent forms of capitalist acquisitiveness, severed the bonds organizing rural England. Against this historical background, Mackenzie's protagonist is singularly impotent. He neither can correct injustice nor advance any political change. It remains for Brockden Brown's man of feeling to solve the problem that Mackenzie's Harley exposes. By submitting to the contract that separates him from the object of his desire, Brockden Brown's Hartley miraculously acquires that object as his reward. Observing this tenet of democratic culture, *Clara Howard* registers moral feeling and contractualism as two sides of the same coin of masculinity. An Englishwoman dictates and sanctions the new society. Indeed, his fidelity to contractualism creates a world at the end of the novel where everyone is not only equal but equally cared for as well. Like Clara and Edward, Sedley and Mary Wilmot will marry. Because Mary turns out to be Clara's British relation, both will see to it that their men head English households. At the same time, because British distinctions of rank have given way to the American ideal of contractualism, those households will be socially and politically American.

The Man of Feeling Returns to England after a Turn in America

The revolutions in America, France, the Caribbean, and, later, Latin America no doubt made it seem as if the world suffered from an excess rather than a deficiency of sensibility. Rather than captive to a rigidly hierarchized social order, one's position appeared to be up for grabs. While such historians as E. P. Thompson and John Barrell have argued that these changes were indeed more apparent than substantive, the fiction of the period nevertheless cast everything readers took for granted in a destabilizing light and then came up with new ways of assuaging the anxiety so generated. A product of the 1770s, Mackenzie's man of feeling was cursed with a sensibility that might have imperiled the old order had he not died of frustration. In the decades following the French Revolution, readers seemed to want more than that, and the hero of Brockden Brown's *Clara Howard* combines the excessive subjectivity required of a compassionate man with the education necessary to convert that excess into self-government. British novels written after the turn of the century adopt the formal strategies by which Brockden Brown converted the one into the other—individual sensibility into citizenship.

Brockden Brown was not the only writer to renew public interest in the man of feeling. William Godwin followed his lead in this respect, and I find the contrast between the two instructive. In 1805 Godwin acknowledged his debt to Mackenzie by subtitling his novel *Fleetwood: Or, the New Man of Feeling*. Initially a misanthrope, Godwin's man of feeling is someone of a "poetical and contemplative character" (73) until he goes off to

Oxford.[14] After a period of sensual indulgence and dissipation, he comes to resemble nothing so much as what one reviewer called "a prosaic Othello" (537) beguiled into jealous suspicion about his wife by an avaricious malcontent who wants to be Fleetwood's heir. In a harshly critical account of *Fleetwood* in the *Edinburgh Review* (April 1805), Sir Walter Scott objects to this misappropriation of Mackenzie's protagonist with these words: "We have been accustomed to associate with our ideas of this character the amiable virtues of a Harley, feeling deeply the distresses of others, and patient though not insensible of his own. But Fleetwood, through his whole three volumes which bear his name, feels absolutely exclusively for one individual, and that individual is Fleetwood himself" (521–22). Objecting to the title of Godwin's novel, another reviewer declares, "By 'A Man of Feeling,' is generally understood a man of warm and active benevolence whose heart is exquisitely sensible to the distresses of every being around him, and whose hand is ever ready, as far as his influence extends, to alleviate or relieve them . . . if the reader expects to find any resemblance between Fleetwood and Harley, he will soon discover his mistake" (525). These two reviewers are not alone in expressing their dismay with Godwin for linking his violent protagonist to Mackenzie's gentle Harley. To a man, these reviewers denounce Godwin for having violated the prototype when he failed to temper his hero's egotistical passions with socially oriented compassion. Such moderation was essential to permissible forms of sensibility by 1805.[15]

When in 1807 the Minerva Press reprinted Brockden Brown's *Clara Howard* in England, under the title *Philip Stanley: or, the Enthusiasm of Love*, it introduced England to the American alternative to Godwin's revision of Mackenzie's Harley—an alternative that soon took hold, I will argue, and flourished in Jane Austen's fiction. William Lane not only built his press to considerable importance over a period of thirty years, but, according to one historian of the Minerva, "also established circulating libraries in all parts of the kingdom for the sale of his novels."[16] Authors and readers alike knew the press as a major publisher of just the sort of novels that the heroine of Austen's *Northanger Abbey* has a taste for.[17] But what Austen herself does to the man of feeling is historically light years beyond both Mackenzie's example and anything Godwin produced. I believe Brockden Brown, or if not he, then some unknown English forebear resembling the American Hartley, enabled this quantum leap. We know that Austen drafted "Elinor and Marianne" in the 1790s and revised it extensively between 1805–10 before first publishing it in 1811 as *Sense and Sensibility*. Her "First Impressions" was on the table in 1797, only to be significantly rewritten and published in 1813 as *Pride and Prejudice*. Whether she actually read *Philip Stanley* during this period—and the likelihood is that she did, given that a Minerva lending library was within five miles of the Austen home—is less important than the fact of a fundamental shift in the kind of masculinity English readers and reviewers were prepared to receive. As I hope to demonstrate, Jane Austen's ideal heroes are cut to the pattern of Brockden Brown's man of feeling.

To succeed as a male in an Austen novel, one must have deep and intense feelings but subject them to rigorous forms of discipline. Before a man can be considered worthy of her heroines, he must wait, much as Edward Hartley had to wait, without any hope of gratification. Austen has little interest in appealing to American readers and even less interest in contract law. But she nevertheless borrows the principle from Brockden Brown that true masculinity expresses itself through a protracted delay, redirection, and sublimation of desire for an original love object. In *Sense and Sensibility*, Austen not only binds Edward Ferrars to a secret pledge of marriage, but also inflicts on Colonel Brandon the loss of his youthful lover. In *Pride and Prejudice* and *Persuasion*, Austen's heroines reject the first offers of marriage from Mr. Darcy and Captain Wentworth, respectively. All of these men appear to grow in sensibility as they suppress their feelings and turn their attention elsewhere—to acts of kindness that do nothing to assuage their profound sense of loss. As a result of the delay or rebuff, furthermore, Austen's man of feeling is given a chance to show compassion and act in some completely selfless way to correct an injustice. The men who finally win the hands of Marianne Dashwood, Eleanor Dashwood, Elizabeth Bennet, and Anne Elliot are men who demonstrate that intense feelings unknown to the heroine lurk behind an exterior of parental concern, extreme reserve, lukewarm affection, and even dislike.[18]

Colonel Brandon is first described as "silent and grave."[19] When Marianne Dashwood performs for guests at Barton Park, he "alone, of all the party, heard her without being in raptures" (28). Lest the reader construe this reticence as a lack of appreciation for Marianne herself, Austen lets it be known what depth of emotion is implied by his self-containment: "He paid her only the compliment of attention; and she felt a respect for him on the occasion, which the others had reasonably forfeited by their shameless want of taste" (28). Not to be outdone in this respect, Edward Ferrars, the secret suitor of Marianne's sister, appears "too diffident to do justice to himself; but when his natural shyness was overcome," Austen assures us, "his behaviour gave every indication of an open affectionate heart" (14).

Mr. Darcy of *Pride and Prejudice* violates the prototype of the man of feeling in a very different way. When the reader first encounters him, Darcy radiates the very opposite of admiration and receives less than his share of that feeling to which rank ordinarily entitles him: "The gentlemen pronounced him to be a fine figure of a man, the ladies declared he was much handsomer than Mr. Bingley, and he was looked at with great admiration for about half the evening, till his manners gave a disgust which turned the tide of his popularity."[20] Add to the fact that he rates very low on an emotional register that Darcy—and Brandon, for that matter—is extremely wealthy and therefore a complete inversion of Harley. Austen as much as dispenses with Harley's coupling of excess emotion with insufficient wealth in order to move on to what she obviously regarded as the more salient feature of the man of feeling—the protracted period of frustration, which in Mackenzie's novel led only to death. Darcy's ability to marry the woman he truly desires has little to do with wealth or position. Austen would convince us that when Elizabeth Bennet agrees to marry him and Marianne Dashwood accepts Brandon's proposal, it is on the basis of emotional compatibility alone. Austen manages to hand over to her heroines the prerogative to decide whether to accept the offers of marriage, and she has these women sound the depth and try the endurance of their partners' feelings before they come to a decision.

Paradoxically, the most direct testimony to the fact that Austen was reworking a form of masculinity that flourished in the 1770s appears in her last and most perplexing novel, *Persuasion*. In the opening pages we learn that the young Wentworth "had no fortune" to back up his initial proposal of marriage to Anne Elliot.[21] Succumbing to social codes not all that different from those prohibiting the marriage of Mackenzie's Harley to the well-born Miss Waltham, Austen's heroine "was persuaded to believe the engagement a wrong thing—indiscreet, improper, hardly capable of success, and not deserving it" (28). And as in the case of Miss Waltham, it is not for lack of love that Anne turns down Wentworth's offer: "Had she not imagined herself consulting his good, even more than her own, she could hardly have given him up" (28). When Wentworth returns to Bath and the society of the Elliots eight years later, however, Austen tells us, "He was rich, and being turned on shore, fully intended to settle as soon as he could be properly tempted" (41). Thus it is no longer lack of money that obstructs his marriage with Anne, who never wavered in her desire for him, despite the various men who parade through Pump Room and parlor, at least one of whom with an eye fixed on her inheritance. Having cleared away all material obstacles standing between two individuals who are entirely suited for one another and already know it, Austen begins a singularly gray novel in which each must re-experience the painful possibility of the other's marriage to someone else. From Anne's point of view, "They had no conversation together, no intercourse, but what the commonest civility required. Once so much to each other! Now nothing!" (42). Exploiting a protracted and futile quest equal only to that composing the second half of Brockden Brown's novel, Austen has both her new man and woman sit in no little agony on the sidelines, each wishing only happiness for the other at the cost of great emotional sacrifice each to him or herself. It is precisely by not expressing desire and the large cloud of small disappoint-ments, and even smaller glimpses of possible gratification, that these char-acters convince us there is so very much feeling there to express.

To drive home her point, Austen populates each of her novels with shal-low characters who use the language of emotion too easily and insincerely and employ it to duplicitous ends. The conventions available for direct expression of feeling have been co-opted by those who misuse them. Rob-ert Ferrars uses the language of feelings to displace his bashful older brother Edward as his mother's sole heir. Robert shares the propensity for "assiduous attention and endless flatteries, as soon as the smallest opening was given for their exercise" (266) with the libertine Willoughby, who "read with all the sensibility and spirit which Edward unfortunately wanted" (38). Marianne succumbs to Willoughby's charm on the assumption "that to the perfect good-breeding of the gentleman, he united frankness and vivacity" (36). But Willoughby's success actually derives from his ability to mirror Marianne's own highly emotive language. Even the usually clear-sighted Elinor is misled when she overhears him speaking to Marianne, "in the whole of the sentence, in his manner of pronouncing it, and in his addressing her sister by her Christian name alone, she instantly saw an intimacy so decided, a meaning so direct, as marked a perfect agreement between them. From that moment she doubted not of their being engaged to each other" (45).

In *Pride and Prejudice*, Austen contrasts Darcy's extraordinary difficulty in expressing his affection for Elizabeth Bennet with his friend Bingley's easy affability, on the one hand, and Wickham's insidious glibness, on the other. *Persuasion*, too, has its linguistically promiscuous types, Captain Benwick and William Walter Elliot. On the one hand, Benwick is so full of the language of Scott and Byron that he strikes Anne Elliot as having "the appearance of feelings glad to burst their usual restraints" (67), while El-liot's verbal facility makes him the proverbial snake in the garden, eager to ensnare the trusting heroine: "Mr. Elliot was not disappointed in the inter-est he hoped to raise. No one can withstand the charm of such a mystery. To have been described long ago to a recent acquaintance, by nameless people, is irresistible; and Anne was all curiosity" (124). In contrast to these abusers of language, the true man of feeling has trouble putting his feelings into words.

Unwilling to sound like their glib but heartless counterparts, Brandon, Edward Ferrars, Darcy, and Wentworth suppress their feelings as if that alone were the only guarantee of sincerity. As Elinor Dashwood explains to her sister Marianne, Edward "believes many people pretend to more admiration of the beauties of nature than they really feel, and is disgusted with such pretensions, he affects greater indifference and less discrimina-tion in viewing them himself than he possesses" (71). As a preamble to his second proposal of marriage, Darcy taunts Elizabeth Bennet with her failure to understand his lack of self-expression as testament to his intense feelings, "You thought me then devoid of every proper feeling, I am sure you did" (253). Wentworth has an even more difficult time expressing his feelings for Anne in the conventions available for that purpose. Cut to the quick by her suggestion that his polite restraint indicates faltering devotion, he blurts out the truth in a note: "You pierce my soul. I am half agony, half hope. Tell me not that I am too late, and that such precious feelings are gone for ever. I offer myself to you again with a heart even more your own, than when you almost broke it eight years and a half ago. . . . I have loved none but you. Unjust I may have been, weak and resentful I have been, but never inconstant." (158) Doubtful even of language so bluntly rendered, he "placed it before Anne with eyes of glowing entreaty fixed on her for a moment" (157), as if to say that words alone will not quite do the trick.

It is the man of feeling's difficult task to find just the right form of cultural expression, as that form testifies to what is not only deep but also unique about his feelings. Darcy cannot be the one to reveal how he rescued the Bennet family name. Brandon is under a similar obligation to rescue Eliza from Willoughby and say nothing of it until forced to do so. Ferrars, too, waits until after he has been released from his obligation to Lucy Steele, while Wentworth is subject to public gossip and rumors of courtship that cast him as the object of desire in plots that contradict his enduring affection for Anne. To prove them adequate, Austen subjects each of her men to trials in which they are required to distinguish themselves by extravagant and prolonged forms of self-containment. By forcing them to wait until they find the right form, the correct setting, and the proper rhetorical moment to give social expression to their deepest desires, Austen creates male protagonists whose depth and consistency of feeling is beyond any doubt.

Even then, there is no adequate medium to reveal the special quality of their affection in a form that is not shot through with conventional phrases available to just about anyone. Consider the case of Captain Wentworth. It would be a mistake to think he is blurting out his feelings when he confesses his love to Anne. The occasion for this revelation is a highly contrived literary topos that under such conditions is *not* available to most other men. Wentworth drafts the note professing his love to her while listening to Anne debate Captain Harville on the ever-so-familiar literary topos of woman's constancy. Having rejected the books, songs, and proverbs Harville offers on behalf of man's constancy, Anne claims only that women love "longest, when existence or when hope is gone" (157). Later, Wentworth confesses that, "[T]hose sentiments and those tones which had reached him while she talked with Captain Harville" vanquished his jealousy of William Elliot. "[U]nder the irresistible governance of which [the debate] he had seized a sheet of paper, and poured out his feelings" (161). It is important to note that the feelings in question are not "poured out" but written in highly formulaic phrases to intervene in the highly conventional debate on constancy: "Unjust I may have been, weak and resentful I have been, but never inconstant" (158). By suppressing his jealousy, on the one hand, and his feelings for Anne, on the other, Wentworth finds a vehicle for emotional expression in one of the most conventional of literary formats.

If Wentworth requires classic literary formulae to express his deepest feelings, we should not be surprised to discover that characters like Brandon, Ferrars, and Darcy are similarly unable to express themselves in the vernacular. Elizabeth Bennet's opinion of Darcy changes when she visits Pemberly with the Gardners and his character is drawn by Mrs. Reynolds, the housekeeper. While gazing at his miniature, the visitors learn from Mrs. Reynolds that rather than a proud and heartless aristocrat, Darcy "was always the sweetest tempered, most generous-hearted, boy in the world." The housekeeper tops off her portrait of Darcy as a man of feeling by describing him as "affable to the poor" (161). This ekphrastic moment transforms him in Elizabeth's eyes: "This was praise, of all others most extraordinary, most opposite to [Elizabeth's] ideas. That he was not a good-tempered man, had been her firmest opinion" (162). When her narrator sees little point in repeating the terms of Darcy's second proposal to Elizabeth, Austen reiterates the point that there is no way for the man of feeling to speak, so hackneyed have the conventions of emotional expression become. She also refuses to provide any dialogue for his response to Elizabeth's acceptance, noting only that: "he expressed himself on the occasion as sensibly and as warmly as a man violently in love can be supposed to do" (239). His face having been transformed by his miniature, that face can now individuate and deepen his otherwise less-than-interesting speech: "Had Elizabeth been able to encounter his eye, she might have seen how well the expression of heart-felt delight, diffused over his face, became him" (239).

Brandon, too, submits to rigid standards of self-expression that deprive him of the means of professing love to Marianne Dashwood. He confesses his desire to her mother instead. For fear that these emotions might sound disingenuous coming from the lips of the man of feeling himself, Austen has Mrs. Dashwood report them to Elinor: "He opened his whole heart to me yesterday as we traveled." She not only reports on the contents of Brandon's feelings, but she also testifies to its genuineness: "It came out quite unawares, quite undesignedly" (238). Paradoxically, it is also by way of second-hand reports that Marianne learns of Brandon's "irresistible feelings." Removed from the heat of the moment, Elinor and Mrs. Dashwood can proceed to analyze his feelings. They observe that their high opinion of Brandon "does not rest on *one* act of kindness" (239) but on many, and his manners are distinguished by "their gentleness, their genuine attention to other people, and their manly unstudied simplicity" (240). Like Darcy, the most expressive moments of this man of feeling occur when he cannot say anything:

> His emotion in entering the room, in seeing her altered looks and in receiving the pale hand which she immediately held out to him, was such, as, in Elinor's conjecture, must arise from something more than his affection for Marianne, or the consciousness of its being known to others; and she soon discovered in his melancholy eye and varying complexion as he looked at her sister, the probable recurrence of many past scenes of misery to his mind, brought back by that resemblance between Marianne and Eliza (241).

By preventing Brandon from speaking what he feels and, at the same time, making his face speak volumes, Austen creates the effect that he is suppressing feelings that exceed the power of words.

Finally, Edward Ferrars resembles those other men of feeling who can speak only hesitantly and in highly restricted forms. Like Philip Stanley, Ferrars fulfills his contractual obligations at great personal sacrifice without hope of gratifying his most deeply held desire. When he reveals to Elinor he is not married to Lucy Steele after all (his brother has fortuitously relieved him of that obligation), she flees the room and he leaves without saying another word. The novel suggests nothing so much as that extraordinary self-denial is the prerequisite for self-gratification: "he was released without any reproach to himself, from an entanglement which had long formed his misery, from a woman whom he had long ceased to love;—and elevated at once to that security with another, which he must have thought of almost with despair as soon as he had learnt to consider it with desire" (255).

In *Clara Howard*, Charles Brockden Brown inscribed the man of feeling within the ideology of the social contract. By so doing, he demonstrated that to secure one's personal interest, one must subordinate his particular interest to that of the community as a whole. Thus we find the form of self-discipline that Clara induces in Hartley transforming those attributes that qualify him for citizenship into the attributes for companionate love. Democracy becomes the natural result of such affection. Where the epistolary novel makes it rather a simple matter for Hartley to express his feelings for Clara, Austen staged an elaborate aesthetic performance to distinguish the revelation of true affection from the abuse of words. Only such self-consciously aesthetic occasions as literary debates, scenes of reading, and discussions about the verisimilitude of a painting provide the terms as well as the rhetoric for true self-expression. Where Mackenzie's man of feeling could speak easily and Goethe's Werther was positively verbose, Austen's men of feeling are placed, as is Brockden Brown's Hartley, in situations where feelings assume an inverse relation to their verbal expression. The verbal constraints placed upon the protagonist become the means of gauging the depth of his feelings. Thus we might credit Austen for transforming the man of feeling from the source of exalted prose to the strong, silent type, a form of masculinity that we now consider uniquely American.

Frontier Feeling

Nowhere is James Fenimore Cooper's debt to the continental version of the man of feeling more apparent than in *Pathfinder*, the novel where the taciturn frontiersman, Natty Bumpo, otherwise known as Hawkeye, falls in love and almost marries. Cooper introduces Hawkeye as the embodiment of "simplicity, integrity and sincerity, blended in an air of self reliance."[22] In this crucial respect, he is the very antithesis of the polygamous conspirator Muir, "whose smooth-tongued courtesy was little in accordance with [Hawkeye's] own frank and ingenuous nature" (424). As if to establish an inverse relation between fullness of feeling and lack of words, Cooper provides numerous occasions on which Hawkeye's feelings exceed his powers of self-expression. "Unwilling, if not unable to say any more," Cooper tells us, "he walked away, and stood leaning on his rifle, and looking up at the stars for quite ten minutes, in profound silence" (190). A hundred pages later, Mabel learns that Hawkeye seeks the companionship of a wife and has her in mind for this role. She refuses his offer on grounds that his age and his familiarity with Indian ways make them too different. This is how Cooper chooses to represent the keen disappointment his protagonist feels: "The pent-up feelings would endure no more, and the tears rolled down the cheeks of the scout, like rain. His fingers again worked convulsively at his throat, and his breast heaved, as if it possessed a tenant of which it would be rid, by any effort, however, desperate" (271). Clearly couched in an exaggerated version of the language of the man of feeling and true to its conventions, this passage shows the taciturn Hawkeye to be capable of extreme emotion—not only unable to free that "tenant" from his heaving breast, but also unfit to be incorporated within a modern household. Unwilling to end their relationship on this note of failure, Cooper spends the second half of *Pathfinder* moving beyond the stalemate created by Hawkeye's role as the strong, silent type. Indeed, we might regard the process by which the novel finally succeeds in marrying off Mabel as something on the order of a descriptive theory of the transformation required before the man of feeling can become a nation-maker, recognizably American and yet receivable in Europe as well. Having turned down

Hawkeye on grounds of cultural incompatibility, Mabel assumes the role of a Clara Howard and insists on Bumpo's strict adherence to the very contract she had earlier rejected. Invoking her father's deal with Hawkeye, she says, "save my father from this dreadful death [at the hands of the Indians] and I can worship you" (376). If Bumpo were to honor the contract with Mabel's father, it would yield a loveless alliance—as would Hartley's marriage of convenience to Mary Wilmot and a far cry from the marriage of an American Adam and Eve. To produce what Doris Sommer terms a "foundational fiction," Cooper has to marry off one English creole to another and to do it while remaining faithful to the contract between Mabel's father and Pathfinder.[23]

If we think that Cooper has painted himself into a conceptual corner in this respect by figuring his hero as a man of feeling, then we must think again. In a scene that might have come from a novel by Henry Fielding were it not so saturated with sentiment, Cooper puts young Jasper Western at the deathbed where Mabel's dying father cements his contract with Hawkeye: " 'Pathfinder'—added the serjeant, feeling on the opposite side of the bed, where Jasper still knelt, getting one of the hands of the young man, by mistake—'Take it—I leave you as her father—as you and she may please—bless you—bless you' " (443). The sergeant's "mistake" is no mistake in terms of the solution Cooper feels compelled to produce and the means available to him for doing so. This "mistake" succeeds in splitting the man of feeling into two component parts—a generous father and an affectionate husband. As surrogate father to Mabel, Hawkeye is in a position to cancel out the first contract based on an outdated patriarchal model and oversee a more American, because consensual, contract. In this regard, he is modeled on the historically earlier man of feeling who was condemned to remain single. At the same time, having this nearly indigenous man as surrogate father makes Mabel something of a Creole who can be at home on the frontier and the perfect mate for Jasper Western. As the new Americans, it is important that neither of them depend on bloodlines or wealth for their value but on something like the cultural capital empowered in Brockden Brown's man of feeling.

Cooper has carefully set the stage for a match to take place on this basis all along. Having been educated by a widow of an officer, as Cooper explains, Mabel "received much more than the rudiments of plain English instruction." With such an education, she "acquired some tastes, and many ideas, ... the results [of which] were quite apparent, in her attire, her language, her sentiments and even in her feelings" (109). Culturally mismatched with Hawkeye, Mabel finds in Jasper her masculine counterpart. When Jasper speaks his feelings, like Hawkeye, he does so "almost unconsciously, but with a truth and feeling that carried with the instant conviction of their deep sincerity" (446). In contrast to Hawkeye, however, Jasper was "brought up under a real English seaman; one that had sailed under the King's Pennant, and may be called a thorough bred: that is to say, a subject born in the colonies" (193). Jasper is Mabel's equal not only in terms of birth and background, but also on the basis of a shared literacy and taste, which achieve a kind of hybridity in Hawkeye. As he tells Mabel, Jasper "is quite a scholar who—knows the tongue of the Frenchers—reads many books. Some, I know, that you like to read yourself—can understand you at all times, which, perhaps, is more than I can say for myself" (456). If American masculinity finds its ideal embodiment in a silent hero who contains a whole world within him, then surely this ideal is deeply indebted to Brockden Brown's revision of Mackenzie's hero.

Brockden Brown transformed the man of feeling into one for whom mere words or the easy expression of feelings were inadequate testimony to his feelings. He made his protagonist delay gratification, journey across the American landscape, and so prove that his depth of feeling for his beloved was evident in his fidelity to a contract. By emphasizing action over words as the best testimony to feelings, Brockden Brown recast as disingenuous any easy expression of masculine sentiment. Taking up the revised type, Jane Austen made it nearly impossible for those males whom she designated as fit mates for her heroines to give voice to their feelings. She made us believe that these men were too full of emotion to do so. The sign of the depth and sincerity of what they felt is expressed, paradoxically, by their near inability to find adequate means of expression except in highly formal and self-consciously artistic settings. Looking at Cooper as the inheritor to Brockden Brown's and Austen's revision of the man of feeling, we may begin to account for his popularity on both sides of the Atlantic. As the first American author to enjoy both American and European followings, it is to Cooper that many look when they seek the example for that stereotype of a distinctive brand of American masculinity. The protagonist—whose legacy extends all the way from Cooper to Melville and Twain to Hemingway—can claim Charles Brockden Brown and Jane Austen for his literary parents.

5

THE GOTHIC IN DIASPORA

LESLIE FIEDLER made the claim, "It is the gothic form that has been most fruitful in the hands of our best writers."[1] From the colonial period to the present day, our fiction has always been Gothic, he declared, "nonrealistic and negative, sadist and melodramatic—a literature of darkness and the grotesque in a land of light and affirmation" (29). Because American literature "is most deeply influenced by the gothic," in Fiedler's view, it "is almost essentially a gothic one" (142). Writing almost thirty years later, Toni Morrison updated Fiedler's contention without really challenging it. She famously found in American fiction "images of impenetrable whiteness" that "appear almost always in conjunction with representations of black or Africanist people who are dead, impotent, or under complete control." This phantom "companion to whiteness" is "a dark and abiding presence that moves the hearts and texts of American literature with fear and longing." Indeed, *Playing in the Dark*, Morrison's own account of American literature, describes the formation of American literature as a "haunting, a darkness from which our early literature seemed unable to extricate itself."[2]

Writing in the heyday of a kind of popular psychological criticism that combined depth psychology with a strain of anthropology that made Freud and Jung equal partners in truth-telling, Fiedler felt authorized to claim that "the guilt which underlies the gothic and motivates its plots is the guilt of the revolutionary haunted by the (paternal) past which he has been striving to destroy" (129). When he identified "the slaughter of the Indians" and "the abominations of the slave trade" as "special guilts" that were projected in the gothic form in America, Fiedler anticipated not only Morrison but also Philip Fisher and a number of other contemporary critics (143).[3] Formulating her argument in the multicultural and historicist environment of more recent decades, Morrison could be much more explicit about the Africanist presence in American literature because she felt it was imperative to be more precise about the historical reasons for guilt. Nor have more recent explanations for this dependency on the gothic abandoned the effort to establish a psychological cause for the phobic fantasy we identify with gothic literature.[4] American literary criticism still proceeds on the assumption that telling one more horrifying story about their inhumanity could drain the reservoir of guilt created by the habitual disavowal of our founding fathers' sadism.

Did the extraordinary crimes that allowed the United States to become a powerful and prosperous nation actually produce a secret past and repository of guilt that expressed itself in a national literary style? If we look to the Armenian Genocide or the Holocaust, we find that survivors, families, and sympathizers of the victims invariably find ways to write about what is justly characterized as the unspeakable horror of these events, but we do not consider it reasonable and necessary to explain the style of contemporary Turkish or German writing as expressions of the unacknowledged guilt concerning these crimes against humanity. My point is not so much to question the efficacy of explanations that want to attribute the prevalence of the gothic in American literature to some unacknowledged guilt as to launch another kind of explanation that begins with the observation that the gothic mode arose in America about the same time as the vogue for gothic fiction appeared in Europe. No one would try to understand the rise of the gothic mode in Europe as a response to the Indian genocide and the horrors of slavery.[5] By understanding American gothic as the appropriation of a European fashion, I believe that we can see how American authors changed the prototype and what in fact they were saying when they did so.

An appetite for the gothic obviously seized hold of the American book trade during the 1790s. Donald Ringe has documented just some of the evidence of the considerable Americans demand both for British gothic novels, short stories, and plays as well as for English translations of German gothic fiction.[6] A brief summary of the contours of the American publication of European gothic texts along with the advertisements for English editions of this same material in catalogues should suffice to indicate that well before American writers began producing gothic fiction in any quantity, American readers were consuming a substantial number of such narratives imported from Europe. In 1794 Matthew Carey came out with an American edition of Stephen Cullen's *The Haunted Priory* in Philadelphia. The following year saw American printings of Radcliffe's *A Sicilian Romance* (Baltimore) and *Mysteries of Udolpho* (Boston). Also in 1795, Radcliffe's *The Romance of the Forest* appeared both in Boston and Philadelphia, Cullen's *Count Roderic's Castle* was printed in Baltimore, and in Philadelphia Charlotte Smith's *Montalbert* was published along with Ann Yearsley's *The Royal Captives: A Fragment of a Secret History*. The following year, readers could purchase American editions of Radcliffe's *The Castles of Athlin and Dunbayne* (Philadelphia), Schiller's *The Ghost Seer* (New York and Charleston), and Richard Warner's *Netley Abbey* (Philadelphia). Clara Reeve's *The Old English Baron* appeared in Philadelphia during 1797. That year also saw printings of Radcliffe's *The Italian* in Mount Pleasant, New York, and Boston, as well as two printings in Philadelphia. Regina Maria

Roche's *The Children of the Abbey* and *Clermont* were published in Philadelphia in 1798, followed in 1799 by *Ambrosio*, the expurgated edition of
Matthew Lewis's *The Monk*. This is just the tip of the iceberg.

As if the proliferation of American editions were not enough, magazine
readers enjoyed serializations of entire gothic novels by British and German
authors along with any number of extracts of gothic texts, and a good
many shorter tales that had originally appeared in English magazines.[7] It
was not unusual during the 1790s for fiction taken from a British source
and published in one American magazine to be reprinted in another. Such
printing and reprinting of gothic fiction clearly responded to an increasing
demand.[8] Advertisements announcing the arrival of the latest British imports and the correspondence and catalogues of lending libraries indicate
the demand for gothic literature exceeded the ability of American printers
to meet it. These British editions were advertised for sale: Ann Radcliffe's
A Sicilian Romance (1790) and *The Romance of the Forest* (1791) in Boston
in 1793; *The Mysteries of Udolpho* (1794) in Philadelphia; and *The Italian*
(1797) in Boston and Baltimore in 1798. British editions of such novels as
Horace Walpole's *The Castle of Otranto* (1764), Charlotte Smith's *The Old
Manor House* (1793) and *Montalbert* (1795), not to mention Lewis's *The
Monk* (1796), were all available for the discerning American consumer. In
addition, German works translated for the British market also sold well in
the United States.[9] If nothing else, this synopsis of publishing history
should remind us that the gothic was not an indigenous American genre
but a highly desirable import.

The obvious enthusiasm of American readers for gothic fiction begs the
question of why the gothic spoke more insistently to the interests of a
diasporic community than any other genre—and did so during the very
decade in British publishing history that has been described as "the effulgence" of the gothic.[10] The fact that American readers were an ocean removed from their cultural home is after all the most important difference
between American and British readerships. In view of this fact, we must
ask ourselves if among the many and different examples of British and
German versions of the gothic available in the new republic, there is not
something distinctive about the gothic fiction eventually written by American authors specifically for an American readership.

Why Things Go Bump in the Night

In England, the gothic came into fashion in the last half of the eighteenth
century alongside and in a cultural dialogue with sentimental fiction.
Where the sentimental novel aimed to create a readership of like-minded
individuals, the gothic, as I shall argue, challenged fiction that aimed at

producing modern individuals of any kind. Where sentimental fiction represented the quality of a character's feelings and his or her ability both to express them and to recognize their manifestations in someone else, gothic fiction initially featured one-of-a-kind aristocrats who were the last of a line threatened with extinction and more often than not seeking a substitute that might continue the bloodline. The individual quality of a character's feelings mattered not a whit; the metaphysics of blood was responsible for directing desire at certain objects whether or not the characters involved shared anything else in common. In this respect, the gothic seemed bent on exhuming cultural material that from the perspective of the late eighteenth and early nineteenth centuries was associated with a much earlier period of history—usually the remains of a culture that housed an older aristocratic model of social relations.

Especially antagonistic to modern realism as articulated by John Locke, Samuel Johnson, Jane Austen, and others, British gothic is populated with characters controlled by what clearly resembles an early modern form of the passions. Gothic fiction habitually brings such figures forth, spells out their barbaric propensities, drives them wild with supernatural occurrences, and then rids the world of its demons, leaving the reader completely, if not smugly, reconciled to a disenchanted modernity.[11] But the appearance of antiquated aristocratic character types living in a world of ghosts and swept away on the tide of passion does not operate as a re-enactment of the past—a period piece of sorts. On the contrary, this material is introduced into the present—or some version of it—in order that we may imagine how modern individuals would feel if suddenly subjected to the condition of an earlier time and marvelous events. As gothic fiction explains away the eruption of passion in the face of apparently supernatural occurrences and banishes such outbursts to the past, it enters into the service of what would later be known approvingly as "realism."[12] Indeed, if we understand the gothic and sentimentalism as two sides of one discursive coin, then we can say that the gothic supplies the emotion over which sentimentalism gains authority in a process of domestication that relegates all magic to the domain of delusion and literature.

Horace Walpole's *The Castle of Otranto* first appeared in December 1764 and still offers a convenient model of the European gothic in all the important respects. Walpole initially introduced the novel as "a story" translated from the "original Italian of Onuphrio Muralto" by William Marshall, who found the manuscript in a library in the north of England.[13] If, as the putative translator informs the reader, "the story was written near the time when it is supposed to have happened," then the events to follow would have occurred between 1095 and 1243 (5). The translator contrasts the rationality of his own time to the irrationality and gullibility he attributes to the original audience: "Miracles, visions, necromancy, dreams and other preternatural events," writes the translator, "are exploded now even from romances. That was not the case when our author wrote" (6). It was perhaps because he was breaking new ground in writing this kind of story that Walpole started it off with such a bang and drops an oversize helmet on the putative heir to Otranto.[14] Witnessing this crushing blow, an unknown young peasant points out that the deadly helmet is exactly like the one atop the marble statue of the dead Alfonso in the Church of St. Nicholas. Already unnerved by these events, Manfred, Lord of Otranto, encounters a portrait come to life and that heaves a sigh, sees three drops of blood fall from a statue, and hails a shrouded figure that suddenly turns to reveal that it is a corpse. His ordeal concludes with perhaps the most spectacular sequence of special effects: a clap of thunder, the collapse of the castle's walls, and the appearance of an immense apparition who names the true heir to the throne before ascending to heaven.

If objects behave like subjects with a life and will of their own, then subjects behave—if not like objects—then certainly as if their lives and their desires were not their own. On discovering his son's limbs protruding from beneath the giant helmet, Manfred immediately decides to marry his ward, Isabella, which means divorcing the princess to whom he has long been married. Such impulsive, even crazed behavior is not restricted to Manfred but moves infectiously through the cast of characters, who are mysteriously "agitated by a thousand passions," (63) and "terrified out of their senses" (102). Matilda, Manfred's daughter, falls in love with Theodore while gazing at his picture in "uncommon" "adoration" (41), and Manfred in a trance accidentally murders his own daughter (108–9). His wife, Hippolyta, patiently endures the prince's worst crimes, even though they leave her stripped of status and childless. Nor do the other characters demonstrate any more complexity of motive and response than she does, despite the fact that their world has been turned quite upside down. In sum, this novel is in every respect antagonistic to the sort of fiction written by either a Richardson or a Fielding, both of whom attribute the outcome of individual deeds to qualities within the individual. But while these turns of event seem nonsensical in the terms we have come to expect of a novel, even ridiculously so, they make perfectly good sense in terms of the propensities and behaviors that Walpole attributes to an older aristocracy.

Contrary to the tenets of Enlightenment thought, such events argue that a kind of magic in the blood of the true prince secures the throne for the legitimate heir, and neither wit nor strength of arms can alter the will of providence on this issue. Each obstacle that stands in the way of Manfred's attempt to legitimate his claim to Otranto works to restore the true heir to his rightful place. None of these obstacles can be explained in terms of human motivation because in Walpole's version of the premodern world, individuals do not count. Manfred sheds not a tear when his son dies but immediately sets about to find someone to produce an heir even if he has to do it himself. Subject to the same logic, Matilda must die even though she and Theodore, the legitimate heir disguised as a peasant, love each other and despite the fact that she has been a dutiful daughter to Manfred in every other respect.

The social body that Walpole imagines is made up of members all of whom share some degree of noble blood. Arranged in vertical chains of dependency, the status of each is determined by his or her proximity by blood to the murdered prince of Otranto. No character can be whole or entire unto itself; each is eminently replaceable by the person next in line. All matter only insofar as they maintain the integrity of the family, and guaranteeing its perpetuity trumps all other forms of motivation. For an equivalent to this concept of the family, we might think of clans or tribes, the members of which belong to a single body, over and against our own model of a contractual society composed of individuals. Why introduce this form of corporate body into a genre dedicated to exploring and expanding the vicissitudes of individualism?

Walpole, as I have suggested, knew very well that he was not writing an early modern romance. He said as much when he published the second edition of his novel in April 1765, just four months after the first edition appeared. For the second edition, he modified the original subtitle from "a Story" to "a Gothic Story," produced a second preface, and revealed himself as the author. By inserting the word "Gothic" he selected a term that during the early eighteenth century conveyed a largely positive meaning.[15] For eighteenth-century Englishmen the gothic style referred to meant the native English tradition in politics, architecture, and religion.[16] To translate this concept into fiction, Walpole places *Otranto* in a tradition going back to Shakespeare and recategorizes it as a blend of two kinds of romance, "the ancient and the modern." Nowhere are the features of the new romance more apparent than in the novel's conclusion. To be sure, old romance prevails in that everyone who does not seem to restore and purify the legitimate lineage of Otranto has either been killed off (Manfred's progeny) or forced to retire from the sociopolitical arena (Manfred and his wife, Hippolyta will spend the last of their days in adjoining convents).

Having removed such characters from the narrative, the novel leaves us not only with the legitimate offspring of Alfonso and Frederick but also with the only two characters who can be said to harbor modern feelings. In the place where the novel uprooted the kind of passion driven by blood and the need to reproduce a family line, a wholly different kind of emotion seems to take root. Although Isabella's father offers his daughter to the new prince, "Theodore's grief was too fresh to admit the thought of another love; and it was not till after frequent discourses with Isabella, of his dear Matilda, that he was persuaded he could know no happiness but in the society of one with whom he could forever indulge the melancholy that had taken possession of his soul" (115). In wedding, they fulfill romance conventions, but their hesitation coupled with their divided and displaced loyalties imply an individuated source of desire and indicate a basis for kinship other than that spontaneous kind of attraction or antipathy that generally indicates the stirring of blood to perpetuate position and power.

I hope it is clear from this brief example that rather than dredge up some deeply buried cause for cultural guilt or trigger the return of the culturally repressed, the English gothic novel is at work producing the machinery of modern culture. Where criticism tends to think of the gothic novel as being something quite separate from the sentimental tradition or to focus, alternatively, on just how the gothic challenges what would become the mainstream British novel, I want to suggest that just the opposite is true. As I see it, the gothic novel works hand and glove with sentimental fiction to banish as obsolete an older model of kinship relations and to propose the modern household as the site where modern social relations are reproduced. Rather than taking up arms against modernity, then, the British gothic plays a necessary part in establishing the cultural prototypes that make it possible.

Forget the Castle

My account of the emergence of the gothic strain in the English novel raises the question of why the gothic should have had so much appeal for an American readership. Even if there had been European immigrants who were still determined to retain their cultural ties to the mother country during the 1790s, such a readership would certainly have been thoroughly Americanized within a generation or two. And still the gothic remained a popular mode of writing well into the nineteenth century in a nation that could have had little or no interest in the fate of an ostensibly indigenous aristocratic body and its way of life. If it is commonplace to say that the gothic is the prevailing mode of American fiction, then it is equally well established—and from an earlier moment in our literary history—that the signature convention of the British gothic made little sense in the United States. In his prefatory note to *Edgar Huntly* (1799), Charles Brockden Brown says as much in explaining the dilemma facing Americans who would write a gothic novel. Where "puerile superstition and exploded manners[,] gothic castles and chimeras are usually employed" by the British novel, American writers have to strive for the same effect "by means hitherto unemployed by preceding authors."[17] Throughout the nineteenth century, men of letters reiterated Brown's claim that where the gothic was concerned American fiction had to depart from the conventions associated with the European novel. Washington Irving and James Kirk Paulding were among those both to ridicule the American use of the European conventions and to devise alternatives.[18]

When he took aim at Isaac Mitchell's now-obscure novel *The Asylum; or, Alonzo and Melissa* (1811) for featuring a gothic manor house, Leslie Fiedler placed himself in a long line of critics who insist that the American gothic could not plausibly use European conventions. Originally published as *Alonzo and Melissa* in serial form by the (Poughkeepsie, New York) *Political Barometer* in 1804, this novel, though American by virtue of its author, audience, and subject matter, violates the prohibition on castles by imprisoning its heroine in

> a large, old-fashioned, castle-like building, surrounded with a moat, crossed by a drawbridge, and with high, thick, wooden walls; the building was almost totally concealed on all sides from view, by irregular rows of large locust and elm trees, dry *Prim* hedges and green shrubbery. The gate which opened into the yard was made of strong hard wood, thickly crossed on the outside with iron bars and filled with old nails and spikes.[19]

This is all Fiedler needs to regard the novel with undisguised contempt: "such a structure in such a place remains not merely unconvincing but meaningless. The haunted castle of the European gothic is an apt symbol for a particular body of attitudes toward the past, which was a chief concern for the genre. The counterpart of such a castle fifty miles from New York City has lost all point" (144–45).[20]

For dabbling in castles, complete with apparitions that carry out their secret and certainly sinister purposes at night, Mitchell's novel has been kept off of most reading lists of gothic fiction, American and British. Calling attention to the publication history of the early novel in America, Cathy Davidson identifies *The Asylum* as "the single most popular gothic novel in early America."[21] In making her point, she takes us through the complicated history of the novel's publication. When Mitchell published the novel in book form in 1811, he tacked on a lengthy sentimental narrative to the version that he had serialized in the *Political Banner*. This sentimental plot became the first of two volumes of the novel. As she explains, most people read "a pirated, uncopyrighted version plagiarized almost verbatim from the newspaper serialization," or what amounted to just the second volume of Mitchell's novel (322). This edition was also published in 1811 by someone who signed his name as Daniel Jackson, Jun. Entitled *A Short Account of the Courtship of Alonzo and Melissa; Setting Forth Their Hardships and Difficulties, Caused by the Barbarity of an Unfeeling Father*, the pirated edition went through at least twenty-five printings over the course of the nineteenth century and continued to sell into the early twentieth century. This edition contained the very episodes that Fiedler considers "not merely unconvincing but meaningless." Judging from the remarkable popularity of *A Short Account*, one can only conclude that nineteenth-century readers either found some meaning in the castle or looked past it to another narrative device to perform the modernizing of gothic fiction.

From Poe's deranged house of Usher to the sickroom in *The Yellow Wallpaper* and the paranoia-inducing apartment in *Rosemary's Baby*, we find that architecture does not have to be a castle in order to indicate that a given narrative is about to take a gothic turn. That Benito Cereno's ship serves the same purpose as not only the castle of Otranto but also the house of seven gables and Rappacini's garden is most obviously suggested by the tendency of these structures to imprison women (or in the case of Cereno's ship, feminized men) and force them to comply with group interests hostile to the captive's feelings and thus to her very existence. Whether a manor house, garden, or ship, the enclosed domicile in European and American gothic fiction allows an overbearing form of patriarchy to further its own interests at the expense of the very differences between genders and generations that sentimental fiction requires in order to form an affective community.

When it confined well-born young women in castles and sought to coerce them into a marriage against their wills, the British gothic was, as I have suggested elsewhere, appropriating the American captivity narrative.[22] Such women as Isabella in Walpole's *The Castle of Otranto* and both Emily St. Aubert and Madame Montoni of Radcliffe's *The Mysteries of Udolpho*—indeed, all of Radcliffe's heroines—are captive to men who might as well be savages and are indeed described in exactly those terms. Who but a savage would dispossess his wife as Manfred does in order to marry the woman intended for his son? Who but a savage would starve his wife into submission as Montoni does and treat his dependents like property? Who but a monster would murder his own niece as the Marquis de Montralt attempts to do in *The Romance of the Forest* (1791)? There is, however, an absolutely crucial difference between the colonial captivity narrative and such novels as *The Castle of Otranto* and *The Mysteries of Udolpho*. The threat of radical endogamy, or incest, hovers over British gothic literature, causing the family to grow claustrophobic, even predatory, in preventing the formation of an affective community.

In setting about to write a gothic novel, an American writer would therefore find him or herself smack in the middle of an ideological contradiction. Such an author would have to be aware, first, of the tradition of the captivity narrative, which works to preserve the diasporic community by representing that form of integration into another culture as something that puts one's very soul in jeopardy; the captive heroine keeps herself scrupulously apart lest she render herself unfit to rejoin and perpetuate the British colony. By turning the phobic thrust of the captivity narrative against the original kin group, on the other hand, the British gothic converts the desire for self-enclosure underlying the captivity narrative into a perverse desire and source of fear. In a situation where intermarriage and assimilation are advantageous, fiction finds it necessary to preserve what might be called the captive's "emotional purity" rather than the purity of her blood. On such purity of mind and soul, as opposed to anything having to do with wealth or position, depends her ability to enter into a consensual marriage. The sentimental ending of *The Castle of Otranto* would seem to demonstrate that a modern consensual society forms at the expense of original kinship relations. But this is in fact far from the truth. The spontaneous and potentially enduring relationship between Matilda and Theodore in peasant guise has to be displaced by a relationship that restores the original bloodline. Any study of American gothic must come to terms with the fact that the British version of the genre resanctifies blood with companionate marriage. Is it perhaps for this reason that American gothic demonizes marriages that value the perpetuity of the original family over and above individual feelings requiring some form of assimilation?

In conspicuous contrast to the secret passages in *Otranto* that inevitably lead one deeper within its interior, the walls of the castle in *The Asylum* are so porous that pirates and smugglers easily come and go through its many secret entrances. In the last pages of the novel, the late night noises that emanate from the rooms below, the dark figures glimpsed about the building, even the resurrected corpse in a blood-stained sheet are revealed as the machinations of Loyalists who used the castle to supply the British troops occupying New York. As castles go, Mitchell's is a red herring as well as a bust. He obviously placed this figure at the heart of his novel in order to signal that the gothic structure, moat and all, should be replaced with a convention that does a better job of imagining social relations for readers in the new United States. Alarmed by the castle's permeability, the heroine's father sends her off to his brother in what would presumably be considered a more inaccessible remove in the American South. As if to say that Charleston has precisely the magical properties lacking in the Connecticut manor house, Mitchell inscribes her in a gothic convention that was no doubt as familiar to readers as the castle, namely, the figure of the veiled woman. Suggesting it is better suited for American fiction than castles, dungeons, or moats, Mitchell offers two quite different examples of the veiled woman in order to distinguish the genuine gothic effect from what Robert Miles terms mere "marketing cues."[23]

The veil declares something lies beneath surface appearances to be discovered. In doing so, the veil transforms the object of desire from something whose value registers on the surface of the body into something whose value cannot be seen. Thus the veil lends the object an interiority that could otherwise not be seen; it makes the invisible visible. In this respect, the veiled woman changes the ontology of the desired object, thus what it means for one character to desire another. In the American literary tradition, the erotically charged figure of the veiled woman appropriates and transforms the captivity narrative. As a whole, what individuates the individual in the American context has less to do with blood than with one's place in an affective community. When someone is removed, the community feels an absence that it compulsively seeks to fill; only the original can repair this hole. Should that original die or "go native," a surrogate will do, as Locke first suggested, to exercise the care-taking function. This brand of individualism not only modifies the early modern model that sought to sustain a blood-based kin group, within the boundaries of which most anyone is substitutable just so long as the familial body itself is rendered internally coherent and whole. The American version of the veiled woman also adapts Adam Smith's model of sympathy to a diasporic situation where no one person necessarily shares the same history with any other.[24]

Let us consider how the veiled woman performs the transformation of the British fantasy of a purified and renewed community into a distinctively American fantasy of community made whole. We might begin with the observation that the veiled woman is linked metonymically to the enshrouded corpse of the first half of *The Asylum* in that both figures perform the return of the dead. Where the resurrected corpse in a bloody shroud is revealed to be mere claptrap invented by Loyalists to scare off Melissa, the second yields the magical element—or lost object—that restores community. Alonzo reads in a newspaper notice that Melissa Bloomfield has died; Melissa's cousin in New London confirms her death. Later on, he visits Charleston to see her grave for himself. After Alonzo learns that the mysterious veiled lady is none other than the very woman presumed to be dead, we learn that Melissa seized the occasion of her cousin's death to take her place in her uncle's family, a practice that would have made perfect sense in eighteenth-century British culture; the interchangeability of the two women allows Melissa the protection of an avuncular surrogate on the order of Clarissa's Uncle Morden. In making this move, she is nevertheless torn from the family history—and in this sense dead—and relocated in another. In "returning" from the dead, morever, she does not reclaim her former state of being as her father's daughter. She is yet again someone else: the missing object of desire that reconsolidates dispersed individuals on the basis of something far more binding than sympathy in the traditional British sense.

What is accomplished by killing off Melissa and then bringing her back from the dead? The short answer is that the return of the dead changes the basis for affective relations. The long answer ties that sentimental tendency to the cultural logic of diaspora. Where initially their relationship observed the patriarchal principle that Melissa's father himself equates with "barbarism" (2:176), Melissa's "return" allows a relationship to form on the basis of a principle resembling the one uniting Walpole's modern couple at the conclusion of the *Castle of Otranto*. To emphasize the point that there can only be one Melissa for Alonzo, Mitchell has him catch a glimpse of his beloved through a window in New London after she has fled the castle. When he first sets eyes on the look-alike, we are told, Alonzo's "heart beat violently" (2:121) and he experienced a "melancholy pleasure" (2:123). On learning it is someone other than Melissa, his affect changes on a dime; he "felt no strong curiosity farther to examine her features" (2:124). Although convinced of her death, Alonzo remains if anything more attached to her, even as her image undergoes decay in his imagination: she lay "stretched on the sable hearse, wrapped in the dreary vestments of the grave—-the roses withered—the lilies faded—motionless—the graces fled—her eyes fixed, and sealed in the glaze of death" (2:138).

In setting the stage for a spectacular scene of sympathetic identification, the novel makes it clear that Alonzo's unwholesome obsession with the dead Melissa has a peculiarly American target in its sights. Summoned to a room in Charleston, Alonzo sees an "elegant" and bejeweled woman wearing a green veil—which is presumably what passes in the United States for an aristocratic body. What marks her as desirable lies beneath the veil. How else do we know she is neither an apparition nor a substitute on the order of Walpole's Isabella? The restoration of the community to a state of imaginary wholeness depends on her being nothing other than the original Melissa. To stress the point, Mitchell intrudes in the narrative to raise the question as to whether this is indeed the original Melissa or "some *female* Martin Guerre or Thomas Hoag—some person from whose near resemblance to the deceased [the author] thinks to impose upon us" (2:219)?[25] We are tipped off that the face beneath the veil will indeed be everything and more that Alonzo hopes for when her voice strikes him as an "enchanting melody" that "thrilled his bosom, electrified his soul, and vibrated every nerve of his heart" (2:217).[26] But when Alonzo actually sees Melissa, it is not with her former social identity restored. What lies behind the veil is the very image of his "own" emotions. Rather than establish the difference between spectator and spectacle as that between subject and object, the lifting of the veil establishes the essential continuity—indeed, indistinguishability—between her voice and his compulsive reciting of her name, his tremors and her tears.[27]

In a novel composed of melodramatic ups and downs, this is the first occasion where Mitchell stages a full-blown encounter between spectator and spectacle that transmits emotion in the manner of sympathy articulated by Adam Smith. According to Smith's *Theory of Moral Sentiments*, on witnessing one of our fellow human beings in agony, we instinctively imagine ourselves in the position of such an object:

> [w]e enter *as it were* into his body, and become in some measure the same person with him, and thence form some idea of his sensations, and even feel something, which though weaker in degree, is not altogether unlike them. His agonies when they are brought home to ourselves, when we have thus adopted and made them our own, begin at last to affect us, and we then tremble and shudder at the thought of what he feels.[28]

This passage finesses the problem that we cannot share another's feelings and still feel only emotions that arise strictly within ourselves in response to certain stimuli. One never runs the risk of becoming other than he was prior to his leap of imagination; he enters only "*as it were* into another's body" (emphasis mine). Thus in feeling for another, one is in effect feeling for himself as if he were that other. His feelings, however moved, are strictly his own. Smith designs this model of sympathy to provide the social glue uniting a group of like-minded but implicitly independent and self-sufficient individuals.

Smith's argument presupposes that one is not dealing with a stranger in becoming in some measure "the same person" with him in enacting the leap of imagination that enables sympathy. *The Asylum* suggests that such a commonality of experience is precisely what could not be taken for granted during the early republic. One could not suppose that those from, say, Charleston, South Carolina, will respond in the same way to the same stimuli as individuals do from, say, New London, Connecticut. In contrast with the kind of community one was called upon to imagine in Jane Austen's England, both Alonzo's family and the Bloomfields are dispersed along with their property across the Atlantic world. What Smith's model offers when stretched to cover this situation becomes something quite different from and alternative to the family. When we feel strongly for another individual, "we enter *as it were* into [his] body," or so Smith claims. According to the American revision of this argument, to feel strongly for another individual, we do in fact enter that individual's body emotionally and his feelings enter ours to transform us into a single body of emotion.

If the unveiling of Melissa consolidates a community in just this way, then the discovery of Alonzo's history disperses the community based on an old (and more British) notion of patriarchy. His father's fortunes were reversed at the outbreak of the Revolutionary War when the British seized ships in which he had invested causing his son to fall below the Bloomfield standard for an acceptable husband. This reversal of fortune was itself secretly reversed by Ben Franklin's intercessions in France. When in France,

Alonzo discovered his father had not only been a childhood friend of Franklin, and later a schoolmate, but also a business partner in the venture that cost Alonzo's father his fortune. Knowledge of this history allows Alonzo to restore what had been lost and in this sense become a father to his father. Indeed, we might say that it takes an entire community to restore this couple to each other, except that a whole spectrum of different individuals leading different lives and pursuing different objectives only becomes a community in doing so. In America, I am tempted to say, public history is always partial. Coming from elsewhere, participating in more than one local community, subject to sudden reversals in fortune and accompanying changes in status, the protagonists of American fiction are never at home until they make a home with one another surrounded by friends whose interwoven histories act as a group and in the common interest. Mitchell invites the reader to join the social body so reimagined: "Our sentimental readers will experience a recurrence of sympathetic sensibilities" (2:218).

The United States of Paranoia

Now that I have challenged Fiedler's too-easy dismissal of *The Asylum* as a mindless imitation of the European gothic, it is time to qualify my position. I would certainly have gone along with Fiedler had he ridiculed Mitchell for writing a protracted sentimental romance. In this novel, as I have demonstrated, conventional gothic machinery does little more than bring about the conditions necessary in establishing what can only be called an "affective community." Gothic fiction, by way of contrast, undermines the fantasy of an expansive community based on feeling alone by throwing into doubt the possibility that one individual can ever truly know another. If in *The Asylum* the revelation of secret histories constitutes a new community by supplying the knowledge necessary to repair the fractured family, then in gothic fiction proper the operations of secret histories raise the question of whether it is possible not just to know another individual but also to be an individual whole and entire unto oneself. It stands to reason that when one cannot know another individual, any sympathetic identification will be misleading, ill founded, or downright dangerous. Indeed, the metonymic tendency and intensity of such feeling can as easily break free of and overturn as consolidate the family.

Charles Brockden Brown participated vigorously in the epistemological debate between the gothic and the sentimental novel.[29] Each of his gothic novels turns on at least one secret history. As a result, each throws into question the possibility of sympathetic identification with someone else no matter how familiar or close in terms of blood. Entitled *Skywalk: The Man Unknown to Himself—An American Tale* in the advertisement (1798), his first abortive attempt at publishing a novel indicates that Brown had in mind the story of a man who could not be a coherent individual, even to himself, because he did not know his history.[30] Brockden Brown's first published novel *Wieland or The Transformation, an American Tale,* is shaped by no less than two secret histories. Here, he goes to some length to suggest that a sinister secret clouds the past of Carwin, whose behavior waxes sometimes pleasant and sometimes suspicious. He arrives in the guise of an American rustic. Next we are led to think he is Spanish and then British. If not an out-and-out imposter, he is at the very least difficult to pin down. But while it is true that Carwin's mastery of the art of ventriloquism makes it difficult for the narrator and her suitor to get together, the problem posed by the secret of his identity is more conceptual than instrumental.

It is worth recalling that when the observer's sense of sight is obscured by a veil in *The Asylum,* the beloved's voice is especially effective in transmitting affect directly from one person to another. In *Wieland,* however, it is precisely voice—through the trick of ventriloquism—that mediates and misdirects affect. Although Carwin is an undoubtedly duplicitous character—intent on seducing Clara, misleading her suitor Pleyel, and for his amusement perversely misdirecting Theodore—the far more frightening and dangerous secret is the secret history harbored by the narrator's brother Theodore who believes he has been commanded by supernatural voices to murder his wife, children, and a female servant. The murder of the family is such a direct blow to the sentimental premise that affect can serve as the basis of community as to cast a pall over the novel's concluding promise of a sentimental ending. Another pair of secret histories generates the gothic dimension of *Edgar Huntly; or Memoirs of a Sleepwalker.* The subtitle might initially cause us to suspect the novel is about Clithro Edny, who apparently murdered Mrs. Lorimer's brother in Ireland while suffering a bout of sleepwalking. More central is the eponymous hero, Huntly himself, who through most of the novel remains completely unaware that he also walks in his sleep. Unbeknownst to himself, while fast asleep he hid the letters of his late friend Waldegrave and did battle with both panthers and Indians. Again, the individual is a mystery even to himself.

In arguing for the solitary singularity of the individual, John Locke raised the philosophical question of whether the sleeping man was the same individual as he was when awake. To push the equation between consciousness or "mind" and identity he offers the example of Socrates: "It is certain, that *Socrates* asleep, and *Socrates* awake, is not the same Person."[31] From this, it follows that "if we take wholly away all Consciousness of our Actions and Sensations," it would be difficult to know "wherein to place personal identity" (II.i.11). There cannot, in other words, be two minds—one unknowable to the other—in one body. Otherwise, we would be strangers to ourselves and incapable of producing, from sensations of the external world, a single, coherent body of knowledge of that world. The coherence that comes with self-reflection—which in turn requires a stable array of ideas based on sensation to reflect upon—is necessarily prerequisite to sympathetic identification. You have to have your own feelings, in other words, before you can share them with another. In putting flesh on the exceptions to this rule, Brockden Brown produces what might be called a sequence of Lockean jokes. He brings to life the very examples by which Locke illustrated the absurdity of humanity in any form other than one mind enclosed in a single body. If one's brother (*Wieland*) or even oneself (*Edgar Huntly*) is fundamentally unknowable and thus a stranger, then with whom and on what basis can one form an affective community? To put it simply, the independent consciousness of the sleep-walker invalidates a model where one has to know how he or she would react in a given situation before that individual can imagine him or herself in another's place. The embezzler in *Arthur Mervyn* and the title figure of *Ormond* pose similar challenges to individual autonomy, thus to the fixity of individual identity and the stability of social relationships that depend on an individual being no one but himself.

From its first appearance in print to this day, Edgar Allan Poe's "Fall of the House of Usher" (1839) has arguably been considered the consummate gothic tale produced by an American author. But if we have dispensed with castles and look to the secret history as the motor of gothic fiction, then, I propose, Nathaniel Hawthorne's earlier short story, "My Kinsman, Major Molineux" (1832) serves as a more useful example of the American gothic. Indeed, in this story, one might say, Hawthorne figures out the aesthetic means of inverting the model of sympathy that concludes a tale like *The Asylum*. Set at some time in the early eighteenth century ("A summer night, not far from a hundred years ago" [68]), the protagonist is initially bound by the cultural logic of patrilineage.[32] He is a second son to a clergyman with "a small salary" and an older son to whom the family farm has been promised. Just as the clients to the king were given the colonial governorships, so children looked to avuncular relations for patronage and protection, as they do in such novels as *Wieland*, *The Asylum*, and the American *Clarissa*. It is this kind of patronage, Hawthorne suggests, that Robin has been led to expect when he ventures from country to town in search of his kinsman: "The Major, having inherited riches, and acquired civil and military rank, had visited his cousin in great pomp a year or two before; had manifested interest in Robin and an elder brother, and being childless himself, had thrown out hints respecting the future establishment of one of them in life" (81).

Where the European gothic stages early modern kinship practices as barbaric and tyrannical in that they pose a fundamental threat to the autonomy of an individual's mind and body, the sentimental narrative on both sides of the Atlantic strives to reconcile a community based on sympathy with one based on ties of blood. Good paternalism displaces bad patriarchy. Such novels as Henry Fielding's *Tom Jones* and Frances Burney's *Evelina* effect much the same kind of resolution as Mitchell's *The Asylum* and Brown's *Clara Howard*. The avuncular figure that often saves the day in American fiction represents just such an attempt at rescue and resolution. By way of contrast, "My Kinsman, Major Molineux" produces what may accurately, if somewhat anachronistically be called a "paranoid community" that makes a group out of disparate individuals by means of a process that disarticulates and parodies the sentimental ending. The moment that Robin, Hawthorne's protagonist, debarks from the boat ferrying him to his kinsman's town is the same transition as Poe's narrator undergoes in taking us across "the tarn" into the house of Usher or, indeed, Amasa Delano effects in climbing from his whale-boat onto the deck of the *San Dominick*. These transitions not only take the protagonists from a simple agrarian world to a more modern, but equally localized, America but also from the possibility of sympathetic identification to the kind of misrecognition that unites individuals in a negative affiliation resembling what we now feel and know as "paranoia." Something of a rube, Hawthorne's Robin finds himself in a baffling set of affiliations that do not observe the rules for deference and respect organizing the community from which he hails. The individuals in the town that Robin encounters—barbers, boatman, mariners, "men who lived by regular and laborious handicraft," an innkeeper, and, yes, prostitutes—are identified according to the labor they perform. As Molineux's kinsman, Robin does have special status—but his status is that of an outsider or stranger, rather than that of proximity to a high-ranking citizen of the town. This reversal of expectations makes Robin someone other to himself as well.

Hawthorne never reveals the secret history of Molineux's reversal of fortune, choosing instead to make us feel the paranoia of immersion in a society that shares a secret history from which we are systematically excluded. But he does see to it that we know a good bit more than the protagonist, who lacks the sense to recognize that something strange is going on and so partake of the paranoia. Where Robin expects to share the deference and cordiality due his kinsman, any mention of Molineux's name provokes anger and incivility. Thus at the door to the barbershop a well-dressed citizen responds to a query about Molineux "in a tone of excessive anger and annoyance" (70). By dropping his kinsman's name in a tavern, Robin causes "a sudden and general movement in the room." The innkeeper seizes this moment to read the notice of a runaway indentured servant, which suggests that Robin could as easily be that fugitive as the relative of a prominent citizen. On leaving the tavern Robin "heard a general laugh" that makes him suspect, however dimly, that he might be the butt of a collective joke (73).

For purposes of this reading, I want to regard the joke, in Freud's famous analysis, as a community-building ploy that inverts sympathetic identification. To establish a triangulated structure, the joke-teller aims derision at a third party in a manner that forces the person to whom the joke is told to form an alliance with the teller at the expense of the other party. In Freud's account, the teller is implicitly masculine and the person at whose expense the joke is told is implicitly feminine. To align oneself with that party is to risk putting oneself in the position of the butt of the joke. There is no halfway ground to occupy in such a structure: one is either on the side of the joke-teller or else aligned with the object of ridicule, meriting exclusion from the alliance among men. In setting up something very much like this unforgiving set of alternatives, the American gothic makes it all but impossible for the protagonist to retain a sentimental identification—even, as in this case, with a noble kinsman—even, moreover, when the paranoid community is comprised of a pretty unsavory group of characters that includes inebriated tavern-goers and prostitutes. What produces this unholy conspiracy?

Where Robin comes face to face with Major Molineux, Hawthorne quite deliberately stages a scene of disaffiliation that recalls those moments in sentimental romance where a protagonist recognizes a kindred spirit and is instantly recognized in turn, each confirming his or her identity in the spectacle of the other's feelings. In the penultimate scene of Hawthorne's story, Robin finally catches sight of Molineux tarred and feathered and about to be ushered out of town in carnivalesque fashion:

> His face was pale as death, and far more ghastly; the broad forehead was contracted in his agony, so that his eyebrows formed one grizzled line; his eyes were red and wild, and the foam hung white upon his quivering lip. His whole frame was agitated by a quick, and continual tremor, which his pride strove to quell, even in those circumstances of overwhelming humiliation. But perhaps the bitterest pang of all was when his eyes met those of Robin; for he evidently knew him on the instant, as the youth stood witnessing the foul disgrace of a head that had grown grey in honor. They stared at each other in silence, and Robin's knees shook, and his hair bristled, with a mixture of pity and terror. (85).

Here, as in the penultimate scene of *The Asylum* is a spectacle of feeling—a "quivering lip," and "tremor" of emotion coursing through the body—and from that body to another: "Robin's knees shook, and his hair bristled, with a mixture of pity and terror."

The scene is no homecoming reunion. Hawthorne makes it quite clear that the feeling they share is the pain Molineux and Robin each experience on seeing the other. Tarred and feathered, Molineux hardly wants to be seen. Nor does Robin want to acknowledge his kinsman, after only the briefest intimation of what it would be like to share the old man's shame. As the scene unfolds, in other words, we witness a spectacular failure of sympathetic identification. When formulating his influential theory of sympathy, Adam Smith definitely meant to use it against a contrary model of feeling that spread directly from one person to another so as to circumvent self-reflection and consolidate a mass or "faction." With the help of Smith, eighteenth-century readers associated this dynamic with the terms "passion" and "contagion," which they understood as dramatically opposed to the kind of feeling that develops when one individual comes to know and share the emotions of another by putting himself imaginatively into the other person's shoes. Addressing the danger of factionalism, Smith admitted of his own country, "In a nation distracted by faction, there are, no doubt, always a few, though commonly but a very few, who preserve their judgment untainted by the general contagion" (219). Obviously indebted to Smith, Hawthorne describes the laughter that unites those bearing witness to Molineux tarred and feathered as, "the contagion . . . spreading among the multitude" (86). The moment when Robin looks at Molineux and sees his kinsman as a stranger is also the moment when Robin becomes something other than himself, overwhelmed by emotions and speaking with a voice that cannot be called his own: "all at once, [the contagion] seized upon Robin, and he sent forth a shout of laughter that echoed through the street" (86).

In approaching the end of this chapter, I want to pause and consider the community formed by contagion and how it differs from one based on sympathetic bonds. *The Asylum* emphasizes the individual, as if to say that only the original will do; no substitute is acceptable. Ben Franklin shares a personal history with Alonzo's father, and he alone can help restore the family wealth. So, too, with the English tar rescued from an American prison who then rescues Alonzo bereft in an English prison so that the sailor can open an English country inn called "The Grateful American." Here, a model of reciprocity based on sympathetic identification—"I am like you and could easily find myself in your shoes"—replaces the early modern exchange of women as the means of imagining affiliations between men. Indeed, it is fair to say that establishing a bond of sympathy between men is the necessary precursor in this novel to the more intense identification between heterosexual partners that founds a home. Marriage is postponed here, as in *Otranto*, until those homosocial relationships have been discovered and reactivated. By way of contrast, the community where Robin encounters his kinsman is formed by the principle of negative affiliation.[33] Individuals are unified in the triangulated manner of the joke—not, that is, on the basis of who they are but on the basis of who they refuse to be.

As I explained in chapter 3, Harriet Beecher Stowe promotes an idealist notion of sympathy capable of cutting across diasporic lines that separate African Americans from European Americans, Quakers from Episcopalians, New Englanders from southerners. In place of blood or nation of origin, Stowe works toward a potentially all-embracing metaphor of the family as a care-taking unit. By ensuring that the family is indeed no more nor less than a metaphor and a state of mind, however, Stowe's model stops abruptly short of practices that violate differences of blood. The American gothic refuses the sentimental gesture towards an ideal unity and culturally coherent nation. Its signature trope, the secret history, is first and foremost a local history. Thus, each locale has its own history that unifies the local group as a single body whole and entire to which everyone else is by definition a stranger until he or she learns and embraces that history as his or her own.[34] Those who take part in such local histories behave like a tribe, mob, cult, or mass body, rather than an aggregate of individuals.

From the 1790s until well into the middle of the nineteenth century, the implication is that American authors more often than not saw the United States as made up largely of local communities with histories that tell members what they cannot be in order to belong. By operating more or less like charivari, the culture of such a community ensures that each of its members be concerned that he or she may be next on the list. Admission into the paranoid community requires novitiates to reject anyone who does not share the principle of negative affiliation that provides him with a local basis of identity. No doubt this is the reason why, at the end of the story, a townsman invites Robin to delay his departure: "if you prefer to remain with us, perhaps, as you are a shrewd youth, you may rise in the world, without the help of your kinsman, Major Molineux" (87).

In *The Asylum*, Mitchell assumes that those reading about the reunion of Alonzo and Melissa "will experience a recurrence of sympathetic sensibilities, and attend more eagerly to the final scene of our drama" (2:217). The negative affiliation produced by gothic fiction extends a more complex invitation to the reader: Do we participate in the group's abjection of Major Molineux or distance ourselves from Robin for turning against his kinsman in his reduced circumstances? Neither position is particularly comfortable, as the knowledge required for a rational decision is withheld. Hawthorne's narrator tells us only that Molineux is "an elderly man, of large and majestic person, and strong, square features, betokening a steady soul" (85). In other words, the narrator does not allow us to see Molineux as Robin and the crowd do, leaving us no choice but to disaffiliate with the protagonist as he comes to epitomize the behavior of the crowd: "every man shook his sides, every man emptied his lungs, but Robin's shout was the loudest there" (86). It is true that to identify with the crowd would be to renounce the individual capacity for sympathy that other kinds of fiction call on us to exercise. But, at the same time, to respond sympathetically to the spectacle of suffering is even less acceptable, as to make such an affiliation would be to set ourselves outside of the community and risk becoming the butt of the joke. We simply do not know enough to invest our sympathy one way or the other.

The secret history calls into doubt the possibility of establishing a community on the assumptions spelled out by Smith's theory of moral sentiments, a theory widely read in the new United States.[35] When he came up with his model of sympathy, Smith was obviously thinking in terms of a nation whose inhabitants were invariably attached to a place where everything one needs to know about them is already known. Thus, he can declare with some confidence that most members of the community have the capacity to overcome the natural tendency to act out their emotions too emphatically if they experience some passion or too quickly identify if they witness the spectacle of another's passion. Ideally, he contends, we learn to see the relationship of spectator and spectacle "neither with our own eyes nor yet with his, but from the place and with the eyes of a third person, who has no particular connection with either" and can therefore "judge impartially between us" (192). Individuals possessing the same standard of judgment will naturally resemble each other more than they differ in responding to emotional stimuli. Each remains perfectly himself—indeed perfects himself—while looking at a contentious situation through the eyes of an impartial "third person."

Before Robin encounters Molineux in all his humiliation, Hawthorne puts his protagonist through a curious dream sequence staged in the moonlight and colored with "romance," where he "could have sworn that a visage, one which he seemed to remember, yet could not absolutely name as his kinsman's, was looking towards him from the gothic window" (81). Here, I would argue, is Smith's "third person" resituated within a gothic framework, which renders inoperative the standard he embodies. The scene where Robin locks his kinsman in a gaze of mutual recognition is contrastingly staged "where the torches blazed the brightest, there the moon shone out like day" (85). As laughter ripples through the crowd, Robin distinguishes "a great broad laugh" which his eyes follow to the gothic window where there stood "the old citizen, wrapped in a wide gown, his grey periwig exchanged for a nightcap, which was thrust back from his forehead, and his silk stockings hanging down about his legs" (86). Rather than apart from the crowd where he can view the scene impartially, the citizen spectator assumes the position of the third party of a joke and echoes the laughter of the crowd. According to Hawthorne, Smith's model fails brilliantly in a community of dispersed individuals cut off from a place of origin and a collective history, because the coherence of such a community will depend on whom that group excludes rather than on how far it can extend its capacity for sympathetic identification.[36]

Poe's "The Fall of the House of Usher"—complete with overly endogamous kinship relations, a dwindling family line, and a hapless maiden imprisoned in a dungeon—is obviously cut from the same cloth as *The Castle of Otranto*, and European authors and critics embraced the story and its author almost as their own. On the assumption that Hawthorne's "My Kinsman, Major Molineux" is the paradigmatic American gothic text, however, I want to read Poe's story in terms of the tropes that Hawthorne identifies with the American gothic. To understand how the paranoid community coalesces to work its magic under the conditions that Poe creates, I must again call on the model of the joke, even though to do so may seem inappropriate, if not tasteless, when the joke concerns a woman being buried alive. Nevertheless, whenever there is a naïve narrator or a well-meaning, if too earnest, spectator to serve as a gull, the basic dynamic of the joke will obtain not only for the narrator-spectator but for the reader of the tale as well. As in "Molineux" and the works of fiction discussed in this chapter, the joke depends upon a secret.

Summoned by a boyhood friend consumed by morbid depression, the narrator assumes that he will soon discover the secret of the Usher family illness. But the secret causing the decline of the Usher family remains to the end as much a secret as the cause of Molineux's disgrace. That secret consequently generates the very kind of paranoia that coalesces a community in gothic fiction. The opening paragraphs make it clear that the narrator is entering an actively malignant environment. Poe indulges his affection for the literary pun in describing the house of Usher in the same terms as its owner—as something on the order of a giant head. Both house and head are famously unwholesome, cracked, and doomed to sink. Their conflation is a dead giveaway that Roderick's mental disorder is one and the same as the general miasma of the place. All the inhabitants participate in his illness. Between him and Madeline, his twin, "sympathies of a scarcely intelligible nature had always existed."[37] Finding that "an irrepressible tremor that gradually pervaded my frame" (330), the narrator can only conclude that his host's "condition [also] . . . infected me" (330). Roderick's contagious state of mind is ascribed to the Ushers' "deficiency of collatoral issue" (319), but this explanation does not offer a cause so much as one more symptom of the same order as Roderick's depression and his sister's wasting away. Their composite body lacks the individuation of the modern body. Founded on a secret, it demands submission to local practices that protect that secret. Thus the doctor is included in the Usher house primarily to be viewed with suspicion: "His countenance, I thought, wore a mingled expression of low cunning and perplexity" (320).

The burial of Madeline sets the stage for a spectacle of sympathetic identification gone wrong. Much like the scene of mutual recognition between Robin and his kinsman, Poe's spectacle inverts the sympathetic model that allows the spectator to put himself imaginatively in the position of another and feel her feelings. As in Hawthorne's story, the spectacle is one that forces the spectator to reject such affiliation suddenly and outright. In so vividly collapsing one into the other, Roderick fails to carry out the separation from Madeline that he already botched by burying her alive. Cast in remarkably similar language, the trembling bodies and fervent embrace of The Asylum's Melissa and Alonzo provide an icon of perfect harmony in which each lover knows what the other is feeling, and it is this reunion in which the sympathetic spectator participates. Poe thwarts that happy sense of oneness. As in a sentimental scene, Poe offers the body quivering with emotion: "for a moment she remained trembling and reeling to and fro upon the threshold." There is the embrace: "with a low moaning cry, [she] fell heavily inward upon the person of her brother, and in her violent and final death-agonies, bore him the to the floor a corpse, and a victim to the terrors he had anticipated" (335). Sympathy, it appears, cannot take place between two individuals if they are not adequately distinguishable to begin with.

This story passes the baton to the narrator. Roderick experiences Madeline's agony step by fatal step until, for all practical purposes, they are quite literally in one another's shoes. For the narrator, on the other hand, the return of the dead is encrypted as a literary romance referred to as " 'The Mad Trist' of Sir Lancelot Canning." In misreading the auditory evidence—namely, "the screaming or grating sound" of Madeline emerging from her tomb—as the fictive "dragon's unnatural shriek" (333), he assumes the role of the reader of a gothic tale. By experiencing the dissolution of another's autonomy vicariously and through the mediation of literature, the narrator preserves his own: "From that chamber, and from that mansion, I fled aghast" (335). It is surely no coincidence that with the death of the daughter of the line of Usher dies not only her brother but the entire and elaborate closed community of the house of Usher as well. In a very deliberate manner, I would argue, the killing off of the daughter of the old line of Usher is Poe's way of putting an end to the sentimental figure of the captive daughter so central to the iconography of the English Diaspora and the sentimental tradition in American fiction.

This is no act of repression signaling some deep and abiding guilt, I would argue, but the means of cutting the ties to an imaginary and artificially reconstituted homeland, the essential elements of which are embodied in the daughter. The gothic narratives of Brockden Brown, Hawthorne, and Poe that I have considered all partake in this break with the past. Accordingly, they represent the originary community, or patriarchal family, as constraining and delusional, even monstrous, as only a formation can be that has outlived its time can be.

Afterword

FROM COSMOPOLITANISM TO HEGEMONY

IN OPENING this book, I raised two questions that I shall now briefly address by way of a conclusion: How did English culture achieve hegemony over other diasporic cultures, including the Spanish, French, Dutch, and German, as well as over Africans, Jews, and the many different indigenous peoples who were forced to relocate from their traditional lands? Can we classify the literature of a group as "diasporic" if that group eventually becomes an imperial power and its literature that of the nation? Written in 1854–55, Melville's *Benito Cereno* raises these very questions and fails to answer them, at least in so many words. Instead of a resolution within the narrative proper, Melville appends his own redaction of the account of the legal proceedings contained in his source, *A Narrative of Voyages and Travels in the Northern and Southern Hemispheres* by Amasa Delano, first published in Boston in 1817. As I see it, the interpolated summary of legal proceedings effectively transforms what might be called "national differences" into "cultural differences" that can be contained and adjudicated within the nation space.

If there's any truth to what I have been saying here and throughout this book, a novella that anticipates this transformation could only have been imagined in the mid-nineteenth century and from an American perspective. Both its narrative structure and literary texture come to us as the product of triangulated relations among three diasporic types— an African slave, a Spanish mercantile captain described as "a sort of Castilian Rothschild, with a noble brother or cousin in every great trading town of South America" (64), and an American sealer from Duxbury, Massachusetts, a town whose name testifies to the English origins of its founders.[1] This encounter takes place in a contact zone where none of the principals can remotely claim indigenous status. If its passengers may accurately be described as displaced persons, then the ship that brings them together is itself "in the condition of a transatlantic emigrant ship" (54) that carries slaves "from one colonial port to another" (48). As this description suggests, each of the three major players in the story to follow can be read as the protagonist of a different narrative tradition that has come from elsewhere to combine and interact in the ongoing circuit of goods, bodies, and texts that turns out to be less transatlantic than hemispheric in scope and character.

The American Amasa Delano steps out of a sentimental narrative. As a man of "benevolent heart" (47), he belongs to the same tradition of fiction as *Uncle Tom's Cabin,* where sympathetic relations seem to bridge the gulf between local cultures by transforming disparate individuals into one extended Christian family.[2] No less obvious and yet unbeknownst to his American counterpart, the Spanish captain Cereno is a figure from the tradition of captivity narratives and such Barbary Coast stories as *The Algerine Captive.*[3] According to the summary of legal testimonies and depositions Melville inserted near the end of his novella, the narrative tradition prevailing on board the Spanish ship has transformed the captain's role from that of maritime adventurer to that of captive, who must nevertheless perform as if he were in charge. Melville offers this extra turn of the screw so that Cereno's performance of mastery can imperfectly veil the slave insurrection destined to shatter Delano's sentimental delusion that all varieties of man can actually coexist harmoniously. It is just such a misperception that the author calls to our attention in a statement that drips with sinister irony, when the American sees the "master and man" standing before him, "the black upholding the white. Captain Delano," the narrator explains, "could not but bethink him of the beauty of that relationship which could present such a spectacle of fidelity on the one hand and confidence on the other" (57). Accounts of such slave rebellions appeared in works so different as Aphra Behn's *Oronooko,* Mrs. Sansay's *The Secret History* (1808), a roman à clef about the rebellion in Santo Domingue, the many news stories about both the *Amistad* affair and the trial that followed, and the various accounts of Nat Turner's rebellion.[4] Melville would have been all too familiar with the tendency of such narratives to turn, as Oulaudah Equianno's autobiography does, on the reversal of the master-slave relationship. Furthermore, the figure of the European captain of a ship ferrying slaves who leans on a black man belongs to the long tradition of abolition literature and poetry in which planters, their children, and all who traffic in slaves are destined to become physically enfeebled and culturally degenerate by virtue of just this relationship.[5]

Of the three narrative traditions, two—sentimental romance and the captivity narrative—here offer starkly opposed models of nation making, each of which actively suppresses the other. The sentimental narrative, I have shown, imagines an infinitely expandable community of individuals who understand themselves as similarly human. Proof of such similarity is their ability to engage in a social relationship based on the principle of sympathetic identification. The captivity narrative, by way of contrast, rejects any universal concept of humanity. In place of the metaphor of one all-embracing family of man, the captivity narrative insists on preserving the group's purity in the face of potential pollution. For the captive to assimilate is not an option, as that would threaten the definition of the group. Thus where the sentimentalist tolerates difference, the captive divides the world into Manichean contenders. There he must, of necessity, maintain his cultural and spiritual superiority, as representative of the kin group, over the false masters who have forced him into servitude. Why, I must ask, would Melville set the captivity narrative and the sentimental figure of the family at loggerheads in this story, if not because the recalcitrant fact of slavery necessarily brings the ideal of inclusiveness into proximity with the threat of pollution and degeneration?[6]

The narrative of insurrection imagines undoing the enslavement that ripped people from their natal homelands, forced them into diaspora, and produced a subjugated population of laborers to cultivate the New World. In so doing, the slave-insurrection narrative activates the master-slave dialectic and has the subordinated population incorporate the master's mastery and either navigate the ship back to the natal homeland or take command of the colonial land that their involuntary labor has cultivated. As part of an insurrection narrative, Cereno's captivity conceals the original captivity of the African slaves whom he set out to sell in South America, endowing the Spaniard with the rhetorical weight that abolition rhetoric had shifted to the side of the African.[7] This act of concealment not only sustains the sentimental view that Delano expresses, as he rhapsodizes on the slave woman dozing on deck with child at her breast—"There's naked nature, now; pure tenderness and love" (73)—but the displacement of African slave by Spanish captive also reveals what is really at stake in both the sentimental and gothic modes, and so exposes the basis of their ultimate collaboration.

Sentimentalism can appear at times to resemble an earlier model of cosmopolitanism in that—here at least—it asks us to tolerate all manner of differences among those it designates as human. At the turn of the nineteenth century, Immanuel Kant famously argued for such toleration, insisting that a stranger ought to have the right "not to be treated as an enemy when he arrives in the land of another."[8] He claims that, on the contrary, "all men have [such a right] by virtue of their common possession of the earth, where as on a spherical surface they cannot disperse and hence finally tolerate the presence of each other" (439). Melville uses practically the same language to suggest the problem with Delano's benevolent view of humanity. When the American captain first sees the *San Dominick*, "the stranger" appeared to show "no colors; though to do so upon entering a haven, however uninhabited in its shores, where but a single other ship might be lying was the custom among the peaceful seamen of all nations"(46–47). Although presumably anyone else—including the reader—would be suspicious of such behavior on the part of a foreign vessel, Delano, we are told, was "a person of a singularly undistrustful good nature" (47). His good nature dispels any uneasiness that would ordinarily be aroused by the curious condition and circumstance of the ship, its fainting captain, its diverse and lackadaisical crew, not to mention the various groups of people gathered on deck sharpening knives and cleaning hatchets. Performing a leap of imagination that requires a wholesale disavowal of the sinister aspects of difference within and between the two ships, Delano is quick to imagine himself in Benito's position, with a faithful servant at his side. On his misperception of the harmonious relation between master and slave rests Delano's conviction that the various groups on board the *San Dominick* can indeed coexist hospitably.

Seeing the world as Delano sees it is to downplay the obvious differences between black and white, European and African, slave and sea captain that characterize strangers who can nevertheless occupy the same ship and share the same history. Thus bound together, to paraphrase Kant, these various peoples cannot disperse and so must respect each other's differences. When recast in sentimental terms and staged as an international encounter in the Americas, however, this fantasy of an extended family of man takes a decisively gothic turn. Having boarded the decrepit vessel, Delano finds himself "in some far inland country; prisoner in some deserted chateau, left to stare at empty ground, and peer out at vague roads, where never wagon or wayfarer passed" (74). Like any gothic castle worth its salt, the *San Dominick* presents the hapless visitor with a sequence of mysterious events, menacing figures disappearing down dark passageways, and inexcusable lapses of discipline along with inexplicable acts of violence, all tolerated by the Spanish captain.[9] As if to dispel any remaining doubt, the novella declares in spectacular fashion that it has gone gothic when it tears the canvas shroud from off the prow of the ship to reveal that its figurehead is a human skeleton.

In a gothic tale like "My Kinsman, Major Molineux," we saw that the charivari unified the town by ridding it of Major Molineux. One of the townspeople offers hospitality to Hawthorne's young protagonist only after he participates in the ritual of exclusion that redefined his kin group. If this story is indeed the exemplary gothic narrative that I take it to be, then it is fair to say that one thing the gothic does is to expose the limits necessary to the cohesiveness of even the most inclusionary society. Similarly, such sentimental novels as *Uncle Tom's Cabin* and *House of the Seven Gables* contain gothic moments where cruel slave owners and mesmerists act out secret histories of lust and rivalry on their dependents. Stowe and Hawthorne confine these moments either to a geographical region—often a location in the past—that at once displaces and acknowledges the deep divisions organizing the nation during the period leading up to the Civil War. Thus objectified and localized, these unbreachable divisions within the new United States could be defined as illusory and relegated to a place that belongs to the nation's prehistory. Such exclusion of the exclusionary is what persuades us to read fiction that identifies itself as gothic in opposition to the apparently inclusionary embrace we expect from a work of sentimentalism. In making this distinction, however, we tend to forget that fiction cannot appear to be all-embracing without the very acts of exclusion that acquire a gothic character in novels by Stowe and Hawthorne.[10] By way of contrast, the gothic in *Benito Cereno* refuses to stage a conflict whose source can be figurally expelled from the story and so pave the way for a complete and unified community.

Melville's alternative is to hurl Don Benito into Delano's whaleboat with Babo after him, knife drawn, and a second knife at hand. In that climactic scene, what began outside the United States as a struggle among European nations for the trade in slaves, territory in the Americas, and domination of the trade routes between colonial enclaves and metropolitan centers has become a conflict among displaced peoples within the narrow confines of an American whaleboat. Melville renders this conflict specific to the Americas by putting it clearly on the other side of the Straits of Magellan and thus beyond the scope of European notions of cosmopolitanism, universal hospitality, and the brotherhood of human beings. Indeed, I would like to suggest, in Melville's novella conflict itself becomes the means of unifying the nation in a way and to a degree not evident in previous fiction.

In considering what it takes to unify a nation, we tend to assume first that it requires the resolution to some conflict that would create unanimity, if not homogeneity, among contending factions. Georg Simmel challenges this assumption. In revising Kant's model of cosmopolitanism, Simmel argues that "a certain amount of discord, inner divergence and outer controversy, is organically tied up with the very elements that ultimately hold the group together; it cannot be separated from the unity of the sociological structure."[11] The social glue that makes disparate groups into a cohesive sociopolitical entity comes from the very antagonisms that give it an identity. After prolonged struggle, each contending group comes to realize the futility of any effort to annihilate the other side and agrees to restrict the expression of mutual hostility. "This formal type of relationship," he claims, "is most widely realized in the enslavement—instead of the extermination—of the imprisoned enemy" (27). Rejecting the model that equates unity with unanimity, thus requiring the expulsion or annihilation of dissidents, Simmel suggests that those divisions that appear most entrenched are paradoxically the most likely to reach an accommodation that both preserves hostility and eliminates the need for violence. Provided, of course, that one side is not exterminated, "animosity actually develop[s] into the germ of future commonness" (26–27), a tendency he ascribes to the fact that the principles of conflict and unification each achieve their "full sociological meaning only through the other" (35).

Simmel considers legal conflict the purest manifestation of this principle. Under the law, ideally nothing—no third parties, no charitable gestures, no acts of vengeance, no extraneous circumstances—enters into the field of contestation except for the elements of the conflict itself. Because of what he calls "its pure objectivity," legal conflict "is grounded entirely on the premise of the unity and commonness of the parties," both of which are equally subordinated to the authority of the law (37). So subordinated, even groups of otherwise disparate standing are rendered potentially equal under the law. This commonness in no way mitigates the conflict among these parties. On the contrary, he contends, "the extreme and unconditional nature of conflict comes to the fore in the very medium of legal conflict and on the very basis of the unity of common norms and conditions" (38). The law as Simmel conceives it takes in and preserves conflicts that threaten the nation, as it redefines and adjudicates contending positions. In this way, the law not only preserves both parties to the conflict but also authorizes the adjudicating discourse that incorporates and redefines those parties in relation to each other.[12]

When the violence that had involved imperial Europe, Africa, and the emergent United States erupts on the *San Dominick*, Melville makes it very clear that this is not primarily a maritime conflict. Originating in Europe, a Spanish ship carries African slaves around the cape from the Atlantic ports of South America to Pacific destinations along the coast of Chile. When the struggle lands in an American whaleboat, what had been a triangulated relationship among European, African, and American suddenly collapses into a violent struggle between white and black, master and slave, citizen subject and property. This conflict cannot be contained by the ship but spreads to and threatens the new nation via Delano's whaleboat. Where in Stowe or Hawthorne the exclusionary operations of the gothic create the condition for sentimental inclusiveness, Melville specifically disallows that possibility. *Benito Cereno* is a peculiarly American story, I am suggesting, precisely because its conflict cannot be resolved within a sentimental economy.

Melville as much as acknowledges his failure in this regard by choosing to break off his fictional narrative and offer a summary account along with extracts of the legal documents from the vice-regal court at Lima translated into English. Given that all these materials appear to be taken from the section entitled "Official Documents" appended to the end of chapter 18 of Delano's *Voyages and Travels*, Melville is more or less handing his narrative over to another and very different kind of author. This gesture on his part is all the more significant for going against audience appeal. George William Curtis, editorial adviser to the publisher of *Putnam's*, provides a clear sense of readers' distaste for Melville's change in registers. He thought it a pity Melville put those "dreary" documents at the end instead of making them "part of the substance of the story" (581). In the wake of critical theory, however, one ought to recover quickly from such disappointment. Melville's decision not to integrate these materials into his fictional narrative should tell us that he in fact used the court documents to think his way toward a kind of resolution of a historically intractable problem that was beyond the cultural scope of the novelistic imagination.

In the first chapter of this book, I drew on Raymond Williams's definition of "hegemony" to help explain how one group could acquire the authority to foist its way of imagining the nation on all other such groups. I identified this authority as primarily cultural, if not entirely linguistic, in character. Williams describes hegemony as "a lived system of meanings and values—constitutive and constituting—which as they are experienced as practices appear as reciprocally confirming."[13] By no means, he insists, does any such "system of meanings and values" account for the totality of experience. The prevailing version of experience is always negotiable. No single group ever commands the territory of the nation and/or its literature. New and different narratives are invariably ready to reshape the given elements of any story—or novel, for that matter—into a history that throws its moral weight behind a residual reading of the raw data of history. But any group that wants to make an alternative narrative out of that material must first insert itself into a field of discourse whose language, modes of cultural production (including print technology), and narrative conventions are all geared to serve other interests and weighted toward repetition rather than change. The narrative that emerges from this conflict will be the one to decide the terms in which the conflict itself shall henceforth be understood and reproduced as law and literature. Thus in order for a subordinated group to make its presence felt within a national culture such as ours, members of the group have to modify the very terms according to which their version of its history is subordinated and subsumed in that culture's master narrative.

The legal extracts edited, summarized, and recast from Amasa Delano's *Narrative of Voyages and Travels* throw important light on something very much like the change I am trying to identify. As Melville uses them to hierarchize the various accounts of the events on board the *San Dominick*, he is, in a very real way, determining which version shall predominate and be repeated. In the interpolated account of court proceedings, the argument of Melville's fictional narrative, or how to resolve the conflict among contending groups, gives way to the question of how the story is told: what information constitutes legal evidence and which version of events should be granted the status of truth? Accordingly, Melville's narrative shifts from a battle of bodies and wits—in which the European and American are each at a decisive disadvantage—onto the terrain of law and language, where print culture and those in charge of its deployment can easily win the day.

On reaching Concepción, according to Delano's *Voyages and Travels*, he restored the ship to Don Bonito, as he is known in this text, along with items taken on board the American ship for safekeeping, which included a bag of doubloons, several bags of dollars, and baskets of watches, "some gold and some silver." Of this booty, Delano insists, "We detained no part of this treasure to reward us for our services we had rendered" (822). In an effort to avoid paying Delano for costs incurred and services rendered in rescuing the Spanish ship from rebellious slaves, the Spaniard nevertheless accuses the American of piracy. Through a sequence of legal skirmishes, Delano is not only exonerated but also paid eight thousand dollars in compensation. Moreover, the account of these negotiations in Delano's *Voyages and Travels* represents his as but one of numerous such cases to come before legal tribunals. Indeed, it is because the legal system must hear each case separately and judge it on its merits that Don Bonito hopes through a series of appeals to delay justice and avoid paying the American for services rendered.

Because Melville asserts power similar to that of the court over the materials of the story that is set in type, *Benito Cereno* provides a stark example of how one diasporic group achieves and maintains its hegemony in relation to others. Melville was obviously aware of the fact that by the time it fell into his hands, Delano's account of the slave rebellion and how it was crushed had not only been transcribed into Spanish for the viceregal court at Lima but subsequently translated into English so that Amasa Delano could include these materials in his *Voyages and Travels*.[14] Since Melville based his novella on Delano's *Voyages and Travels*, relatively few American readers have felt compelled to go back to the earlier versions of the court proceedings. Indeed, it was only in the 1920s, with the revival of interest in Melville, that scholars looked into the source material for *Benito Cereno*.[15] Melville's interpolation of Delano's account had seen to it that subsequent readers understood the historical encounter as the account of a slave insurrection that was almost—and fatally—mistaken for a sentimental account of the symbiotic relationship of master and slave. Conflict rather than hospitality organized international relations in the contact zone. As far as Delano was concerned, the law resolved that conflict, exonerating him of the unwarranted charge of piracy and compensating him for his services. According to Melville, however, the law failed to resolve the conflict between African and European, black and white, and he incorporates that failure into his novel with a few additional flourishes that make this failure apparent.

Delano's *Voyages and Travels* never suggests that the historical figure named Don Bonito retired to a monastery after he lost his legal battle with

Delano. Evidently feeling that his novella required a solution outside as well as inside the law, Melville resolves the problem of Spanish treachery by means of the same convention that Walpole included in the repertoire of gothic literature when he packed off Manfred to a convent at the end of *The Castle of Otranto*. By so dispatching Cereno, one might argue, Melville succeeds in consigning the conflict among European diasporas to the past. But in effecting this double defeat of the Spaniard, *Benito Cereno* forces its reader to confront the fact that the law has solved but half the problem posed by the twin figures of master and slave. Thus another, more intractable problem eludes both the court proceedings included in his source and Melville's additional gesture of banishing Delano's Spanish competitor to a monastery. These proceedings open up the conflict between Anglo and African diasporas and the question of whether slaves can be dealt with under the terms of property law.

I hardly need call attention to how effectively the interpolated court documents silence Babo, criminalize the insurrection narrative, and in true gothic form, abject the African. Poised between an older notion of unity that depends on eliminating one side in a conflict of this magnitude and a newer concept of the nation as an apparatus capable of incorporating and legitimating virtually any struggle among contending groups, Melville turns to legal discourse to provide the terms with which to rethink the possibility of national unity. Presumably there it could be grounded, as Simmel claims, "entirely on the premise of the unity and commonness of the parties." A conflict so grounded would no longer challenge national unity but, quite the contrary, authorize the language of law that contains and deals with conflicts between hostile groups on a case-by-case basis. But there is clearly a problem in drawing this analogy between Melville's mid-nineteenth-century narrative and Simmel's early twentieth-century theory. To maintain unity through conflict, Simmel implies, the structuring conflict has to be *fully* incorporated under the law. In adjudicating the conflict between Spanish and American commercial interests, the court avoids the entire issue.

The legal proceedings, as Melville presents them, fail to include Babo's narrative of captivity and rebellion, the very narrative that his novella establishes as the rock bottom of contending versions of truth. By putting Cereno in a monastery and allowing Delano to sail blithely off at the end of his story, Melville leaves the problem that landed in the American whaleboat staring us squarely in the face. Indeed, he stages that problem as a grotesque reminder of barbarism past and to come: "Some months after, dragged to the gibbet at the tail of a mule, the black met his voiceless end. The body was burned to ashes; but for many days, the head, that hive of subtlety, fixed on a pole in the Plaza, met, unabashed, the gaze of whites"(116). In condemning the silent insurgent to the gibbet, the court at Lima also fails to address a problem then brewing within the United States, one that posed a certain threat to national unity. To allow that conflict into Delano's whaleboat was apparently as far as Melville could go. Incorporating the conflict fully under the law would have to be put off until a later moment.

By reading *Benito Cereno* as a conflict among diasporic cultures, we can address the questions with which I began. Having occupied a minority position, those who sought to reproduce English culture outside of Great Britain were no more or less in diaspora than any other such group. Once a group achieves cultural hegemony, as Melville's story suggests, the conflict among the competing groups does not disappear. On the contrary, that conflict persists and so lends our national culture its distinctive identity. At the same time, in order to make a national culture accommodate their respective differences and account for alternative historical perspectives, other diasporic groups have to master the terms of that conflict. To negotiate within the categories of the dominant culture, each such group must reproduce the very discourse that distorts and displaces its distinctive way of making sense of America. In this way, diasporic groups not only acquire the status of subjects under the law, but in using the law to oppose the dominant culture, also think with, and ultimately within, the dominant categories.

With the benefit of hindsight, we know that the century and a half following the publication of *Benito Cereno* was given over to the violence of war, the turbulence of Reconstruction, the influx of new immigrant groups, uplift movements, and an ongoing struggle for civil rights. As integral parts of this process, the literature of the United States grew more pluralistic, the educational system more diversified, and the institution of the law more sensitive to racism and attuned to cultural difference. An argument can be made that the gradual disappearance of what Simmel calls "repulsive energies" (18) through this period was accompanied by a gradual loss of the culturally specific differences such groups bring with them to the United States. If the English determined the language, the legal apparatus, and the cultural categories in terms of which other groups had to negotiate for equal citizenship in the United States, is it reasonable, then, to call the English in America a "diasporic" group? The most accurate answer is both yes and no.

The question assumes that a disaporic group must of necessity occupy a minority position. Initially, the English indeed understood themselves as precisely that. Once theirs became the legal language of the land, however, only a truly reactionary imagination would be willing to put the group who identified that language as their own and felt it served their interests in the position of a subordinated group. At the same time, unless we are willing to see the English in America as one transplanted culture among

others, and in no way preordained to establish theirs as the reigning culture, we cannot hope to understand how one group did in fact achieve a
position of cultural dominance in relation to others. What I have been
describing is a chapter in the process by which one group—the English—
went from being just one among several such groups who attempted to
make a home in an utterly alien place to the group who established the
basis for a culture unique to the new United States. As I have suggested, it
is through the transformative process of repetition, with a difference, that
the culture of British America became specifically American such that none
of us thinks of American literature as British.

This transformation was not accomplished by British Americans alone,
although they certainly set the process in motion. As other groups reproduced the language and literary forms equated with Englishness, their revisions were incorporated in the differential system comprising our national
culture. Just as the Dutch and the French before them, so, too, the African
and the Chinese acquired the ability to represent themselves in English as
not English and claim the rights of American citizenship even so. Thus
what began as the shape and substance of English culture in a diasporic
setting, itself a revision of what quickly became an imaginary original,
necessarily underwent a transformation over time. Under the circumstances I have associated with the principle of hegemony, some degree of
assimilation is required of any group who claims the rights accompanying
citizenship—the right not to be violated in one's body, the right to be
represented under the law, and thus implicitly the right to speak for oneself,
the right to be different within specified limits. But such a cultural negotiation, as Paul Gilroy suggests, is never a one-way street. The various versions
of literacy in American English that necessarily emerged and continue to
emerge from this process irreversibly change the culture that provides the
terms of negotiation. As a result, it is fair to say English culture not only
ceased to be diasporic but ceased to be English as well.

NOTES

Chapter One: Diaspora and Empire

1. That there is a problem with assuming a clean separation of American from British literature is born out in the confused way that American universities have institutionalized research and teaching in the areas of American literature, history, and culture. American literature tends to be nestled within departments of English literature. American history, on the other hand, is housed in history departments, along with other national histories, and requires entirely different training from a specialization in European history. A number of universities have created programs and departments of American Studies devoted to the cultural, ethnic, and social history of the United States—but not its literary traditions. English departments teach survey courses that assume the two literatures were separate and distinct at least from the late seventeenth century on. Indeed, the major literary anthologies in the field reflect this division. Thus in present-day institutional terms, American literature, in contrast with American history, is both separate from, and yet somehow still attached to, British literature. It is this peculiar relationship that I mean to explore.

2. Among the growing tradition of scholarship that addresses transatlantic literary relations are Paul Giles, *Transatlantic Insurrections: British Culture and the Formation of American Literature, 1730–1860* (Philadelphia: University of Pennsylvania Press, 2001); Julie Ellison, *Cato's Tears and the Making of Anglo-American Emotion* (Chicago: University of Chicago Press, 1999); Steven Fink and Susan S. Williams, eds., *Reciprocal Influences: Literary Production, Distribution and Consumption in America,* (Columbus: Ohio State University Press, 1999); David Shields, *Oracles of Empire: Poetry, Politics, and Commerce in British America, 1690–1750* (Chicago: University of Chicago Press, 1990); Michael Kraus, *The North Atlantic Civilization* (Princeton: Van Noostrand, 1957); William L. Sachse, *The Colonial American in Britain* (Madison: University of Wisconsin Press, 1956); and Clarence Gohdes, *American Literature in Nineteenth-Century England* (New York: Columbia University Press, 1944).

3. *A Literature of Their Own: British Women Novelists from Brontë to Lessing* (Princeton, N.J.: Princeton University Press, 1977).

4. Or so Philip Gura saw the field when he surveyed two decades of scholarship. He made the point then that while historians had by the mid-1980s abandoned that notion of exceptionalism, literary scholars still clung to it. The overwhelming tendency today is to read colonial American literature as if it were sui generis and to look for an unbroken line of development within a field constituted only by American texts. Philip F. Gura, "The Study of Colonial American Literature, 1966–1987: A Vade Mecum," *William and Mary Quarterly,* 3d ser., 45 (1988): 309.

5. See William C. Spengemann, *A New World of Words: Redefining Early American Literature* (New Haven: Yale University Press, 1994), and *A Mirror for Americanists: Reflections on the Idea of American Literature* (Hanover, N.H.: Published for Dartmouth College by The University Press of New England, 1989).

6. This nomenclature is admittedly and significantly confusing, but I am not using the terms "English" and "British" interchangeably. As I explain in this and the following chapter, a number of Britons outside of England wanted to emulate what they understood English taste and English writing to be. At the same time, a number of Englishmen back in England were unwilling to be lumped together with the Scots, the Welsh, and other British subjects. Where Eighteenth-century Englishmen would have used the word "British" to describe those in Great Britain who were not born in England, Americans tended to use the word "English" to describe various British folkways, cultural practices, and writing. Linda Colley discusses the resistance on the part of many eighteenth-century Englishman to have "England" and "English" give way to "Great Britain" and "British" in *Britons: Forging the Nation 1707–1837* (New Haven: Yale University Press, 1992). This situation looks ahead to the formation of a Celtic periphery in the early nineteenth century. As Catherine Hall points out, during the early nineteenth century, "Englishness marginalizes other identities," particularly the Scots, the Welsh, and the Irish. "In constructing what it meant to be English," Hall writes, "a further claim was constantly being made—that Englishness was British, whereas those on the margins could never claim the right to speak for the whole . . . an English identity could claim to provide the norm for the whole of the United Kingdom, and indeed the Empire" (Hall, *White, Male and Middle Class, Exploration in Feminism and History* [New York: Routledge, 1992], 206). I use "English" in two senses, then: to refer to the idea of Englishness produced in the colonies by the diaspora, as well as to those Englishmen who were indeed native to England and remained English citizens. "British" or "Briton" refers to those from the English periphery, and those who emigrated from the British Isles to British North America or their offspring who claimed British identity.

7. Franklin to Lord Kames, January 3, 1760, *Papers of Benjamin B. Franklin*, ed. Leonard W. Larabee (New Haven, Conn.: Yale University Press, 1966), 9:6–7. Max Savelle, "Nationalism and Other Loyalties in the American Revolution," *American Historical Review* 67 (1962): 901–23. In his "Observations Concerning the Increase of Mankind, Peopling of Countries, etc." (1755), Franklin predicted that within a hundred years, the population of the English-speaking colonies in America would exceed that of Great Britain and that the largest number of Englishmen in the world would be in America. *Papers of Benjamin B. Franklin*, ed. Leonard W. Larabee (New Haven, Conn.: Yale University Press, 1961), 4:227–34, esp. 233.

8. John Adams, "Dissertation on the Canon and Feudal Law," in *The Works of John Adams*, ed. Charles Francis Adams (Boston: Charles C. Little and James Brown, 1851), 3:461. Jack P. Greene makes a strong case for an antinationalist position on the grounds that there are few signs of a national consciousness emerging before the 1780s. *Peripheries and Centers: Constitutional Development in the Extended Polities of the British Empire and the United States, 1607–1788* (New York: Norton and Company, 1990), 153–80.

9. T. H. Breen, "Ideology and Nationalism on the Eve of the American Revolution: Revisions Once More in Need of Revising," *Journal of American History*, 84 (1997): 13–39, discusses the confusing and contradictory perceptions of national identity within the empire held by Americans during the years running up to the Revolution. He asks, "Did being 'British' mean that one was also 'English,' or that people who did not happen to live in England could confidently claim equality with the English within the larger empire?" (23).

10. Michael Zuckerman, "Identity in British America: Unease in Eden," *Colonial Identity in the Atlantic World, 1500–1800*, eds. Nicholas Canny and Anthony Pagden (Princeton, N.J.: Princeton University Press, 1987), 157. Before the 1770s, Jack P. Greene writes, "The central cultural impulse among the colonists was . . . [to] think of themselves and their societies—and be thought of by people in Britain itself—as demonstrably British," (Greene, *Pursuits of Happiness: The Social Development of Early Modern British Colonies and the Formation of American Culture* [Chapel Hill: University of North Carolina Press, 1988], 175). See also Colley, *Britons: Forging the Nation, 1707–1837*, 132–45 and Colin Kidd, *British Identities Before Nationalism: Ethnicity and Nationhood in the Atlantic World, 1600–1800* (Cambridge: Cambridge University Press, 1999), 261–79.

11. On the use of postcolonial theory to describe the culture of the new republic, see Malini Johar Schueller and Edward Watts, "Introduction: Theorizing Early American Studies and Postcoloniality," in *Messy Beginnings: Postcoloniality and Early American Studies*, ed. Malini Johar Schueller and Edward Watts (New Brunswick, N.J.: Rutgers University Press, 2003), 1–28; Lawrence Buell, "Postcolonial Anxiety in Classic U.S. Literature," in *Postcolonial Theory and the United States: Race, Ethnicity, and Literature*, ed. Amritjit Singh and Peter Schmidt (Jackson: University of Mississippi Press, 2000), 196–219, as well as his "American Literary Emergence as a Postcolonial Phenomenon," *American Literary History* 4 (1992): 411–42; Richard King, ed. *Postcolonial America* (Urbana: University of Illinois Press, 2000); and Edward Watts, *Writing and Postcolonialism in the Early Republic* (Charlottesville: University of Virginia Press, 1998).

12. Because I am interested in literature and other imaginative cultural products, the concept of creolization fails to describe the phenomena I wish to address. For an account that uses the notion of creolization to explain the persistence of British practices in colonial Maryland, see Trevor Burnard, *Creole Gentlemen: The Maryland Elite 1691–1776* (New York: Routledge, 2002).

13. For the debate over the definition of the concept of diaspora, see William Safran, "Diasporas in modern Societies: Myths of Homeland and Return," *Diaspora* 1 (1991): 83–99; James Clifford, "Diasporas," *Cultural Anthropology* 9 (1994): 302–38; Robin Cohen, "Diasporas and the Nation-State: From Victims to Challengers," *International Affairs* 72 (1996): 507–20; Khachig Tölölyan, "Rethinking Diaspora(s): Stateless Power in the Transnational Moment," *Diaspora* 5 (1996): 3–36; Vijay Mishra, "The Diasporic Imaginary: Theorizing the Indian Diaspora," *Textual Practice* 10 (1996): 421–47; Steven Vertovec, "Three Meanings of 'Diaspora,' Exemplified Among South Asian Religions," *Diaspora* 6 (1997): 277–99; Dominique Schnapper, "From the Nation-State to the Transnational World: On the Meaning and Usefulness of Diaspora as a Concept," *Diaspora* 8 (1999): 225–54; Kim Butler, "Defining Diaspora, Refining a Discourse," *Diaspora* 10 (2001): 189–219.

14. Cotton Mather, "Introduction," *Magnalia Christi Americana, or The Ecclesiastical History of New-England, from First Planting in the Year 1620, unto the Year of our Lord, 1698* (London: Thomas Parkhurst, 1702), 1:4.

15. "What's Colonial about Colonial America?" *Possible Pasts, Becoming Colonial in Early America*, ed. Robert Blair St. George (Ithaca, N.Y.: Cornell University Press, 2000), 65.

16. Nancy Armstrong, "Why Daughters Die," *Yale Journal of Criticism* 7 (1994): 1–24.

17. Jonathan Boyarim and Daniel Boyarim, *The Powers of Diaspora: Two Essays on the Relevance of Jewish Culture* (Minneapolis: University of Minnesota Press, 2002), 11.

18. *The Black Atlantic, Modernity and Double Consciousness* (Cambridge, Mass.: Harvard University Press, 1993). All references are to this edition and have been included in the text. Gilroy has been criticized for marginalizing modern Africa and African intellectuals in the process of showing how a generic homeland displaces the actual place of origin. See, for example, Yogita Goyal, "Theorizing Africa in Black Diaspora Studies: Caryl Phillips' *Crossing the River,*" *Diaspora* 12 (2003): 5–38.

19. Rowlandson writes. "I saw a place where English Cattle had been. That was comfort to me, such as it was. Quickly after that we came to an English path which so took with me that I thought I could have freely laid down and died" (Rowlandson, *The Soveraignty and Goodness of God*, from *Puritans Among the Indians: Accounts of Captivity and Redemption, 1676–1724*, ed. Alden T. Vaughn and Edward W. Clark [Cambridge, Mass.: Harvard University Press, 1981], 45).

20. T. H. Breen, "An Empire of Goods: the Anglicization of Colonial America," *Journal of British Studies* 25 (1986): 467–99. In *The Marketplace of Revolution: How Consumer Politics Shaped American Independence* (New York: Oxford University Press, 2004), Breen writes that the major cities of colonial America "contained many men and women who defined taste as English taste, fashion as English fashion, and polite conversation as but a provincial echo of the learned and witty talk they believed regularly occurred in cosmopolitan centers. The shopkeepers who advertised in the colonial newspapers appreciated the allure of Britishness" (166–67).

21. As Colin Kidd explains, differences among colonists were coming to matter less because of this process of re-Anglicization: "Only in the eighteenth century did a process of Anglicising homogenisation" draw together "the shared interests of Englishmen in America" (Kidd, *British Identities Before Nationalism*, 263).

22. Partly in response to a generation of critics who argued that American literature came into its own with the American Renaissance, for more than two decades scholars have examined American literature for signs of growing cultural independence and autonomy. Emory Eliott, for instance, announces quite self-consciously that his would be one of the first books to show that Emerson, Thoreau, Hawthorne, and Melville were indebted "of their precursors: those unsung poets and novelists of the late eighteenth century such as Joel Barlow, Hugh Henry Brackenridge, Charles Brockden Brown, Timothy Dwight, and Philip Freneau" (Eliott, *Revolutionary Writers: Literature and Authority in the New Republic, 1725–1810* [New York: Oxford University Press, 1982], 6).

23. James Raven, *London Booksellers and American Customers: Transatlantic Literary Community and the Charleston Library Society, 1748–1811* (Columbia: University of South Carolina Press, 2002), 6.

24. I am indebted to Peter Stallybrass and James N. Green for this observation and for allowing me to consult a portion of their forthcoming book on Benjamin Franklin as printer.

25. David D. Hall and Hugh Amory, "Afterword," in *The History of the Book in America: The Colonial Book in the Atlantic World*, ed. Hugh Amory and David D. Hall (Cambridge: Cambridge University Press, 2000), 482.

26. James Raven, "The Importation of Books in the Eighteenth Century," in *The History of the Book in America: The Colonial Book in the Atlantic World*, 183.

27. Raven, "The Importation of Books," 196.

28. James N. Green writes that in the 1760s those who began to emigrate from Britain "were more likely to be master printers or even booksellers, and many were from Scotland and Ireland, bred to the trade of reprinting English books" (Green, "English Books and Printing in the Age of Franklin," in *The History of the Book in America*, 283).

29. Calhoun Winton, "The Southern Book Trade in the Eighteenth Century," in *The History of the Book in America*, 233.

30. Richard Beale Davis, *A Colonial Southern Bookshelf: Reading in the Eighteenth Century* (Athens: University of Georgia Press, 1979), 14. See also his *Intellectual Life in Jefferson's Virginia, 1793–1830* (Chapel Hill: University of North Carolina Press, 1964), 71–84, and his, "Books, Libraries, Reading, and Printing," in *Intellectual Life in the Colonial South, 1585–1763* (Knoxville: University of Tennessee Press, 1978), 2: 491–626.

31. James N. Green, "English Books and Printing in the Age of Franklin," 282.

32. Reilly and Hall, "Customers and the Market for Books," 389.

33. David D. Hall and Hugh Amory, "Afterword," 482.

34. *Imagined Communities: Reflections on the Origin and Spread of Nationalism* (London: Verso, 1983).

35. Raymond Williams, *Marxism and Literature* (Oxford: Oxford University Press, 1977), 108–14

36. It is for this reason, I suspect, that we rarely find England explicitly mentioned as " a site of nostalgia or of reactionary longing" in early American novels. See Cathy N. Davidson, *Revolution and the Word: The Rise of the Novel in America*, 2nd ed. (New York: Oxford University Press, 2004), 22.

37. Ernst Robert Curtius, *European Literature and the Latin Middle Ages*, trans. Willard R. Trask (New York: Pantheon, 1953), 28–30.

38. See, for example, Suvir Kaul, *Poems of Nation, Anthems of Empire: English Verse in the Long Eighteenth Century* (Charlottesville: University of Virginia Press, 2000), 77–97; William Levine, "Collins, Thomson, and the Whig Progress of Liberty," *Studies in English Literature* 34 (1994): 553–77.

39. Alexander Pope, *Poetical Works*, ed. Herbert Davis (London: Oxford University Press, 1966), lines 683–84.

40. George Berkeley, "Verses by the Author on the Prospect of Planting Arts and Learning in America," in *A Miscellany Containing Several Tracts on Several Subjects* (London: J. and R. Tonson and S. Draper, 1752), 186–87.

41. See, for example, William C. Dowling, *Poetry and Ideology in Revolutionary Connecticut* (Athens: University of Georgia Press, 1990), 56–68; Robert Weisbuch, *Atlantic Double-Cross: American Literature and the British Influence in the Age of Emerson* (Chicago: University of Chicago Press, 1986), 71–72; Elliott, *Revolutionary Writers*, 29–30; and Lewis P. Simpson, "Introduction," in *The Federalist Literary Mind* (Baton Rouge: Louisiana State University Press, 1962), 32–34.

42. Leo Lemay crosslists *translatio studii* with nationalism in his *Calendar of American Poetry* (see 346). James Kirkpatrick's *The Sea Piece* (1750) and James Sterling's poem to Arthur Dobbs (1752) championing his efforts to find a northwest passage is not nationalist in any conventional sense; Sterling identifies himself as a gentleman writing from America but who is first and foremost a British subject. For a discussion of the volume and an excellent discussion of Francis Bernard's "*Epilogus*," see John C.

Shields, *The American Aeneas: Classical Origins of the American Self* (Knoxville: The University of Tennessee Press, 2001), 89–95. As Shields notes, before the 1770s there are few if any poets who fantasize that political independence would produce a national culture superior to any found in Europe (95).

43. In *Cato's Tears*, 142–47, Julie Ellison discusses the differences between the two versions of Freneau's *The Rising Glory of America*.

44. Arguing from quite different evidence, Gordon Wood has made the claim that the colonists were behaving like a British Diaspora: "During the first half of the eighteenth century the growth and consolidation of a colonial elite . . . had led to an increasing imitation of English manners and customs. By 1760, the American colonies were more English in their culture than at any time since the first settlements; in fact, to some observers the Americans seemed more English than the English themselves" (Wood, ed. *The Rising Glory of America 1760–1820*, rev. ed. [Boston: Northeastern University Press, 1990], 2). See also Michael Zuckerman, "Identity in British America," *Colonial Identity in the Atlantic World, 1500–1800*, 115–57.

45. *The Works of George Berkeley Bishop of Cloyne*, ed. A. A. Luce and T. E. Jessop (London: Thomas Nelson and Sons, 1956), 8:152. He claimed with the false modesty common among members of a coterie in the letter of February 10, 1725/26 that the poem was "written by a friend," and should be "shown to none but your family." Berkeley acknowledged his authorship of the poem when he published the revised version in his *Miscellany Containing Several Tracts* (1752).

46. *The Works of George Berkeley Bishop of Cloyne* 7:345.

47. Anthony Pagden observes that Berkeley's claim was made "with a degree of cynicism rare even among seventeenth-century Anglican divines" (Pagden, *Lords of All the World: Ideologies of Empire in Spain, Britain and France, c. 1500–1800* [New Haven, Conn.: Yale University Press, 1995], 204).

48. "American Liberty," in *The Poems of Philip Freneau, Poet of the American Revolution*, ed. Fred Lewis Pattee (Princeton, N.J.: The University Library, 1901), 1:145. Citations of Freneau's poems are to this edition.

49. *New Travels Through North America in a Series of Letters* (Philadelphia: Robert Bell, 1783).

50. Timothy Dwight, *The Major Poems of Timothy Dwight, 1752–1817*, ed. William J. McTaggart and William K. Bottorff (Gainesville, Fl.: Scholars' Facsimiles and Reprints, 1969), lines 49–55.

51. "Oration, Delivered July 4th, 1783," (Boston, Mass.: John Gill, 1783), 19.

52. Although it was important for the Americans to disavow the practice of conquest and forced conversion because it resembled those of "the rapacious Spanish," as Reginald Horsman notes, "In the years immediately following the Revolution the Americans assumed that they could secure Indian lands simply as a result of their victory over the British" (Horsman, *Expansion and American Indian Policy, 1783–1812* [Norman: University of Oklahoma Press, 1992: East Lansing, Michigan State University Press, 1967], 5). This, despite the fact that many native peoples either were allies of the Americans or sought to remain neutral. While Washington's Indian policy formulated by Henry Knox recognized the Indian right of soil, Horsman writes, the Indians were expected to abandon their cultures and adopt "the lifestyle of American pioneer farmers" (Horsman, "The Indian Policy of an 'Empire for Liberty,' " in *Native Americans and the Early Republic*, ed. Frederick E. Hoxie, Ronald Hoffman, and Peter J. Albert

[Charlottesville: University of Virginia Press, 1999], 45). These policies, however, were largely ignored by backcountry settlers who poured into Indian territories to seize land and drive off the native peoples. See Colin G. Galloway, *The American Revolution in Indian Country: Crisis and Diversity in Native American Communities* (Cambridge and New York: Cambridge University Press, 1995)

53. "A Poem on the Future Glory of the United States of America," in *The Miscellaneous Works of David Humphreys (1804)* (Gainesville, Fla.: Scholars, Facsimile and Reprints, 1968), lines 555–56. Citations of Humphreys's poems are to this edition.

54. "An Oration in Commemoration of the Independence of the United States of America," in *Political Sermons of the Founding Era, 1730–1805*, ed. Ellis Sandoz (Indianapolis, In.: Liberty Press, 1991), 1181.

Chapter Two: Writing English in America

1. Although this position is most forcefully argued in postcolonial theory and criticism, its assumptions find their way into many discussions of American post–Revolutionary War culture. The unstated assumption is that postcolonial theory, which developed to account for the political, economic, and cultural conditions of twentieth-century cultures emerging into a world of transnational capitalism, can be transposed onto the relationship between first- and second-world cultures in the eighteenth century.

2. Nancy Armstrong and Leonard Tennenhouse, *The Imaginary Puritan: Literature, Intellectual Labor, and the Origins of Personal Life* (Berkeley: University of California Press, 1992), 47–50, review eighteenth-century theories of revolution. For an extended discussion of the term "revolution" in eighteenth- and nineteenth-century historical writing, see R. C. Richardson, *The Debate on the English Revolution Revisited* (London: Routledge, 1989), 65–86.

3. David Simpson, *The Politics of American English, 1776–1850* (New York: Oxford University Press, 1986), 46–47. Throughout this chapter, I am indebted to Simpson's groundbreaking study of the language debate in America.

4. Raymond Williams, *The Long Revolution* (New York: Columbia University Press, 1961), 180–81.

5. Michael Warner, *The Letters of the Republic: Publication and the Public Sphere in Eighteenth-Century America* (Cambridge, Mass.: Harvard University Press, 1990), 32.

6. Simpson, *Politics of the American English*, notes, "Except for Samuel Johnson, no one in 1776, on either side of the ocean, seems to show much concern for a standard spelling practice, whether in personal drafts or printed texts" (23).

7. Donald Greene, ed., *The Oxford Authors: Samuel Johnson* (Oxford: Oxford University Press, 1984), 307; hereafter cited parenthetically in the text.

8. Noah Webster, *Dissertations on the English Language, 1789* (Menston [Yorks.]: Scolar Press, 1967), 36–37.

9. John Howe, *Language and Political Meaning in Revolutionary America* (Amherst: University of Massachusetts Press, 2004), 80–81

10. Thomas Gustafson, *Representative Words: Politics, Literature, and the American Language 1776–1865* (Cambridge: Cambridge University Press, 1992), 21–60, discusses

the debate in America about the relationship between representative government and representation in language.

11. Stephen Gill, ed., *The Oxford Authors: William Wordsworth*, ed. (Oxford: Oxford University Press, 1984), 591; hereafter cited parenthetically in the text.

12. William Keach, "Poetry, after 1740," in *The Cambridge History of Literary Criticism*, ed. H. B. Nisbet and Claude Rawson (Cambridge: Cambridge University Press, 1997), 4: 117–66, reminds us that "Wordsworth was not alone in his effort to derive from the primitivist, emotivist and nativist strands characteristic of so much mid- and late-eighteenth-century critical theory a new agenda for poetic language. A series of essays that appeared in the 1796 *Monthly Magazine,* signed 'The Enquirer' and written by William Enfield, cites Hugh Blair's *Lectures on Rhetoric and Belles Lettres* and various French (rather than German) theorists in claiming that poetry has its origins in a 'rude state of nature' when language was inherently 'bold and figurative'." (139).

13. Joel Barlow, *The Vision of Columbus; A Poem in Nine Books* (Hartford: Hudson and Goodwin, 1787), vii; hereafter cited parenthetically in the text.

14. Oliver Goldsmith, *The Collected Works of Oliver Goldsmith,* ed. Arthur Friedman, (Oxford: Clarendon Press, 1966), 4: 287, lines 1–4; hereafter cited parenthetically in the text.

15. Timothy Dwight, *The Major Poems of Timothy Dwight (1752–1817)* (Gainesville, Fla.: Scholars' Facsimiles & Reprints, 1969), lines 1–4; hereafter cited parenthetically in the text.

16. Hugh Henry Brackenridge, *Modern Chivalry,* ed. Claude M. Newlin (New York: Hafner, 1962), 3; hereafter cited parenthetically in the text.

17. Even as he calls for a simple American style, the narrator of *Modern Chivalry* brandishes examples from Greek, Latin, French, or English literature, along with American examples. Because he also describes what he is doing as pure nonsense, playful satire, and adventure, one should not be surprised to find Brackenridge ultimately claiming for the book almost as many purposes as the various dialects, spoken and written, it includes. As Cathy Davidson observes, "In effect, the narrative, like the hero, is a farrago, a hodgepodge, an adventure in discourse on a whole range of political opinions regarding the operations of democracy and the failures and the triumphs of the new Republic, and all bound up in one continuous, shape-shifting saga" (Davidson, *Revolution and the Word: The Rise of the Novel in America,* 2d ed. [New York: Oxford University Press, 1986], 265–66).

18. Although neither makes the specific argument of this chapter, Grantland Rice in *The Transformation of Authorship in America* (Chicago: University of Chicago Press, 1997), 125–43, describes Brackenridge's deployment of dialects as a way of criticizing an implicit trust in print, while Christopher Looby, *Voicing America: Language, Literary Form, and the Origins of the United States* (Chicago: University of Chicago Press, 1996), 202–65, sees the novel thematizing the very linguistic diversity and attempting to establish "a monolingual standard to aid in [America's] . . . self-constitution" (204).

19. John Locke, "An Essay Concerning the True Original, Extent and End of Civil Government," in *Two Treatises of Government,* ed. Peter Laslett (New York: Cambridge University Press, 1990), V.49; hereafter cited parenthetically in the text.

20. John Locke, *An Essay Concerning Human Understanding,* ed. Peter H. Nidditch (New York: Oxford University Press, 1979), III.x.34; hereafter cited parenthetically in the text.

21. Sandra M. Gustafson, *Eloquence is Power: Oratory and Performance in Early America* (Chapel Hill: University of North Carolina Press, 2000), 140–71.

22. *An Inquiry Into the Original of Our Ideas of Beauty and Virtue in Two Treatises,* ed. Wolfgang Leidhold (Indianapolis: Liberty Fund, 2004), 19; hereafter cited parenthetically in the text.

23. Francis Hutcheson, *An Essay on the Nature and Conduct of the Passions and Affections with Illustrations on the Moral Sense,* ed. Aaron Garrett (Indianapolis: Liberty Fund, 2002), 12; hereafter cited parenthetically in the text.

24. Norman Fiering, *Moral Philosophy at Seventeenth-Century Harvard: a Discipline in Transition* (Chapel Hill: University of North Carolina Press, 1981), 5 and 198–206. See also Franklin E. Court, "The Early Impact of Scottish Literary Teaching in North America," in *The Scottish Invention of English Literature,* ed. Robert Crawford (Cambridge: Cambridge University Press, 1998), 134–63.

25. John Witherspoon, "Lectures in Moral Philosophy," in *The Selected Writings of John Witherspoon,* ed. Thomas Miller (Carbondale: Southern Illinois University Press, 1990), 159. All citations of the text are to this edition.

26. Although he does not cite Locke here, Witherspoon is making a distinction that is quite compatible with the way Locke describes the difference between passive and active power; see *An Essay Concerning Human Understanding,* II.21.

27. George Puttenham's *The Arte of English Poesie* (1589), for example, insisted that copiousness was the means by which the courtier succeeded at court. For discussions of the importance of rhetoric to the courtier's success and the figure of allegory and copiousness to the role of the courtier, see Daniel Javitch, *Poetry and Courtliness in Renaissance England* (Princeton, N.J.: Princeton University Press, 1978), and Frank Whigham, *Ambition and Privilege: the Social Tropes of Elizabethan Courtesy Theory* (Berkeley: University of California Press, 1984).

28. Witherspoon, "Lectures in Moral Philosophy," 251. See, also, Sandra Gustafson, *Eloquence is Power,* 251.

29. Jay Fliegelman, *Declaring Independence: Jefferson, Natural Language and The Culture Of Performance* (Stanford, Calif.: Stanford University Press, 1993), 34.

30. In a different context, Jay Fliegelman notes, "Writing in the 1750's and 1760's, a host of rhetoricians, all of whom were widely read in America—James Burgh, Thomas Sheridan, and John Rice among them—proposed a redefinition of the very function and nature of rhetoric, of oratory, and of language itself" (*Declaring Independence,* 29–30). Of the three, Burgh was a Scot trained at St. Andrews and Sheridan was an Irishman who lectured in Dublin and Edinburgh as well as Oxford and Cambridge. Thus even some of those rhetoricians who became famous in England would more accurately have been seen as British. Indeed, Sheridan's first book on oratory was entitled *British Education* (1756).

31. There were more than fifty-six American printings between 1802 and 1827 of Blair's *Lectures,* at least two dozen of which were abridged editions. As for Campbell's *Philosophy of Rhetoric,* Winifred Bryan Horner and Shelley Aley write, that between 1800 and 1825, it "was the second most commonly adopted textbook in American colleges, surpassed only by Hugh Blair's popular *Lectures*" ("George Campbell," *Eighteenth Century British and American Rhetorics and Rhetoricians: Critical Studies and Sources,* ed. Michael G. Moran [Westport, CT: Greenwood Press, 1994], 52).

32. According to Bernard Bailyn, *Voyagers to the West: A Passage in the Peopling of America on the Eve of the Revolution* (New York: Vintage, 1986), between 1760 and 1775 "over 55,000 Protestant Irish emigrated to America; approximately 40,000 Scots, and over 30,000 Englishmen." The number of Scots was equivalent to 3 percent of the population of Scotland in 1760 (26).

33. Robert Crawford, *Devolving English Literature* (Oxford: Oxford University Press, 199), 22.

34. Clifford Siskin, *The Work of Writing: Literature and Social Change in Britain, 1700–1830* (Baltimore: The Johns Hopkins University Press, 1998), 79–99. Howard D. Weinbrot argues in *Britannia's Issue: The Rise of British Literature From Dryden to Ossian* (Cambridge: Cambridge University Press, 1993) that from the mid-1660s to the 1760s "the naïve view of Anglo-Saxon heritage polished by expanding Rome is modified to include Scottish Celtic and Hebrew Jewish cultures" (1).

35. Janet Sorensen, *The Grammar of Empire in Eighteenth Century British Writing* (Cambridge: Cambridge University Press, 2000).

36. See Crawford, *Devolving English Literature*, 36–38, on William Barron's summary account of the Scots' view.

37. Horner and Aley, "George Campbell," 52.

38. David Foxon, *Pope and the Early Eighteenth-Century Book Trade*, rev. ed., ed. James McLaverty (Oxford: Oxford University Press, 1991), 18–23, 42, and 52.

39. For an account of the publication and sale of Pope's *An Essay on Man* in America, see Agnes Marie Sibley, *Alexander Pope's Prestige in America, 1725–1835* (New York: King's Crown, 1949), 22–56 and 137–43.

40. Richard L. Bushman, "Caricature and Satire in Old and New England before the American Revolution," *Massachusetts Historical Society Proceedings* 88 (1976): 19–34.

41. Lewis P. Simpson, "Introduction," in *The Federalist Literary Mind: Selection from the Monthly Anthology and Boston Review, 1803–1811* (Baton Rouge: Louisiana State University Press, 1962), 38.

42. William C. Dowling, *Poetry and Ideology in Revolutionary Connecticut* (Athens: University of Georgia Press, 1990), 57.

43. Kenneth Silverman, *Timothy Dwight* (New York: Twayne, 1969), 22.

44. Sibley, *Alexander Pope's Prestige in America*, 25.

45. Ibid., 58.

46. Quoted in ibid., 62.

47. Douglas Sloan, *The Scottish Enlightenment and the American College Ideal* (New York: Teachers College Press, 1971), 80–81.

48. This particular American edition is one-third the length of the edition published in London by William Strahan in 1783. Hugh Blair, *Lectures on Rhetoric and Belles Lettres* (Philadelphia and Richmond: Jacob Johnson, 1808), 245.

49. Étienne Balibar, "Subject and Subjectivation," in *Supposing the Subject*, ed. Joan Copjec (London: Verso, 1994), 1–15.

50. David Humphreys, *The Miscellaneous Works of David Humphreys*, ed. William Bottroff (Gainesville, Fla.: Scholars' Facsimile and Reprints, 1968), 122.

51. Laurence Buell, *New England Literary Culture: From Revolution to Renaissance* (Cambridge: Cambridge University Press, 1989), 90.

52. Paul Giles, *Transatlantic Insurrections: British Culture and the Formation of American Literature, 1730–1850* (Philadelphia: University of Pennsylvania Press, 2001), 29.

53. "The Midnight Consultations or a Trip to Boston," in *The Poems of Philip Freneau, Poet of the American Revolution,* ed. Fred Lewis Pattee (Princeton, N.J.: University Library, 1901), lines 71–74; hereafter citations of Freneau's poetry are to this edition.

54. Lewis Leary has written that the marginalia in the two volumes of Pope that Freneau used at Princeton "help create . . . vividly the picture of an apprentice, serious-minded and reverential, sitting before a master" (Leary, *That Rascal Freneau: a Study in Literary Failure* [New Brunswick: Rutgers University Press, 1941], 23).

Chapter Three: The Sentimental Libertine

1. See, for example, the essays in Shirley Samuels, ed., *The Culture of Sentiment: Race, Gender, and Sentimentality in Nineteenth-Century America* (New York: Oxford University Press, 1992), particularly Laura Wexler's, "Tender Violence: Literary Eavesdropping, Domestic Fiction, and Educational Reform," 9–38; Elizabeth Barnes, *States of Sympathy: Seduction and Democracy in the American Novel* (New York: Columbia University Press, 1997); Julia A. Stern, *The Plight of Feeling: Sympathy and Dissent in the Early American Novel* (Chicago: University of Chicago Press, 1997); Dana D. Nelson, *The Word in Black and White: Reading "Race" in American Literature, 1638–1867* (New York : Oxford University Press, 1992), 66–86; and Jane Tompkins, *Sensational Designs: The Cultural Work of American Fiction, 1790–1860* (Oxford: Oxford University Press, 1985).

2. This account draws from Nancy Armstrong, *Desire and Domestic Fiction: A Political History of the Novel* (New York: Oxford University Press, 1987).

3. Bernard Bailyn notes that of the emigrants from Britain in 1773–76 period, "By far the largest category—over two-thirds of the entire emigration—is that of emigrants traveling alone" (Bailyn, *Voyagers to the West: A Passage in the Peopling of America on the Eve of the Revolution* [New York: Knopf, 1986], 134).

4. Cathy N. Davidson, *Revolution and the Word: The Rise of the Novel in America,* 2d ed. (New York: Oxford University Press, 2004), 215.

5. *Amelia: or the Faithless Briton. An Original Novel, Founded Upon Recent Facts,* for example, was serialized in part or in whole in the following magazines: *Columbian Magazine* 1 (October 1787): 667–82 and 877–80; *Massachusetts Magazine* 1 (October–December 1789): 649–51, 645–51 [mispaginated], and 750–54; *New York Magazine or Literary Repository* 6 (October–December 1795): 627–32, 652–56, and 715–20; *Philadelphia Minerva* 3 (June–July 1795): 125–30; and *The New-York Weekly Magazine* 3 (August 1797): 53–54 and 61–62 [excerpted text].

6. A Hollywood film such as Stephen Spielberg's *E. T.* is a case in point.

7. John Locke, "An Essay Concerning the True Original Extent, and End of Civil Government," in *Two Treatises of Government,* ed. Peter Laslett, 2nd ed. (Cambridge: Cambridge University Press, 1967), II.vi.65.

8. "Lothario: or, The Accomplished Villain," *Massachusetts Magazine* 1 (July 1789): 443–45. This story is signed "Chrisiphanes" and originally appeared under the title "Instance of the Deadly Consequences of Cruelty and Lust," in *The London Magazine* 38 (April 1769): 171–73. See Edward W. R. Pitcher, *Fiction in American Magazines Before 1800* (Schenectady, N.Y.: Union College Press, 1993), entry A1571.

9. "Innocent Simplicity Betrayed. The Story of Sir Edward and Louisa," *Massachusetts Magazine* 1 (August–September 1789): 470–73 and 539–42. By Henry Mackenzie, this story first appeared in 1780 in the *Mirror* and was also reprinted as "The Story of Louisa Venoni," in the *Boston Magazine* 1(November–December 1784): 562–65 and 611–13; as "The Story of Sir Edward and Louisa," in the *New York Magazine or Literary Repository* 1(October 1790): 597–602 and in the *Literary Miscellany* 1 (1795): 3–14.

10. Both "A Copy of a Letter From a Young Lady to her Seducer" and "The Melancholy Effects of Seduction" attribute the heroine's seduction to a gullibility stemming from her lack of education. "Melancholy Effects of Seduction. A Letter from a Gentleman to his Friend, Relating the Melancholy Effects of Seduction," *Massachusetts Magazine* 7 (1795): 467–73. "Copy of a letter from a Young Lady to her Seducer" was particularly popular in America. It was first published in the London *Town Magazine* 3 (April 1771): 181–82, under the title of "Miss P. of M___, Somersetshire to the Honorable Mr.___." It was then reprinted as "From a Late London Paper. Miss L___ to Mr.___" in *Pennsylvania Chronicle and Advertiser* 5 (1771): 140. Subsequently, it was published under various titles including: "A Copy of a Letter From a Young Lady to Her Once Pretended Admirer," *New Haven Gazette* 2 (1785): 58, and "Copy of a Letter From a Young Lady to Her Seducer," *Massachusetts Magazine* 3 (1791): 678–79. Two years later, this version was reprinted in *Impartial Gazetteer, and Saturday Evening Post* 5 (January 26, 1793): 246. It then appeared as an "Animated Letter, From the Hon. Miss B___ to Sir Richard P___. From an English Paper," *New York Weekly Magazine* 2 (21 December 1796): 193, and as "A Letter From a Once Celebrated Juliet to the Honorable Mr___ of Somerset," *Thespian Oracle; or Monthly Mirror* 1 (1798): 17–20.

11. In "The Story of Edward and Maria," *Massachusetts Magazine* 3 (March 1791): 146–47, the heroine is soon seduced even though her father "bestowed" an education on her "superior to her humble situation" (147). Indeed, she labels her father's desire to educate her as the cause for the vanity that made her vulnerable to seduction: "I fell a victim to my own vanity, the foundation of which was innocently laid by my poor father" (147).

12. "The Duellist and the Libertine Reclaimed," in *Massachusetts Magazine* 1 (April 1789): 205. This story was reprinted from the London *Lady's Magazine* 14 (March 1783): 180–83.

13. Hugh Kelley, "*The Babbler* No. V: The Sentimental Libertine; a Story Founded Upon Fact," in *Massachusetts Magazine* 2 (1790): 173–74.

14. William S. Kable summarizes the various claims to the first American novel in his introduction to *The Power of Sympathy* (Columbus: Ohio State University Press, 1969), xi–xv. Cathy N. Davidson offers a particularly useful account of the problem in *Revolution and the Word*, 143–73.

15. William Hill Brown, *The Power of Sympathy*, and Hannah Webster Foster, *The Coquette*, ed. Carla Mulford (New York: Penguin, 1996), 11. See Philip Gould, *Covenant and Republic: Historical Romance and the Politics of Puritanism* (Cambridge: Cambridge University Press, 1996) for an account of why this form of republican masculinity might at first strike Harrington as repugnant (27). See also Jan Lewis, "The Republican Wife: Virtue and Seduction in the Early Republic," *William and Mary Quarterly* 44 (1987): 689–721.

16. The transformation from a British to an American model of the family can be seen in the change from the captivity narrative of a Mary Rowlandson to one like that of

Mary Jemison. For accounts of this transformation, see Ezra Tawil, "Domestic Frontier Romance, or, How the Sentimental Heroine Became White," *Novel* 32 (1998): 99–124, and Nancy Armstrong and Leonard Tennenhouse, *The Imaginary Puritan: Literature, Intellectual Labor, and the Origins of Personal Life* (Berkeley: University of California Press, 1992).

17. Several scholars have noted the extensive use of the libertine as a figure in Early American Letters. Bryce Traister, "Libertinism and Authorship in America's Early Republic," *American Literature* 72 (2000): 1–30, argues that this figure "embodied the political anxieties of the age; libertinism negotiated the tensions between republican and liberal visions of the United States" (8). My argument is concerned with the qualities of affect that the libertine produced rather than those feelings that sought expression in the populace. I do not disagree with the argument that the libertine may have created anxiety in the reader as he violated the law of the father. I will insist, however, that the libertine also relieved anxiety by violating the law of the father.

18. Foster, *The Coquette*, 131.

19. In 1798, Malthus was appalled at American disregard for the more economically sensible British kinship rules. According to Malthus, this indiscriminate breeding had not yet brought misery to the English in America, where the food supply seemed boundless, but bring misery it surely would—in proportion to the appetites uncurbed by economic exigency. See Thomas Malthus, *An Essay on The Principles of Population* (1798), ed. Philip Appleman (New York: Norton, 1976).

20. For discussions of the figure of the libertine in the French literary tradition, see Marcel Hénaff, *Sade: The Invention of the Libertine Body,* trans. Xavier Callahan (Minneapolis: University of Minnesota Press, 1999); Pierre Saint-Amand, *The Libertine's Progress: Seduction in the Eighteenth-Century French Novel,* trans. Jennifer Curtis Gage (Hanover, N.H.: University of New England Press, 1994); Peter Cryle, *Geometry in the Boudoir: Configurations of French Erotic Narrative* (Ithaca, N.Y.: Cornell University Press, 1994); and Joan DeJean, *Libertine Strategies: Freedom and the Novel in Seventeenth-Century France* (Columbus: Ohio State University Press, 1981).

21. As Michel Feher notes, in the introduction to *The Libertine Reader: Eroticism and Enlightenment in Eighteenth-Century France* (New York: Zone, 1997), it is a given in French libertine literature that marriage is the means by which church and state first delay, and then dissipate, desire (10).

22. Samuel Johnson, *A Dictionary of the English Language: In Which the Words are Deduced from their Originals* (London: W. Strahan, 1755; New York: AMS, 1967), s.v. "Libertine."

23. Gordon Wood, The *Radicalism of the American Revolution* (New York: Knopf, 1992), 112 .

24. The publication information that follows, except where noted, is drawn from Charles Evans, *American Bibliography,* 14 vols. (Chicago: Blakely, 1903–1959), and Clifford K. Shipton [and] James E. Mooney, *National Index of American Imprints Through 1800,* 2 vols. (Worcester, Mass.: American Antiquarian Society, 1969). I list those texts I have seen and do not include the bibliographical ghosts in Evans that were identified by Shipton and Mooney.

25. William Merritt Sale Jr. finds that the American editions of Richardson's novels published after 1786 "were all written with an eye very closely fixed on the edition of *The Paths of Virtue,* 1756" (Sale, *Samuel Richardson: A Bibliographical Record of*

his Literary Career with Historical Notes [New Haven, Conn.: Yale University Press, 1936], 134).

26. Remarks on flyleaves of several of the copies I have examined indicate the ages of some owners. The inside cover of a 1795 edition of *Clarissa* in the John Carter Brown Library indicates that the owner was eighteen. Samuel Pickering Jr. argues in "The 'Ambiguous Circumstances of a Pamela': Early Children's Books and the Attitude Towards Pamela," *Journal of Narrative Technique* 14 (1984): 153–71, that a text such as "The History of Little Goody Two-Shoes" must have been indebted to something like the abridged version of *Pamela* and both were intended for the same audience. It may well be that Richardson's text inspired many a moral tale, but the form peculiar to the abridgment popular in the United States suggests that this text was quite different from the sort of children's book Pickering has studied.

27. James Raven, *Judging New Wealth: Popular Publishing and Responses to Commerce in England, 1750–1800* (Oxford: Clarendon Press, 1992), 38, and James Raven, "The Publication of Fiction in Britain and Ireland, 1750–70," *Publishing History* 24 (1988): 30–47.

28. Mary M. Pollard, *Dublin's Trade in Books 1550–1800* (Oxford: Clarendon Press, 1989), 135–53.

29. See Victor Neuburg, "Chapbooks in America: Reconstructing the Popular Reading of Early America," in *Reading in America*, ed. Cathy N. Davidson (Baltimore: The Johns Hopkins University Press, 1989), 81–113.

30. Jay Fliegelman, *Prodigals and Pilgrims: The American Revolution Against Patriarchal Authority, 1750–1800* (New York: Cambridge University Press, 1982), 79–83.

31. The locus classicus is Leslie Fiedler's comment: "It is the nature of American scriptures to be vulgarizations of the holy texts from which they take their cues; and just as The Book of Mormon caricatures the Bible unawares, so Charlotte Temple is an unwitting travesty of Clarissa Harlowe" (Fiedler, *Love and Death in the American Novel* [New York: Anchor, 1966], 97).

32. Ian P. Watt, *Rise of the Novel: Studies in Defoe, Richardson, and Fielding* (Berkeley: University of California Press, 1957).

33. Nancy Armstrong, "Why Daughters Die: The Racial Logic of American Sentimentalism," *Yale Journal of Criticism* 7 (1994): 10.

34. Annette Weiner, *Inalienable Possessions: The Paradox of Keeping-While-Giving* (Berkeley: University of California Press, 1992).

35. Armstrong, "Why Daughters Die," 11.

36. James E. Seaver, *A Narrative of the Life of Mrs. Mary Jemison*, ed. June Namias (Norman: University of Oklahoma Press, 1992). Jemison's capture occurred in the late eighteenth century; her story was recorded in 1824.

37. Armstrong, "Why Daughters Die," 12.

38. Samuel Richardson, *Clarissa or the History of a Young Lady* (Boston: Samuel Hall, 1795), 28.

39. Samuel Richardson, *Pamela, or Virtue Rewarded*, ed. William Merritt Sale Jr. (New York: Norton, 1958), 245.

40. [Samuel Richardson], *The Pleasing History of Pamela* (Boston: Samuel Hall, 1793), 20. No author is listed on the title page. The edition entitled *The History of Pamela or, Virtue Rewarded* (Philadelphia: William Gibbons, 1794) does not reproduce

the scene in which Mr. B dresses up as a serving girl as a ruse by which to make his way undetected into Pamela's bed.

41. For example, the abridged editions do not reproduce any of the letters, but rather describe briefly what influence her writing had on her master: "Mr. B. being extremely moved at her description of her distress, behaved with more tenderness and respect" (Richardson, *The History of Pamela or, Virtue Rewarded* [Philadelphia: William Gibbons, 1794], 62).

42. [Richardson], *The Pleasing History of Pamela* (Boston, 1793), 1.

43. In the unabridged text, Richardson printed Letter 261, Paper X, as a seemingly random assemblage of scraps of verse, several stanzas of which are set askew and in a haphazard fashion. By this typographical device, he manages to call attention to the effect of the rape on the writing subject, while saying not a word about her physical condition.

44. Richardson, *Clarissa* (Boston, 1795), 80–81.

45. Samuel Richardson, *Clarissa, or The History of a Young Woman*, ed. Angus Ross (London: Penguin, 1985), 1011.

46. Moll Flanders may be regarded as the exception that proves the rule, in that she must go to the colonies in order to transform herself from a promiscuous woman into a member of the respectable classes.

47. Susannah Rowson, *Charlotte Temple*, ed. Cathy N. Davidson (New York: Oxford University Press, 1986), 118.

48. Richardson, *Clarissa* (Boston, 1795), 112.

49. Charlotte was tutored by a French woman who later betrayed the girl and was instrumental in her corruption. In that Charlotte came under this French influence, she could be regarded as less English, in American terms, than her daughter will turn out to be as a result of the young girl's English upbringing.

50. Wood, *The Radicalism of the American Revolution*, 222.

51. Doris Sommer, *Foundational Fictions: The National Romances of Latin America* (Berkeley: University of California Press, 1991), 77–78.

52. Harriet Beecher Stowe, *Uncle Tom's Cabin or Life Among the Lowly*, ed. Ann Douglas (New York: Penguin, 1986), 512; hereafter, citations in the text are to this edition.

53. Nathaniel Hawthorne, *The House of the Seven Gables*, in *Nathaniel Hawthorne: Novels*, ed. Millicent Bell (New York: Library of America, 1983), 515; hereafter, citations in the text are to this edition.

Chapter Four: The Heart of Masculinity

1. Mackenzie's *Man of Feeling*, for instance, went through nearly forty editions in the eighteenth century. See the appendix in Harold W. Thompson, *The Scottish Man of Feeling* (Oxford: Oxford University Press, 1931), 417–18.

2. My interest is specifically in how American literature revised the figure of the man of feeling. Most studies of American sentiment and masculinity do not address the problem. Of those I have found particularly useful are Julie Ellison, *Cato's Tears and the Making of Anglo-American Emotion* (Chicago: University of Chicago Press, 1999); *Sentimental Men: Masculinity and the Politics of Affect in American Culture*, ed. Mary

Chapman and Glenn Hendler (Berkeley: University of California Press, 1999); and Dana D. Nelson, *National Manhood: Capitalist Citizenship and the Imagined Fraternity of White Men* (Durham: Duke Universtiy Press, 1998).

3. In an insightful reading of the novel, Bruce Burgett has pointed out that "Brown's naming of his protagonist Hartley alludes to Mackenzie's Harley" (Burgett, *Sentimental Bodies: Sex, Gender, and Citizenship in the Early Republic* [Princeton, N.J.: Princeton University Press, 1998], 193n.20). Burgett goes on to read this novel as an account of male masochism. In addition to Burgett's discussion of Brockden Brown's borrowings from Mackenzie, I would also note that near the end of *Clara Howard*, Brockden Brown invents a benefactor named Sedley—the same name Mackenzie assigned a similar character in one of the last episodes of his novel.

4. Dorothy Blakely, *The Minerva Press, 1790–1820* (London: Bibliographical Society at the University Press, 1939 [1935]). Mackenzie's narrator alerts us from the outset that he thinks of Harley's memoirs as something on the order of *Pamela* when he writes, "had the name Marmontel, or a Richardson, been on the title-page—'tis odds that I should have wept" (Henry Mackenzie, *The Man of Feeling*, intro by Kenneth C. Slagle [New York: Norton, 1958], xv). Citations of the text are to this edition.

5. Henri Petter has speculated that "Edward Hartley may have been rejected as unsuitable for a title because of its resemblance to Edgar Huntly" (Petter, *The Early American Novel* [Columbus: Ohio State University Press, 1971], 184). If that were the case, why change the title from *Clara Howard*?

6. G. J. Barker-Benfield, *The Culture of Sensibility: Sex and Society in Eighteenth-Century Britain* (Chicago: The University of Chicago Press, 1996), 141. For the Samuel Richardson, quote see his *A Collection of the Moral and Instructive Sentiments, Maxims, Cautions, and Reflections Contained in the Histories of "Pamela," "Clarissa," and "Sir Charles Grandison"* (1755) (Delmar, N.Y.: Scholars' Facsimiles and Reprints, 1980), 204–5.

7. John Locke, "Of Paternal Power," in *Two Treatises of Government*, ed. Peter Laslett (Cambridge: Cambridge University Press, 1988), II. iv.

8. Ian Watt, *The Rise of the Novel, Studies in Defoe, Richardson, and Fielding* (Berkeley: University of California Press, 1957).

9. Anna Laetitia Barbauld, *British Novelists with an Essay and Prefaces Biographical and Critical* (1810) consisted of fifty volumes and Sir Walter Scott's *Ballantyne's Novelist's Library* (1821–24) was a collection of fourteen authors in ten volumes. For a discussion of the importance of these two collections in establishing the canon of the English novel, see Homer O. Brown, *Institutions of the Novel* (Philadelphia: University of Pennsylvania Press, 1997), 181–84.

10. Mackenzie's own essays on novel writing in *The Lounger* 1785–86—specifically no. 20, June 18, 1785 and no. 100, December 30, 1786—make clear that the symbolic capital acquired through novel reading enhances one's business and induces the virtues of justice, prudence, economy, benevolence, and compassion. John Mullen notes that eighteenth-century readers were surprised to discover the industrious Henry Mackenzie was himself not at all like the pensive Harley; see Mullen, *Sentiment and Sociability: The Language of Feeling in the Eighteenth Century* (Oxford: Clarendon Press, 1988), 118.

11. For a discussion of this problem, see Donald J. Ringe, "The Historical Essay," in Charles Brockden Brown, *Clara Howard in A Series of Letters and Jane Talbot, A Novel:*

The Novels and Related Works of Charles Brockden Brown, ed. Sydney J. Krause, S. W. Reid, and Donald J. Ringe (Kent, Ohio: Kent State University Press, 1986), 5:433–36; hereafter citations of the text are to this edition.

12. Benjamin Franklin, "Information to Those Who Would Remove to America," in *The Autobiography and Other Writings on Politics, Economics, and Virtue*, ed. Alan Houston (Cambridge: Cambridge University Press, 2004), 341–48.

13. Gillian Brown, *The Consent of the Governed: The Lockean Legacy in Early American Culture* (Cambridge, Mass.: Harvard University Press, 2001) discusses the feminizing of consent in America.

14. William Godwin, *Fleetwood: Or, the New Man of Feeling*, ed. Arnold A. Markley and Gary Handwerk (Toronto: Broadview Press, 2000), 73; hereafter citations of the text are to this edition.

15. Hannah More's "Sensibility: An Epistle to the Honourable Mrs. Boscawen" (1782), for example, warns specifically against confusing sensibility with mere feeling, an error that critics so deplored in *Fleetwood*.

16. Blakely, *The Minerva Press*, 21.

17. Ibid., 57, 69.

18. I have not discussed the problem of masculinity in *Emma*, because Claudia L. Johnson has covered the topic so well and in a manner that is compatible with my argument; see Johnson, *Equivocal Beings: Politics, Gender, and Sentimentality in the 1790s: Wollstonecraft, Radcliffe, Burney, and Austen* (Chicago: University of Chicago Press, 1995), 191–203.

19. Jane Austen, *Sense and Sensibility*, ed. Claudia L. Johnson (New York: Norton, 2002), 27; hereafter citations of the text are to this edition.

20. Jane Austen, *Pride and Prejudice*, ed. Donald Gray (New York: Norton, 2001), 8; hereafter citations of the text are to this edition.

21. Jane Austen, *Persuasion*, ed. Patricia Meyer Spacks (New York: Norton, 1995), 2; hereafter citations of the text are to this edition.

22. James Fenimore Cooper, *The Pathfinder, or The Inland Sea*, ed. Richard Dilworth and intro. by Kay Seymour House (New York: Penguin, 1989), 48; hereafter citations of the text are to this edition.

23. Doris Sommer, *Foundational Fictions: The National Romances of Latin America* (Berkeley: University of California Press, 1993), 52–82.

Chapter Five: The Gothic in Diaspora

1. Leslie Fiedler, *Love and Death in the American Novel* (New York: Anchor, 1992), 28.

2. Toni Morrison, *Playing in the Dark: Whiteness and the Literary Imagination* (New York: Vintage, 1993), 33.

3. Philip Fisher, *Hard Facts: Setting and Form in the American Novel* (Oxford: Oxford University Press, 1987), 22–86. See also Renée L. Bergland, *The National Uncanny: Indian Ghosts and American Subjects* (Hanover, N.H.: University Press of New England, 2000).

4. Chris Baldick and Robert Mighall offer an excellent review of the literary criticism of gothic fiction and sum up the situation of the last seventy-five years this way: "The

collapse of history into universal psychology has been a consistent feature of Gothic Criticism since at least the 1930s" (Baldick and Mighalla, "Gothic Criticism," in *A Companion to the Gothic*, ed. David Punter [Oxford: Basil Blackwell, 2005], 218).

5. There is a tradition of looking at the European gothic as a political language for either the excesses of revolution or the monstrosity of the ancien regime. See, for example, Ronald Paulson, *Representations of Revolution, 1789–1820* (New Haven, Conn.: Yale University Press, 1983). For a critique of that allegorical reading of the gothic, see David H. Richter, *The Progress of Romance, Literary Historiography and the Gothic Novel* (Columbus: Ohio State University Press, 1996), 53–65.

6. Donald Ringe, *American Gothic: Imagination and Reason in Nineteenth-Century Fiction* (Lexington: University Press of Kentucky, 1982), 13–35. I am indebted to Ringe's discussion in this section.

7. From August to November of 1795 *New-York Weekly Magazine* published Friedrich von Schiller's *The Ghost-Seer* in serialized form. The magazine then ran the serialization of Cajetan Tschink's *The Victim of Magical Delusion*, which appeared in seventy-two parts from December 2, 1795 to April 12, 1797.

8. Thus, for example, "The Castle of Costanzo" appeared originally in the *Universal Magazine* in August 1784, then in *Boston Magazine* in 1785, the *Impartial Gazeteer, and Saturday Evening Post* in 1795, and *Philadelphia Minerva* in 1796 and 1798 while the "Origin of the Priory of the Two Lovers" was first published in the *Universal Magazine* in February 1784 and appeared in *Massachusetts Magazine* in 1792, *New York Magazine or Literary Repository* in 1795, and *Philadelphia Minerva* in 1796.

9. Among German novels were such titles as Christiane Naubert's *Herman of Unna* (1794), Schiller's *The Ghost-Seer* (1795) and Cajetan Tschink's *The Victim of Magical Delusion* (1795).

10. Robert Miles, "The 1790s: the Effulgence of Gothic," in *The Cambridge Companion to Gothic Fiction*, ed. Jerrold E. Hogle (Cambridge: Cambridge University Press, 2004), 41–62.

11. The gothic novel participated in what Max Weber, borrowing from Frederick Schiller, called "the disenchantment of the world." While Weber is more interested in how empirical science stripped the magic and the supernatural from material objects, I would argue that the novel did more to make the process of disenchantment seem only normal and rational. See *From Max Weber: Essays on Sociology*, trans. and ed. H. H. Gerth and C. Wright Mills (New York: Oxford University Press, 1946), 155.

12. See Samuel Johnson, *Rambler 4* (March 31, 1775) on the new realistic novel that appeals to British readers Johnson, *The Major Works*, ed. Donald Greene. (Oxford: Oxford University Press, 2000), 175–78. In his review of Jane Austen's *Emma*, Sir Walter Scott contrasts the fantastic writings of the gothic that he equates with the older style of novel to the realism of Austen, which interests a more modern and mature reader. See "Review of *Emma* by Jane Austen," in *Sir Walter Scott on Novelists and Fiction*, ed. Ioan Williams (London: Routledge and Kegan Paul, 1968), 225–36.

13. Horace Walpole, *The Castle of Otranto*, ed. W. S. Lewis with an intro. by E. J. Clery (Oxford: Oxford University Press, 1996), 5. The names Onuphrio Muralto and William Marshall are mentioned only on the title page of the first edition.

14. Although Walpole was attempting something new in fiction, he knew well enough that his own contemporaries took considerable interest in apparitions, as sug-

gested by the persistence of apparition narratives throughout the eighteenth century. See Jayne E. Lewis, "Spectral Currencies in the Air of Reality: *A Journal of the Plague Year* and the History of Apparitions," *Representations* 87 (2004): 82–101.

15. For discussions of association of the gothic and Whig politics, see Colin Kidd, *British Identities Before Nationalism, Ethnicity and Nationhood in the Atlantic World: 1600–1800* (Cambridge: Cambridge University Press, 1999), 75–98; Christine Gerrard, *The Patriot Opposition to Walpole: Politics, Poetry, and National Myth, 1725–1742* (Oxford: Clarendon Press, 1994); R. J. Smith, *The Gothic Bequest: Medieval Institutions in British Thought, 1688–1863* (Cambridge: Cambridge University Press, 1985); J.G.A. Pocock, *The Machiavellian Moment: Florentine Political Thought and the Atlantic Republican Tradition* (Princeton, N.J.: Princeton University Press, 1975); and Samuel Kliger, *The Goths in England: a Study of Seventeenth- and Eighteenth-Century Thought* (Cambridge, Mass.: Harvard University Press, 1952).

16. Following Tacitus, Whig politicians insisted on their right to remove a king based on the ancient, or "Gothic" constitution, a right they claimed their Germanic forebears, the Saxons, introduced into Britain. When used to describe architecture, "Gothic" meant something barbaric and wild, but it was also an honorific term in a protonationalist climate where an indigenous style was aesthetically preferable to the classical model.

17. Charles Brockden Brown, *Three Gothic Novels: Wieland, or, The Transformation; Arthur Mervyn or, Memoirs of the Year 1793; Edgar Huntly or, Memoirs of a Sleep-Walker* ed. Sydney J. Krause (New York: Library of America, 1998), 641.

18. Ringe, *American Gothic*, 102–27 shows that although a handful of American writers of the 1820s and 1830s tried to use one or two European gothic conventions, most "drew on sources closer to home" (102).

19. Isaac Mitchell, *The Asylum; or, Alonzo and Melissa: An American Tale, Founded on Fact* (Poughkeepsie, N.Y.: Joseph Nelson, 1811) 2:58–59.

20. Despite the fact that it was one of the most popular Gothic novels in the nineteenth century, most critics either ignore it altogether in their discussions of the gothic in American literature or mention it only derisively to note the use of the castle. See, for example, Alexander Cowie, *The Rise of the American Novel* (New York: American, 1948), 107–8.

21. Cathy N. Davidson, *Revolution and the Word: The Rise of the Novel in America*, 2d ed. (New York: Oxford University Press, 2004), 322.

22. Leonard Tennenhouse and Nancy Armstrong, "The American Origins of the English Novel," *American Literary History* 4 (Fall, 1992): 386–410. See also Nancy Armstrong, "Why Daughters Die: The Racial Logic of American Sentimentalism," *Yale Journal of Criticism* 7 (1994): 1–24.

23. Robert Miles discusses these cues in "The 1790s, the Effulgence of Gothic," 41–42.

24. In a country of immigrants, it was presumably not always possible to recognize kin. Moll Flanders, for example, discovers only accidentally that she had mistakenly married her own brother in America.

25. Reprinted from the British *Westminster Magazine* 6 (September–October 1778): 465–66, 521–23, the story of Martin Guerre was reported in "Two Husbands to one

Wife," *Impartial Gazetteer, and Saturday Evening Post*, 9 (July 16, 1796): 420. Stories of Thomas Hoag had been in magazines in 1797 and 1805.

26. At the conclusion of *The Mysteries of Udolpho*, Radcliffe describes the moment when the protagonist, returned from his lengthy detour, bursts into the room and reunites with the heroine in similarly auditory terms: "[His] features were veiled in the obscurity of twilight; but his voice could not be concealed for it was the voice of Valencourt! At the sound, never heard by Emily without emotion, she started, in terror, astonishment and doubtful pleasure . . . [and] sunk into a seat, overcome by the various emotions" (Ann Radcliffe, *The Mysteries of Udolpho*, ed. Bonamy Dobrée [Oxford: Oxford University Press, 1998], 667).

27. In her still illuminating analysis of the veiled figure, Eve Kosofsky Sedgwick argues for its centrality in gothic fiction on grounds that this figure perfectly captures the paradox of the novel form itself: "[T]he human face and body always insist on being recognized as such. But at the same time the fascination with the code [of human identity] in Gothic novels is so full and imperious that it weakens the verbal supports for the fiction of presence" (159). Is this not what happens when Melissa moves her veil aside? Sedgwick's conclusion is not all that different from my own, though cast in different terms: "The issue of what constitutes the character—what internecine superposition of the length of words, the image of a body, a name, and, on the countenance, an authenticating graphic stamp—had never before the Gothic been confronted so energetically in those terms" (Kosofsky Sedgwick, *The Coherence of Gothic Conventions* [New York: Methuen, 1980], 170).

28. Adam Smith, *The Theory of Moral Sentiments* (Amherst: Prometheus, 2000), 4; emphasis mine.

29. William Godwin's model of the philosophical novel Brockden Brown imitated has been discussed by a number of scholars. See, for example, Pamela Clemit, *The Godwinian Novel: The Rational Fictions of Godwin, Brockden Brown, and Mary Shelley* (Oxford: Clarendon, 1993); Robert Miles, "What Is a Romantic Novel?" *Novel* 34 (2001): 180–201; and Jon Klancher, "Godwin and Republican Romance," in *Eighteenth-Century Literary History: An MLQ Reader*, ed. Marshall Brown (Durham, N.S.: Duke University Press, 1999), 68–86.

30. The prospectus was published in the *Weekly Magazine* 1 (March 17, 1798): 202.

31. John Locke, *An Essay Concerning Human Understanding*, ed. Peter H. Nidditch (Oxford: Oxford University Press, 1979), II.i.11. Citations in the text are to this edition.

32. Nathaniel Hawthorne, *Tales and Sketches, Including Twice-Told Tales, Mosses from an Old Manse, and The Snow-Image*, notes by Roy Harvey Pearce (New York: Library of America, 1996), 68. Citations in the text are to this edition.

33. For a discussion of this concept in American literature, see Amanda Emerson, "From Equivalence to Equity: the Management of an American Myth," *differences* 14 (2003): 78–105.

34. Although one might think that Ichabod Crane, Irving's famously bookish schoolmaster, would have mastered the local history, his ignorance of whom is intended to marry whom makes him the butt of a joke that drives him quite literally from the community.

35. See Franklin E. Court, *The Scottish Connection: the Rise of English Literary Study in Early America* (Syracuse, N.Y.: University of Syracuse Press, 2001); Terence Martin, *The Instructed Vision: Scottish Common Sense Philosophy and the Origins of American Fiction* (Bloomington: Indiana University Press, 1961); Roy Harvey Pearce, *The Savages of America: A Study of the Indian and the Idea of Civilization* (Baltimore: The Johns Hopkins University Press, 1953), 88–89.

36. In *The Black Atlantic, Modernity and Double Consciousness* (Cambridge, Mass.: Harvard University Press, 1993), 11–15, Paul Gilroy speaks directly to the problem of disparate and broken histories in discussing the relationship between the histories produced by the African diaspora and the nationalist histories of Great Britain and the United States. As a result of this relationship, he contends the narratives of Black Britons and African Americans are broken up and woven into the larger fabric of a cosmopolitan history.

37. Edgar Allan Poe, *Poetry, Tales, and Selected Essays*, notes by Patrick F. Quinn and G. R. Thompson (New York: Library of America, 1996), 329; hereafter citations in the text are to this edition.

Afterword: From Cosmopolitanism to Hegemony

1. Referring to Cereno as a Castilian Rothschild makes him a diasporic figure twice over: first as a kind of mercantile Jew whose sojourn in Spain was as a member of the Diaspora, and after 1492, as a member of the community that either fled Spain or remained and submitted to conversion. Many new Christians, or *conversos*, relocated to the Americas where they were less likely to come under the scrutiny of the Inquisition while secretly practicing Judaism; hereafter citations of the text are to Herman Melville, *Benito Cereno, The Piazza Tales and Other Prose Pieces 1839–1860: The Writings of Herman Melville*, with a Historical Note by Merton J. Sealts (Evanston and Chicago: Northwestern University Press and the Newberry Library, 1987), 9:47–117.

2. Sarah Robbins makes the case that Melville assumed that his readers would read his story in relation to Stowe's novel because *Putnam's* was running editorials attacking Stowe's style during the same time it was serializing *Benito Cereno*. See Robbins, "Gendering the History of the Antislavery Narrative: Juxtaposing *Uncle Tom's Cabin* and *Benito Cereno, Beloved* and *Middle Passage*," *American Quarterly* 49 (1997): 531–73. For an important discussion of Melville's criticism of Stowe's racialism, see Ezra Tawil, *The Making of Racial Sentiment: Slavery and the Birth of the Frontier Romance* (Cambridge: Cambridge University Press, 2006), 191–208.

3. The German legal theorist Carl Schmitt was particularly fond of Melville's story and signed a letter on his birthday in 1938 as Benito Cereno. Since the novella, according to Tracy Strong, was widely read and discussed in Germany with specific attention to the contemporary situation, there has been much speculation as to what this famous theorist of sovereignty intended by that self-designation. Did he want others to think of him as the unwilling participant in the Nazi legal apparatus or even their helpless victim? At the very least, we can say that Schmitt seems to have ignored the fact that the various narrative traditions cancel each other out, and he instead reads the novella as a captivity narrative, in which the plight of the captive Cereno should

arouse one's moral and sympathetic identification. See Tracy B. Strong's foreword, "The Sovereign and the Exception: Carl Schmitt, Politics, Theology, and Leadership," in Carl Schmitt, *Political Theology, Four Chapters on the Concept of Sovereignty*, trans. George Schwab (Chicago: The University of Chicago Press, 2005), vii–xi.

4. *Secret History: or, the Horrors of St. Domingo, in a Series of Letters Written by a Lady at Cape Francois, to Colonel Burr, Late Vice-President of the United States, Principally during the Command of General Rochambeau* (Philadelphia: Bradford and Inskeep, 1808). Eric Sundquist reminds us that "in changing the name of Benito Cereno's ship from the *Tryal* to the *San Dominick*, Melville gave to Babo's slave revolt a specific character that has often been identified" (Sundquist, *To Wake the Nations: Race in the Making of American Literature* [Cambridge, Mass.: Harvard University Press, 1993], 140). For a discussion of Melville's views on slave revolts, see Carolyn Karcher, *Shadow of the Promised Land: Slavery, Race, and Violence in Melville's America* (Baton Rouge: Louisiana State University Press, 1980).

5. In *Barbaric Traffic: Commerce and Antislavery in the Eighteenth-Century Atlantic World* (Cambridge, Mass.: Harvard University Press, 2003), 43–85, Philip Gould discusses how the trope of degeneracy is used in abolitionist writing.

6. I have argued elsewhere that during the colonial period the gothic and the captivity narrative worked hand in glove. See Nancy Armstrong and Leonard Tennenhouse, *The Imaginary Puritan: Literature, Intellectual Labor, and the Origins of Personal Life* (Berkeley: University of California Press, 1992), 196–216.

7. Melville is ironically appropriating the tactic of role reversal found in antislavery writing. As Gould explains, "In order to preserve the logic of the humanitarian argument," antislavery writing "called upon readers to 'see' themselves as African slaves" (*Barbaric Traffic*, 48–49).

8. Immanuel Kant, "Perpetual Peace: A Philosophical Sketch," in *Kant, Selections*, ed. and trans. Lewis White Beck (Englewood, N. J.: Prentice-Hall, 1988), 439.

9. In *The Emergence of American Literary Narrative 1820–1860* (Cambridge, Mass.: Harvard University Press, 2005), 219, Jonathan Arac has called attention to the use of gothic rhetoric in Melville's story.

10. Even Kant's model of universal hospitality unwittingly performs one act of exclusion. To imagine universal tolerance, Kant implicitly excludes those who cannot tolerate certain cultural differences.

11. Georg Simmel, *Conflict* and *The Web of Group-Affiliation*, trans. Kurt H. Wolff and Reinhard Bendix (New York: The Free Press, 1964), 20.

12. A number of critics have argued that in maintaining slavery, the American Constitution and legal apparatus was itself a formidable impediment to freedom. Taking a different view, Deak Nabers has shown that in such a novel as *Clotel*, William Wells Brown, however critical of "law's role in limiting natural rights," is "fundamentally committed to pursuing those rights through legal activities" (Nabers, "The Problem of Revolution in the Age of Slavery: *Clotel*, Fiction, and the Government of Man," *Representations* 91 [2005]: 86–87). Brown presumably understood that despite the limitations of the law, freedom came from conflicts waged within the law.

13. Raymond Williams, *Marxism and Literature* (Oxford: Oxford University Press, 1977), 110.

14. The historical Amasa Delano apparently went on to include an accurate translation in his account. He calls the court translator "a bad linguist," complaining that "the

Spanish captain's deposition, together with Mr. Luther's and my own, [had to be] translated into English again" (825). It is clearly a matter of some importance to make the text both conform to the legal proceedings and yet put those documents into perfectly legible English.

15. Harold H. Scudder, "Melville's *Benito Cereno* and Captain Delano's Voyages," *PMLA* 43 (1928): 502–32. See also Merton J. Sealts, "Historical Note," in Benito Cereno, *The Piazza Tales and Other Prose Pieces 1839–1860*, 9:511.